Change Leadership:
A Practical Guide to Transforming Our Schools

Readers are invited to review and download full-size versions of the exercises in *Change Leadership* to use with their own groups and teams.

If you would like to download and print out an electronic copy of the exercises, please visit http://www.gse.harvard.edu/clg/news1a.html or http://www.josseybass.com/go/changeleadership

Thank you,
Change Leadership Group

# Change Leadership:
# A Practical Guide to
# Transforming Our Schools

Tony Wagner
Robert Kegan
Lisa Lahey
Richard W. Lemons
Jude Garnier
Deborah Helsing
Annie Howell
Harriette Thurber Rasmussen

Foreword by Tom Vander Ark

JOSSEY-BASS
A Wiley Imprint
www.josseybass.com

**Library of Congress Cataloging-in-Publication Data**

Wagner, Tony.
    Change leadership: a practical guide to transforming our schools / Tony Wagner, Robert Kegan; foreword by Tom Vander Ark.—1st ed.
        p. cm.
    ISBN-13: 978-0-7879-7755-9
    ISBN-10: 0-7879-7755-1
1.  School management and organization—United States. 2.  Education—Aims and objectives—United States. 3.  Educational change—United States. I. Kegan, Robert. II. Title.
    LB2805.W315 2006
    371.200973—dc22                                                           2005027613

Printed in the United States of America

FIRST EDITION
*PB Printing*   10  9  8  7  6  5

The Jossey-Bass Education Series

# CONTENTS

Foreword                                                                 xi
Preface                                                                  xv
Acknowledgments                                                          xxiii
About the Authors                                                        xxvii


**ONE** Introduction: Reframing the Problem                               1

A Knowledge Economy Requires New Skills for All Students                  3
Greater Supports for Learning in a Changing Society                       6
Reform or Reinvention? Technical Challenges Versus
    Adaptive Challenges                               8
Organizational Beliefs and Behaviors                                     12
Individual Beliefs and Behaviors                                         14
Accepting the Challenge and the Risks: Moving Toward Communities
    of Practice via Collaborative Learning          16


**PART ONE** Improving Instruction                                       21


**TWO** Creating a Vision of Success                                     23

Challenges to Improving Instruction                                      24
Seven Disciplines for Strengthening Instruction                          27
Using the Seven Disciplines                                              32
Launching an Instructional Improvement System: The Critical
    First Conversations                              34

Developing a Shared Vision                                          35
Defining a New Framework for Effective Instruction                  38
Linking the New 3 R's of Instruction                                43


**THREE** Committing Ourselves to the Challenge                     51

Identifying Your Commitment                                         51
Spotting Your Obstacles Through Self-Reflection                     54


Reflections                                                         59


**PART TWO** Why Is This So Hard?                                   61


**FOUR** Generating Momentum for Change                             63

Obstacles to Improvement Versus Momentum for Improvement            64
Generating the Momentum for Systemic Change                         74
Communities of Practice as a Strategy                               74


**FIVE** Exploring Individual Immunities to Change                  83

Attending to Countering Behaviors                                   83
A Deeper Look                                                       85
Finding the Competing Commitment                                    87
Taking the Next Step                                                90


Reflections                                                         93


**PART THREE** Thinking Systemically                                95


**SIX** Relating the Parts to the Whole                             97

Arenas of Change                                                    98

Toward Transformation: Using the 4 C's      110
Another Use for the 4 C's      120

**SEVEN** The Individual as a Complex System      **123**

Hidden Commitments and Personal Immunities      124
Big Assumptions and Immunities      127

Reflections      130

**PART FOUR** Working Strategically      131

**EIGHT** The Ecology of Change      **133**

Phases of Whole-System Change      133
Change Levers: Data, Accountability, and Relationships      134
Strategic Change in Action      137
Putting the Pieces Together: The Ecology of Educational Transformation      162
Measuring Success and the Challenge of High-Stakes Test Scores      163

**NINE** Overturning Your Immunities to Change      **167**

Steps Toward Individual Change      168
Considering Steps for the Most Powerful Learning      184
Phases in Overturning Your Immunities      185
Becoming Fully Released from Immunities to Change      187

Reflections      191

**TEN** Conclusion: Bringing the Outward and
Inward Focus Together      **193**

Hold High Expectations for All Our Students      196
Involve Building and Central Office Administrators in Instruction      198

Choose a Priority and Stay Relentlessly Focused on It            202
Foster a Widespread Feeling of Urgency for Change               207
Encourage a New Kind of Leader                                  209
Develop a New Kind of Administrative Team                       214
Shining a Broader Light on Change                               218
Implications for the Change Leader: Toward Adaptive Work        221
Concluding . . . or Commencing?                                 227

## APPENDIXES

**A**. Team Exercises                                           231

**B**. Recommended Reading                                      255

Index                                                           257

**By Tom Vander Ark**
*Executive Director, Education*
*Bill & Melinda Gates Foundation*

After spending a long weekend attempting to summarize what I thought we had learned about leading high-performing districts, I read this book and drew three conclusions. First, this work is hard—it's complicated, technical, personal, and political. Second, with so few people studying what may be the most important domestic issue of our time, we're all fortunate that the Change Leadership Group (CLG) has spent the last five years working on educational success at scale and on the leadership necessary to create it. And third, it wasn't the architectural blueprint I expected five years ago, but probably better and more appropriate to the challenge.

School districts are a complicated American anachronism. Despite the recent aggregation of control to the state and federal level, we rely more heavily on local educational authorities than any other developed country. Although many state constitutions acknowledge public education as the paramount duty of the state, we rest the responsibility for policy, service delivery, employment, and real estate development with local districts. Our history of local control has proven to be a blessing and a curse—a building block of democracy and a stumbling block (at least in some cases) to creating a system of public education of consistently high quality. Today, many principals are subjected to six accountability systems: local, state, and federal compliance regulations, and local, state, and federal outcome requirements. The potential of new data systems, the challenges of school choice, and budget problems add to the confusion. The difficult process of aligning and streamlining these policies and systems will (or should) occupy the second half of this decade. This policy debate could easily take place without improving teaching.

That's where this book comes in handy. It's only about instructional leadership. It doesn't debate policy, doesn't contemplate the role or architecture of districts, and it doesn't tell you how to make AYP (average yearly progress) (but you will if you do what it says). It tells you how to improve the quality of instruction by becoming an effective instructional leader.

I wish it were simple, but it's not. When I made this grant five years ago, I wasn't quite sure what to expect (I've since hired a bunch of people who ask far more specific questions than I did). I thought it would result in a training program for people trying to help improve schools, and assumed there would be a methodology behind it—a "how-to" guide. To some extent CLG has done both, but this isn't a school improvement cookbook. It's a framework full of pointed questions that thoughtful groups of education leaders should ask themselves about their work.

This book does suggest that there is a necessary progression to the work of system improvement:

1. Preparing for change by answering the "why change?" question
2. Including others and building the systems capacity for improvement
3. Improving instruction

It emphasizes the danger of jumping to doing without preparing. This point is important enough that it warrants a short story.

As Dick Elmore frequently does, this book highlights the important work that Tony Alvarado did in District 2 in New York. It's one of the best examples of instructional leadership in the country. Tony promoted adult learning about instruction, which resulted in powerful agreements, which led to the development of strong instructional practices. When Alan Bersin lured Tony to San Diego, he imported a decade of learning about instructional leadership and encapsulated it in a Blueprint. They "jolted" the system by jumping right into phase three, implementation, while quickly building capacity to improve instructional leadership (phase two). The "bet" was that early results would build support for the radical surgery being done on the system. A regime of what has come to be called "managed instruction" was implemented with major budget realignments (which means hundreds of people lost their jobs) and a new set of priorities. Five foundations invested over $50 million in the most elegant instructional improvement plan ever devised. Several years later they were both out of work and the board was dismantling the plan. In between, teachers and some parents complained bitterly about the top-down reforms, and results failed to gain the expected level of community support.

What can we learn from this case? First, best practices don't travel well. At least not without a culture of engaged adult learners and the commitments that they are able to make. Second, change won't happen unless you help the community answer the question, "why change?" Third, context matters—a lot.

There may be a fourth lesson. Being president of the United States may be the only job that's tougher than being a school superintendent. Roy Romer will tell you that it's harder than being governor. John Stanford said it's harder than being a general. I know it's harder than running a big corporation.

More than a money problem or a people problem, I think we have a design problem. As the CLG team points out, superintendents have to run the system we have while leading the creation of the system we need. We group kids by age and march them through the same experiences through sixth grade assuming most will get what they need, then we increasingly allow them to assemble courses of optional degrees of difficulty taught by people who hardly know each other, much less the 150 kids they see every day. And we wonder why all kids aren't reaching high standards. This appeared to me to be primarily an architecture problem. With many of our early grants, I encouraged people to fix the architecture. Several years later many of those folks are stuck in architectural arguments and never got to the heart of the issue—teaching for learning. If, as this book suggests, you take the time to prepare and include, and then focus on improving instruction, you'll tackle the architecture as needed and do it with a sense of purpose. You'll have the momentum of engagement and improvement behind you when you get there.

Tony Wagner sent me a poem a few years ago that describes a great learning environment better than anything else I've read before or since. Rabindranath Tagore wrote it as a prayer for his country. It captures my hopes and aspirations for the schools and districts we work with.

> Where the mind is without fear
> And the head is held high,
>   Where knowledge is free;
> Where the world has not been broken
> Up into fragments by narrow domestic
>   Walls;
> Where words come out from the
> depth of truth;
> Where tireless striving
> Stretches its arms towards
>   perfection;
> Where the clear stream of reason
> Has not lost its way into the
> dreary desert sand of dead habit;
> Where the mind is led forward
> By thee into ever-widening
>   Thought and action—
> Into that heaven of freedom,
> My Father,
>   Let my country awake.
>                     Rabindranath Tagore, "Gitanjali 35"

Thank you for awakening and for reading this book. You must care about or be involved in educational leadership. Making systems of schools work for all kids is the most important economic development, social justice, and civil society issue of our time. It's complicated and difficult work, but it's the most important thing you could be doing with your life.

# PREFACE

The need for a dramatically more skilled and highly educated workforce in a global knowledge economy—combined with profound changes in students' and families' life circumstances—have created unprecedented demands on education leaders. Although it is increasingly clear that schools and districts must change fundamentally, not just incrementally, most leaders in education are understandably uncertain how they might go about their work differently.

Working to ensure that no child be left behind, struggling to overcome long-standing achievement gaps among racial and ethnic groups, dealing with the expectation that every school make progress annually—school leaders are being asked, in essence, to perform two very different jobs simultaneously.

Imagine being asked to rebuild an airplane—*while you are flying it*. Doing so would be difficult under any circumstances, but even more so if you—as all other hard-working, conscientious pilots—had received all your training in flying the plane *as it is*, rather than also learning how to transform the plane itself. Rebuilding it may require an entirely different set of skills.

Our goal in *Change Leadership* is to help school leaders, and leadership teams, better understand and develop the capacities needed to succeed at their second job of rebuilding the school system—while it operates. We offer a new *systems change* framework for education and a set of tools for leaders who are hard at work rebuilding the plane—while keeping it in the air, loaded with passengers.

The Change Leadership Group has spent the years since 2000 with school and district leaders from all over the United States—in urban, suburban, and rural districts; in districts with thirty-seven high schools and districts with one; in districts with decent financial resources and those forced to reduce personnel each year despite rising student populations. As different as these settings were, we never found an administrative team that was not working as hard as it could. What we've learned is that "improving our schools" on the scale now demanded cannot simply be added to the set of routine responsibilities and activities with which leadership teams in schools and districts are normally occupied. The problem is not lack of hard work, good intentions, or initiative.

We believe the successful leadership of transformational improvement processes in schools and districts requires sharpening capacities in two quite different directions at the same time:

1. Leaders need to see more deeply into why it is so hard for our organizations to change, even when there is a genuine, collective desire to do so. More than just seeing why, leaders need to learn how to take action effectively to help our organizations actually become what they need and want to be.

2. Leaders need to see more deeply into why it is so hard for individuals to change, even when individuals genuinely intend to do so. Beyond this merely diagnostic self-understanding, we as leaders need to learn how to take action effectively to help ourselves become the persons we need and want to be in order to better serve the children and families of our communities.

We must sharpen our capacities in both directions because, in the end, each depends on the other. It may be impossible for us to change at work in the ways we need to without new organizational arrangements, and it may be impossible to bring about significant changes in our organizations without considering deeply the possibility of our own change.

It is precisely this simultaneous attention to cultivating both a greater organizational savvy and a deeper self-awareness that distinguishes our approach. Not just ends unto themselves, these new forms of organizational and personal knowing are tightly linked to bringing about new results. We deliberately formed the Change Leadership Group to bring together an unusual collection of people knowledgeable about (1) the world of educational reform, (2) organizational development, and (3) adult learning because it was our judgment that many improvement efforts founder on the limitations of a naïve approach to the complications of either organizational or individual change or both. Our goal here is to clearly illuminate what we at the Change Leadership Group call the dual focus—simultaneously sharpening our outward and inward attention. Like any discipline, this dual focus can be learned and develops gradually over time. In *Change Leadership*, we present a variety of ways to help you develop it.

## HOW DOES *CHANGE LEADERSHIP* WORK?

As much as possible, we have structured this book to permit you to experience the kinds of learning we seek to promote in our "Learning Labs." To introduce another metaphor, we often refer to these three-day, interactive learning institutes as a kind of "school improvement fitness center." We invite leadership teams into a novel environment that will put them to work, individually and collectively, developing new muscles to accomplish their improvement goals.

A natural question is: What can you reasonably hope to accomplish through a single three-day visit to a fitness center? Obviously, the muscles are not going to be developed in that time. The more reasonable expectation is that you will meet a series of "machines" (tools for development), begin to familiarize yourself with how they work and how to use them, and experience a comprehensive workout routine. Truth be told, you might also expect to be a little sore after the first exposure from all the stretching. But adhere to your new routine, use the tools, and over time, you will develop new capacities.

This metaphor of the fitness center should help make clear both what this book is and what it is not. It is not another treatise—a ten-chapter analysis, argument, or illustration of what is "wrong with our schools." ("Here's why they don't work. Here's what they should look like. You take it from here.") Nor is it a point-to-point road map to guide you through an improvement process. Rather, it is a guide to help you develop the capacities that we believe—based on experience—will better enable you to lay down your own best road to the transformation of your school or district.

As a guide to the development of leadership capacities for transforming our schools (what we mean by "change leadership"), this book combines the conceptual with the practical, the thinking with doing. We present a set of practical concepts, invite you to "think about them by doing," and then, in your own change leadership work, to "do by thinking" of the concepts that will gradually become more familiar to you.

Our framework includes several concepts that we introduce one by one, in paired chapters. Throughout the book, you are invited onto different "exercise machines," each chapter exercising a different "muscle group" of the single "body." This is why we really mean it when we say that if you are tired after the work of one chapter, you should rest and recharge before you go on to the next. It is best to come to each chapter fresh and energized, because each is "working you out" in a different way. We urge you not to race through the book or merely skim for the developing ideas. Instead, take the time to assimilate the concepts and to complete the exercises. With this combined effort, you will develop the capacities to make full use of the concepts.

## HOW IS THE BOOK ORGANIZED?

In Chapter One, we provide background for the lessons of the book. We consider some of the fundamental economic and social changes of the last quarter century as they relate to education, and make the case that the nature of these changes transforms what has been described as the education "problem" from one of mere failure demanding "reform" to obsolescence requiring "reinvention." At the end of this chapter, we invite you to frame your school's or district's education "problem" as a challenge that you can work on throughout the book, using the tools in successive chapters.

In the four sets of paired chapters that follow, we describe key organizational improvement challenges for schools and districts. In these core chapters, we provide you with a series of diagnostic tools and exercises to help you identify more clearly what you want to work on in your school or district and how you can go about this work in a new way. To explore the dynamic, interdependent relationship between individual and organizational change, we describe the experiences of a superintendent, whom we call Arthur. We describe in detail how he uncovered—and worked to overcome—those personal beliefs and behaviors he discovered stood in the way of his being a more effective leader of educational change. We also provide stories from a variety of schools and districts across the country. In each of these chapters, we present a progressive series of exercises that can lead you to deeper insights into your own personal learning challenges as they connect to your school's or district's ability to improve. Separate exercises are designed to exercise your "outer" and "inner" attention, the organizational and personal learning aspects of the theme for each set of chapters.

Chapter Two makes the case for a laserlike focus on the improvement of teaching as the goal of a change process, and describes what a system that is designed for continuous improvement of instruction and instructional leadership might look like. The chapter is designed to help you assess the current status of your work related to improving teaching. In Chapter Three, we introduce the first step of an unfolding process designed to illuminate your own personal learning challenge, your inner challenge, as it relates to improving teaching and learning in your school or district.

Chapter Four takes up the question of what often gets in the way of change in schools and districts and, conversely, what generates the momentum and energy for successful initiatives. In Chapter Five, we ask you to take a second step in developing your personal learning curriculum by identifying what may be getting in the way of your working more effectively.

Chapter Six lays out a systemic model for thinking about the arenas of change in education and the ways in which they are interdependent and overlap as a system. We discuss competencies, conditions, culture, and context as necessary parts of transformation. In this chapter and in Chapter Seven, we help you create a sharper picture of your own system, organizationally and personally, to see more deeply into these outer and inner dimensions.

Chapter Eight outlines critical elements of a more strategic approach to the change work—starting and intervention points, and the sequencing of important steps. We describe the phases of a successful, sustainable change process, and we explore the importance of data, accountability, and relationships in each phase. These concepts are presented through case studies of two districts illustrating the different elements of our model and showing how they look in practice. Chapter Nine provides ways to help you work strategically at overturning your own individual immunities to change. It concludes with recommendations for how to enable success in your self-learning curriculum.

Chapter Ten explicitly brings together the two parallel outer and inner threads that we discuss throughout the book—the twin challenges of organizational change and personal growth. In this concluding chapter, we consider the implications of the dual focus for education leaders in the twenty-first century.

Throughout *Change Leadership*, we include diagnostic tools, exercises, and links to additional materials to further your understanding of both the system at large and your personal system. All the tools intended for individual use only are marked with an "individual" icon 🯄; many of the tools are also adaptable for group use, and where that is the case you will also find a group icon, which is your signal that, in Appendix A, you will find this same tool modified for use in groups or teams. It is our belief that you will gain more from this book if you actively engage the exercises included throughout the chapters. To aid this process, you can download full-page templates of each exercise that provide space for your own writing from both the Change Leadership Group (http://www.gse.harvard.edu/clg/ news1a.html; click on "Exercise Templates") and Jossey-Bass (http://www. josseybass.com/go/changeleadership). Additionally, because you might want to put colleagues or other district members on these "workout machines," we highlight a few exercises that we have learned may be especially challenging for an unskilled user to help a fellow first-time user with. We mark these exercises with a "caution" icon to signal the importance of your taking stock of your comfort and skill level with the material in order to decide whether to ask someone else to engage it. We also provide a variety of examples from our practice. When we identify people with their full name and affiliation it is with their permission. In other cases, either to preserve privacy or because the person is an amalgam of real people with whom we have worked, we have used a first name only. Appendixes provide exercises to use in groups, as well as a list of recommended readings, grouped by topic.

## HOW TO MAKE BEST USE OF THIS BOOK

We recognize that many people will read this book on their own and have therefore designed the activities so that they will be meaningful and valuable to the individual reader. But, for the same reasons that we strongly encourage people to come to our Learning Labs in teams, we encourage you to engage in this work together with others. You might form an ad hoc group, where you gather interested colleagues in your school or district and use this book as the focus of a study group. You can then all benefit from trying on ideas, learning from your discussions, and encouraging each other.

For those of you who are in a leadership team, we recommend that you and your whole team read *Change Leadership* together. Individually and as a group, you will get even more out of this book if you read it, complete all of the exercises, and take the time to collectively think through the implications of what you are learning for how to lead. This suggestion of a "group read" follows from our understanding that to meet the new challenge of reaching all students with new skills, we need to work in fundamentally new ways ourselves. No one person can solve this new challenge; neither can individuals working alone. We need each other, and we need to work together in new ways. Reading and learning together is a start.

Although you may already serve on some kind of central office or school-based management team, our observation is that meetings of these groups usually deal with administrative matters or "crisis management" rather than with the more substantive problems of change leadership—much in the way that most faculty meetings are often taken up with announcements rather than discussions related to improvement of teaching and learning. The work in education at every level remains highly isolated, compartmentalized, and increasingly crisis driven.

A central idea throughout this book concerns the way leadership teams themselves may need to reorganize the way they operate when they are at work on their second job—that of remaking the school or district at the same time they are running it. Because these groups will need to create new individual and organizational capacities (not merely apply existing capacities to a new task), they may need to reflect the features of a learning community, such as we see in the growth of teachers' professional learning communities, critical friends groups, or the Japanese lesson study process. But they need to be something more, as well.

Looking at the profound transformation in how work is organized in most other professions over the last quarter century, we can see additional qualities an effective team must have. From law to law enforcement, to business, to medicine, individuals increasingly work in teams to solve problems, improve services, and collaboratively create new knowledge. The simple reason why most work is now organized around team structures is that focused, disciplined groups are far more likely to generate a better result than can individuals working alone. Communities of practice—groups "bound together by shared expertise and shared passion for a joint enterprise"[1]—are increasingly used in a wide variety of workplace settings to enable individuals and organizations to learn new skills and processes and to identify and address ongoing problems of practice. According to Wenger and Snyder, communities of practice help drive strategy, start new lines of business (or inquiry), solve problems quickly, transfer best practices, develop professional skills, and recruit and train talent.[2]

Thus, the leadership teams we are advocating are not voluntary groups, nor are they focused on their own learning as an end unto itself. They exist to transform the larger system, the school or district. This may well require individual learning and change. But it is always tightly connected to their charge—to make something valuable happen in the schools or districts they lead. As such, they must also reflect the features of high-performing executive teams at work on transformational change. We call these new kinds of leadership groups, which combine the work of leaderly learning with effective execution for systemwide improvement, leadership practice communities.

However you approach the information we present, we welcome you. We hope you will experience us as with you all along the way, encouraging your workout. May *Change Leadership* work for you as a renewable resource—more than a structured single visit to the gym, a guide to a new kind of ongoing leadership practice.

### Endnotes

1. Etienne Wenger and William Snyder, "Communities of Practice: The Organizational Frontier," *Harvard Business Review* (January-February 2000): 139.
2. Ibid., 140–141.

## ACKNOWLEDGMENTS

Were it not for the bold generosity of the Bill & Melinda Gates Foundation, there would be no Change Leadership Group at the Harvard University Graduate School of Education. Because of the foundation's support, and particularly that of its director of education, Tom Vander Ark, an interdisciplinary team has been at work for the last five years seeking to develop practical knowledge that will be of immediate use to school leaders working at systemwide improvement. We thank Tom for his many contributions, especially his consistently constructive impatience, and his thoughtful Foreword to this book.

In developing and "field-testing" the change concepts and practical tools you will encounter in this book, our group became indebted to a host of colleagues and district settings. Although none should bear any responsibility for the limitations of what you will find here, all have contributed to strengthening our framework and the means for applying it.

In our first years we gathered two groups of distinguished practitioners to try on, react to, and make suggestions about our developing ideas. We met several times on either coast, and they came to be called our "West Coast Fellows" and our "East Coast Fellows." For their many contributions to our thinking and our spirits, we want to thank East Coast Fellows Rebecca Bradley, Gerry House, Steve Jubb,

Bob Mackin, Bob McCarthy, Gene Thompson-Grove, and Ron Walker; and West Coast Fellows Sally Anderson, Roger Erskine, Chuck Hayward, Judy Heinrich, Connie Hoffman, Kent Holloway, Jim Huge, Rick Lear, Michele Malarney, Judy Ness, Harriette Thurber Rasmussen, George Woodruff, and Leslie Rennie-Hill.

We also had the privilege of working over several years with the brave leadership teams of three generous districts that were willing to partner with us as "beta sites" to try on and test out earlier versions of the materials you will find here. We are deeply grateful to the school districts of West Clermont, Ohio; Corning, New York; and Grand Rapids, Michigan, and to all the leaders in each of these districts who became, in effect, our collaborators. We especially want to acknowledge our collaboration with West Clermont Superintendent Michael Ward and Assistant Superintendent Mary Ellen Steele-Pierce; Corning-Painted Post District Superintendents Donald Trombley and Judy Staples; Corning District's Quantum Leap Project Executive Committee, including Assistant Superintendent Ellen Robinson (Committee Chair), Billie Gammaro, Mike Ginalski, Cheryl Jordan, Rick Kimble, Bill Losinger, Mat McGarrity, and Bob Rossi; and Grand Rapids Superintendent Bert Bleke, Director of Organizational Learning Mary Jo Kuhlman, Deputy Superintendent Charles Sturdyvant, Chief Academic Officer John Harberts, and Chief Operations Officer Ben Emdin.

We learned a great deal from our relationship with "change leaders" from ten districts or district-serving organizations, each of which sent small, continuing teams to our Change Leadership Program, twice a year, a week at a time, over two years. We stayed connected with these leaders between "residencies" throughout the two years, and a form of this colearning network continues to this day. This group engaged and improved every concept and tool you will find in this book. We want to thank these colleagues from the Connecticut Center for School Change; the Corning-Painted Post Area School District of Corning, New York; Deer Park City Schools of Cincinnati; EdVisions, Inc., of Henderson, Minnesota; the Evergreen School District of Vancouver, Washington; Gloucester, Massachusetts, Public Schools; Hamilton County Public Schools of Chattanooga, Tennessee; Houston Independent School District; Kent Intermediate School District and Grand Rapids Public Schools of Eastern Michigan; and the Stonington, Connecticut, Public Schools.

Throughout our work we have been well served by a highly eclectic advisory board drawn from the worlds of practice and scholarship in the fields of education, business, organizational development, and leadership studies. We very much want to thank Advisory Board members Katherine Boles, James P. Comer, John E. Deasy, Linda Darling-Hammond, Richard F. Elmore, Linda Greyser, Ronald A. Heifetz, N. Gerry House, Michael Jung, Diana Lam, Katherine K. Merseth, Richard Murnane, Jerome T. Murphy, Pedro A. Noguera, Thomas W. Payzant, Hillary Pennington, Robert S. Peterkin, Robert B. Schwartz, Peter M. Senge, Nancy Faust Sizer, Theodore R. Sizer, Ron Walker, and Patricia A. Wasley.

We could not have done the work that led to this book without superior institutional support for the Change Leadership Group. We want to thank former Harvard University Graduate School of Education deans Jerome Murphy and Ellen Lagemann; former Programs in Professional Education leaders, Clifford Baden and Linda Greyser; and our own outstanding administrators over these years, Genet Jeanjean, Elena Demur, Kathrine Livingston, Shelley Lawson, and Rebecca Udler.

Our doctoral fellows, Dana Wright and Elizabeth Zachry, read every line of this book several times over and, through their suggestions, made the final product a better one. We are also very grateful to Lesley Iura at Jossey-Bass for the many ways in which she has expressed her belief in, and support for, this project and to freelance developmental editor Jan Hunter for her excellent work. Together, Lesley and Jan have helped make this book more readable and appealing to a broader audience.

Finally, we want to acknowledge the collaborative nature of our own work leading up to, and throughout, the creation of this book. Initially we drew conceptually on Tony Wagner's previous work on school improvement, and Robert Kegan and Lisa Lahey's previous work on adult learning (and where we borrow from those works most directly we indicate in the text). However, over our time together, *all* the authors contributed to reconstructions, elaborations, and modifications of the starting ideas until we collectively created a single integrative framework we are each certain no one of us could have brought about on his or her own. Every chapter has had multiple authors and been rewritten a number of times, and every author has weighed in on every part of the book. Because the book itself calls on its readers to try out new kinds of collaboration, we feel ethically bound to admit that our own collaboration has not always been easy, but we also want to say that, in the end, we have found it to be a rewarding one, and we hope you will find the result rewarding as well.

## ABOUT THE AUTHORS

**Tony Wagner** is codirector of the Change Leadership Group (CLG) at the Harvard Graduate School of Education. An initiative of the Bill & Melinda Gates Foundation, CLG prepares teams to be effective change leaders in schools and districts. Tony also consults widely with schools, districts, and foundations around the country and internationally and is senior advisor to the Bill & Melinda Gates Foundation. He is a frequent speaker and widely published author on education issues. Routledge Falmer recently published Tony's latest book, *Making the Grade: Reinventing America's Schools,* as well as a new edition of Tony's first book, *How Schools Change: Lessons from Three Communities,* with a foreword by Theodore R. Sizer. Before assuming his current position at Harvard, Tony was a classroom teacher for twelve years, a school principal, project director for the Public Agenda Foundation, cofounder and first executive director of Educators for Social Responsibility, and president and CEO of the Institute for Responsive Education. Tony earned his M.A.T. and Ed.D. at the Harvard University Graduate School of Education. His Web site for New Village Schools is http://www.schoolreinvention.org.

**Robert Kegan**, codirector of the Change Leadership Group, is the Meehan Professor of Adult Learning and Professional Development at the Harvard Graduate School of Education and educational chair of Harvard's Institute for Management and Leadership in Education. His research and writing examines the possibility of continued psychological development in adulthood, and its necessity if professionals are to deliver on the complex challenges inherent in twenty-first-century work. Kegan is author of *The Evolving Self: Problem and Process in Human*

*Development; In over Our Heads: The Mental Demands of Modern Life;* and (with Lisa Laskow Lahey) *How the Way We Talk Can Change the Way We Work: Seven Languages for Transformation.* The recipient of numerous awards and honors, including four honorary doctorates and the Massachusetts Psychological Association's Teacher of the Year award, he is also codirector of a joint program undertaken by the Harvard Medical School and the Harvard Graduate School of Education to bring principles of adult learning to the reform of medical education. A former junior and senior high school English teacher, Kegan is also an airplane pilot, a rabid poker fan, and the unheralded inventor of "the Base Average," a more comprehensive statistic for gauging a player's offensive contributions in baseball.

**Lisa Lahey** is associate director of the Change Leadership Group at the Harvard Graduate School of Education. Her current professional interests focus on adult development within school districts, and tightly connecting individual development with districtwide goals for improved student performance. Lisa coaches leaders on how to create, facilitate, and maintain conditions to support individual, group, and organizational development. She also coaches individuals and groups on transforming communications for improved collaboration, work performance, and decision making. She has extensive experience in designing and facilitating processes that promote deep adult learning and that serve organizational goals. Lisa's clients have included Lexington Public Schools, Acton Public Schools, the Fleet Initiative for Boston Public Schools, The Winsor School, McKinsey & Company, Columbia University Center for New Media Teaching and Learning, and The Dalton School. She is cofounder and senior consultant at MINDS AT WORK, a consulting firm specializing in school and workplace learning in the United States and Europe. A former principal and high school teacher, Lisa has also taught extensively in graduate school programs in several Boston-area schools and professional development programs. Coauthor of numerous articles on adult development, Lisa's first book, *How the Way We Talk Can Change the Way We Work: Seven Languages for Transformation* (coauthored with Robert Kegan), was published by Jossey-Bass in 2001. She earned her M.Ed./Ed.D. in human development from the Harvard Graduate School of Education.

**Richard W. Lemons** is associate director of the Change Leadership Group at the Harvard Graduate School of Education. In the field of education, Richard has been a high school teacher, a community college administrator, a researcher, a literacy coach, and a change coach/consultant. His current research and professional interests revolve around high school transformation, leadership development, and the large-scale improvement of teaching and learning. As a coach and consultant, Richard works with individual leaders and teams to assist them in being more reflective, purposeful, and strategic in their day-to-day work. In addition, he works with schools and school districts to develop systems for and a practice of instructional improvement.

Richard's clients have included Boston Public Schools, Boston Plan for Excellence, Massachusetts Department of Education, Connecticut (CT) Department of Education, Farmington Public Schools (CT), Stonington Public Schools (CT), Farmington Valley Superintendent's Association (CT), Connecticut Assistant Superintendent's Association (CT), Connecticut Center for School Change, Kent Independent Superintendents Association (MI), Pfizer, Inc., and Pick 'N Pay (South Africa). Richard is also the senior consultant for leadership development and school improvement at the Capitol Region Education Council (CREC) in Connecticut. Richard is the coauthor of "Leadership and the Demands of Standards-based Accountability," in *The New Accountability: High Schools and High-Stakes Testing*, published in 2003. He earned his M.Ed. and Ed.D. in administration, planning, and social policy from the Harvard Graduate School of Education.

A sixteen-year veteran teacher and founding member of the Change Leadership Group, **Jude Garnier** is currently director of adult learning at the Small Schools Project, where she helps support the learning of schools and districts in the state of Washington involved in significant reinvention funded by the Bill & Melinda Gates Foundation. She holds a Ph.D. in Educational Leadership/Systems from the Union Institute and University where her research focused on the transformation of schools and districts into learning communities.

**Deborah Helsing** is a senior program associate at the Change Leadership Group. In addition to lecturing at the Harvard Graduate School of Education, Deborah teaches the course Models of Teacher Decision Making, and coordinates the course Thinking Like an Educator. Her background in teaching includes primary school TESOL instruction and teacher training in the Kingdom of Tonga as well as secondary English literature and writing instruction at an alternative high school in

Kansas City. She holds an M.A.C. from the University of Michigan and an Ed.D. in Learning and Teaching from the Harvard Graduate School of Education.

**Annie Howell** is a senior doctoral fellow at the Change Leadership Group as well as an advanced doctoral student at the Harvard Graduate School of Education (HGSE). Her research as a doctoral student and her practice as a coach focus on adult development and transformational learning in the context of professional development. Annie also works for the Boston Public School District, where for five years she coordinated the Preparation for Principalship Program, and she is now a faculty member of the Boston Principal Fellows Program teaching the subject of adult learning to aspiring leaders. Before her work with the Change Leadership Group, Annie helped design and initiate an independent, expedition-based high school in Massachusetts called Shackleton Schools. At HGSE, she has been a teaching fellow for courses in Adult Development and Teaching and Learning, a facilitator for the Harvard Institute for School Leadership, and a cochair of the Harvard Educational Review where she coedited *Race and Higher Education: Rethinking Pedagogy in Diverse College Classrooms,* published in 2003. In the summer months, Annie leads adult sailing trips for Outward Bound off the coast of Maine. Annie holds a B.A. from Princeton University and a M.Ed. from Harvard Graduate School of Education.

**Harriette Thurber Rasmussen**'s commitment to build a new education system for the twenty-first century spans the past decade and the opportunity to interact and influence every level of the system—from the building to the statehouse and through public and private arenas. Her intimate work with one elementary school's seven-year restructuring effort offered a vision of possibilities and led to involvement in creating Washington State's standards and innovative performance assessment system. Its implementation has reconfirmed the caveats of whole systems change and the dangers inherent in high-stakes testing without adequate attention to the relationships on which student success is ultimately based. After participating in a six-year initiative to research the connection between collaborative staff development practices and student learning, she integrated her experiences into a focus on school and district redesign. Harriette currently serves as project coach for four Washington districts undergoing whole systems reinvention, an initiative funded by the Bill & Melinda Gates Foundation. She also acts as a senior consultant to the Change Leadership Group at Harvard University. Based in Portland, Oregon, she is author of numerous publications on parental involvement.

# Introduction: Reframing the Problem

O ur education system was never designed to deliver the kind of results we now need to equip students for today's world—and tomorrow's. The system was originally created for a very different world. To respond appropriately, we need to rethink and redesign.

In 1983 a government-appointed, blue-ribbon commission published a report entitled *A Nation at Risk* proclaiming a "crisis" in American public education. It described a "rising tide of mediocrity" in our country's public schools. It argued that America's economic security was threatened by a low-skill labor force that was no longer competitive in the global marketplace. The report launched a heated debate, inspiring three national summits on education where many of the nation's governors and business leaders met to discuss the education crisis. A bipartisan national consensus on the importance of ensuring that all students have access to quality schools and a rigorous academic program began to emerge, as did a host of new initiatives and reforms at the local, state, and national levels. By the early 1990s, "education reform" had become the top priority for state governments. And in 2001, with the passage of No Child Left Behind legislation, the federal government assumed unprecedented authority over our nation's public schools.

What has been the result of these efforts thus far? Data from the National Assessment of Educational Progress (NAEP) tests suggest some progress in raising students' math scores at all grade levels in the last dozen years. However, the data on our accomplishments in reading and writing are very sobering. A long-term analysis of the average reading scores of both elementary and secondary school–age students shows virtually no change since 1980.[1] And although writing scores increased slightly for fourth and eighth graders, the percentage of twelfth graders who scored "below basic" *increased* from 22 to 26 percent![2] More disturbing still are the data about the percentage of students who graduate from high school, the percentage of those who graduate "college-ready," and the persistent gaps in achievement among different ethnic groups. According to recent research conducted by Jay Greene and Greg Forster at the Manhattan Institute for Policy Research, in 2001 only about 70 percent of all high school students who started ninth grade in public schools actually graduated—a figure substantially lower than what has been assumed in the past and well below the graduation rates of half a dozen other industrialized countries. The graduation rate for Asian students was 79 percent; for white students, 72 percent; but barely 50 percent of all black and Latino students left high school with a diploma. Further, those who do finish high school are not necessarily college-ready. Only a little over a third of white and Asian students complete the necessary college preparation classes and possess the literacy skills required for success in college. Only 20 percent of black high school students and 16 percent of Latino students meet these qualifications.[3]

---

Do you know how the figures for your district stack up in comparison?

We find that many educators do not know the cohort graduation rates for their districts, perhaps for understandable reasons. Nonetheless, we think it is important that you be familiar with these numbers and how they compare with the national figures.

- How many students who begin ninth grade graduate within four years?
- How does your graduation rate for white and Asian students compare with that for black and Latino students?
- Do your graduation requirements match the entrance requirements for college in your state?

---

What you may well be pondering is this: Why has there been so little progress, despite all the good intentions and hard work of talented people, not to mention significant expenditures of time and money? It is our view that the "failure" of education reform efforts in the past twenty years is primarily the result of a misunderstanding of the true nature of the education "problem" we face. We focus here on the problem because, as Einstein reminds us, "The formulation of the problem is often more essential than its solution."[4] As we see it, the problem is less about a "rising tide of mediocrity" than about a tidal wave of profound and rapid economic and social changes, which we believe are not well understood by many educators, parents, and community members.

Misunderstanding the problem has, in turn, led to the selection of strategies at the national, state, and local levels that have not met the challenge head-on. To extend the analogy, we have been using gradualist strategies to solve the "slow-moving" problem of a "rising tide" when what is called for is a set of more dramatic and systemic interventions commensurate with the challenge of a tidal wave. The purpose of this chapter, then, is to reframe the education challenge so as to create a different understanding of the nature and range of solutions that are required for real results.[5]

## A KNOWLEDGE ECONOMY REQUIRES NEW SKILLS FOR ALL STUDENTS

In the 1970s, our graduation and college-readiness rates were even lower than they are today, but this was not considered a "crisis." It has become a crisis because of the nature of the skills needed in today's knowledge economy. Our economy has transitioned from one in which most people earned their living with skilled hands to one in which all employees need to be intellectually skilled if they hope to make more than minimum wage. In nearly every industry today, companies are hiring the most highly educated people they can find or afford. For the past decade, CEOs like David Kearns (*Winning the Brain Race*) and academics like Richard Murnane and Frank Levy (*Teaching the New Basic Skills* and *The New Division of Labor*) have described the significant competitive advantages of a highly educated labor force.[6] Employees must know how to solve more complex problems more quickly, and must create new goods and services if they are to add significant value to virtually any business or nonprofit organization, no matter what size. And those who don't have these skills are not being hired.[7]

Because this change came so quickly, many people are surprised to learn that the skills required in most workplaces today directly correspond to those that are needed for success in college. Although not all young people need to have a college education to get a decent job, employers are increasingly expecting that new employees will have skills comparable to students who do attend college. Figure 1.1, drawn from a 2002 Public Agenda Foundation study, shows the ranking of the skills and habits of mind in which high school graduates are *least* well prepared for

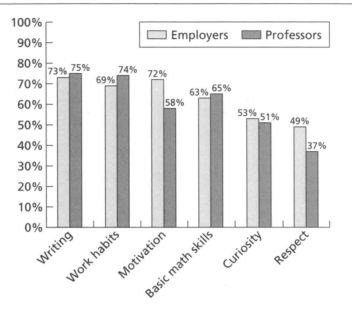

**Figure 1.1**

**Percentage of Employers and Professors Saying High School Graduates are Unprepared**

work and college.[8] Notice the agreement on the skills that employers and college professors now demand: writing, work habits, motivation, basic math skills, curiosity, respect. In light of this, the differences seem minor. For example, employers say that their new hires lack adequate skill in writing; college professors find that entering students do not write adequately. The difference is a mere 2 percent; even more striking is how high those percentages are: 73 and 75, respectively.

The competencies that academics and business leaders now demand are not just "the basics—the 3 R's." When they talk about good writing skills, for example, both groups are associating effective writing with a person's ability to reason, analyze, and hypothesize; find, assess, and apply relevant information to the solution of new problems; and, of course, write and speak clearly and concisely. All these, plus the ability to use a range of information and communication technologies, are the new literacy demands of a knowledge economy that go far beyond basic reading and writing skills. The math skills demanded, similarly, go beyond computation to include a working knowledge of statistics, probability, graphing, and spreadsheets. Finally, the expectation that young adults will come to college or the workplace knowing how to organize and motivate themselves to learn independently, do quality work, and team with others represents a shift toward the increasing importance of what Daniel Goleman calls emotional intelligence.[9]

In a new report written for the Educational Testing Service, Anthony P. Carnevale and Donna M. Desrochers summarize the key competencies needed by workers in today's new economy:[10]

- **Basic Skills:** Reading, Writing, and Mathematics
- **Foundation Skills:** Knowing How to Learn
- **Communication Skills:** Listening and Oral Communication
- **Adaptability:** Creative Thinking and Problem Solving
- **Group Effectiveness:** Interpersonal skills, Negotiation, and Teamwork
- **Influence:** Organizational Effectiveness and Leadership
- **Personal Management:** Self-Esteem and Motivation/Goal Setting
- **Attitude:** Positive Cognitive Style
- **Applied Skills:** Occupational and Professional Competencies

---

*The realities of today's economy demand not only a new set of skills but also that they be acquired by all students.*

---

So when studies reveal that the overwhelming majority of today's public high school students leave school "unprepared for college," they also indicate a lack of preparation to access most jobs in our economy and to assume responsible roles as informed citizens in a democracy. An eighteen-year-old who is not college-ready today has effectively been sentenced to a lifetime of marginal employment and second-class citizenship. The realities of today's economy demand not only a new set of skills but also that they be acquired by all students.

Although this information may not be new to you as an education leader, evidence suggests that there is a serious "perception gap" between majorities of high school parents and teachers, on the one hand, and professors and employers on the other. According to a recent Public Agenda Foundation national survey, 67 percent of high school parents and 78 percent of high school teachers believe that public school graduates have "the skills needed to succeed in the work world." However, only 41 percent of employers in the same survey thought that these graduates had what was needed to do well in the workplace.[11] This finding suggests that the first task in a successful systemic change process is to generate greater understanding and urgency for change (which we discuss in Chapter Eight).

## GREATER SUPPORTS FOR LEARNING IN A CHANGING SOCIETY

So we educators have a new challenge, one that could be considered both formidable and unprecedented in any context because we have not had to educate all students to this skill level before. But the problem we face extends even beyond the "all students, new skills" challenge. For when we ask teachers to name the greatest hurdles they face in classrooms, they talk most frequently about students who appear less motivated to learn traditional academic content and lack of family support for learning. More than eight out of ten teachers in a recent study cite as a serious problem "parents who fail to set limits and create structure at home for their kids and who refuse to hold their kids accountable for their behavior or academic performance."[12]

Strikingly, in this same study, a majority of parents agreed they need to be doing more to ensure that their children do their best in school. Many parents also say that supporting their children's learning is a significant challenge for which they feel largely unprepared. Despite the fact that more than 75 percent of all parents in one Public Agenda study reported being more involved in their children's education than were their parents, less than one in four agreed that they "know a lot about how to motivate their own children."[13] In another recent Public Agenda study, more than 75 percent of the parents surveyed said that raising children is a lot harder today, compared with when they were growing up.[14]

These findings point to profound changes in our society that have significant impact on teaching and learning: today's young people are growing up with a very different relationship to authority and self-control. First, in an increasingly consumer-oriented society, a substantial majority of parents agree that children are growing up overindulged and lacking in self-control and self-discipline.[15] Second, young people today show less deference toward authority. More than nine out of ten Americans surveyed agreed that young people's lack of respect for adults is a problem; more than half see it as a significant problem.[16]

At the same time, more and more children are growing up "home alone." With the increasing numbers of mothers who now hold full-time jobs outside the home and the high rates of divorce, the traditional two-parent, single-wage-earner family is fast becoming a relic of the past. In a landmark study of American adolescence, Mihaly Csikszentmihalyi and Reed Larson found that teenagers spent only about 5 percent of their free time in the company of their parents    and the majority of that time was spent with their mother.[17] Is it any wonder that young people who spend so little time in the company of their parents or other adults do not learn respect for authority? Similarly, how are today's youth supposed to understand the value of self-discipline and self-control without substantial contact with caring adults?

This is not to suggest in any way that today's students and families are at fault. In fact, growing up in an age of instant access to information, many of today's students know much more at an earlier age than their counterparts of a few decades ago, and they are certainly more adept at and motivated to learn new technologies than most adults. When interviewed in focus groups, the majority of high school students acknowledge that they are often bored in class, but they insist that they want to succeed and say they plan to attend college. Most adolescents today also say that in order to be motivated to learn and to do well in school, they need many more opportunities for hands-on learning, as well as closer relationships with their teachers, who can serve as academic coaches and advisors. Similarly, many parents welcome offers of help and advice on how to support their children's learning and attend school or church-sponsored parent support groups, when available.

This question of how to motivate all students to want to learn new skills is rarely raised in the national debate about education reform, even though students are very clear (when asked) about what motivates their learning. Overlooking this critical ingredient—motivation—to reforming education is, we believe, a serious omission. The reality is that students who lack self-control and who have less respect for authority are far more difficult to teach and to motivate by traditional means. Respect for authority and belief in the value of hard work have been the engines of school success for generations of students—engines that may no longer work in the same ways for many of today's young people. These are more pieces of the puzzle that must be considered in a full examination of the problem of a "failed" education system. Their omission often leads to finger-pointing and blame.

Indeed, terms like *fault* and *failure* obscure a clear view of the problem and, in fact, are part of the problem. Feeling victimized by the stigma of being part of a profession labeled by many as "failing," some teachers are quick to blame parents, students, and their colleagues (who must have ill-prepared their students in earlier grades), and the real problem often remains obscured. The important point here is that the economic transformation to a knowledge economy has been accompanied by deep-seated and less visible social changes that are having significant effects on students and families. These changes must be taken into consideration as we try to better understand the education challenge facing us. No one is to blame, and all of us who are concerned with education today need to work together to understand the new challenges for teaching, learning, and parenting in the twenty-first century.

---

*Terms like* fault *and* failure *obscure a clear view of the problem and, in fact, are part of the problem.*

---

## REFORM OR REINVENTION?
## TECHNICAL CHALLENGES VERSUS ADAPTIVE CHALLENGES

Up to this point, we have portrayed a multifaceted problem that contributes to and holds in place an education system that no longer fosters a healthy economy or democracy—or the individuals they are intended to support and represent. The hurdles of teaching *all* students *new* skills in this environment where there are more distractions and fewer supports for traditional classroom-based learning represent an extraordinary set of challenges for educators. Now add to this picture the profound shifts in both student and adult demographics of our public schools—such as the divide between a predominantly white teaching force and an increasingly diverse student body, and the high turnover rate of new teachers, nearly half of whom now leave the profession within the first five years—and one begins to understand how our education problem is much more one of obsolescence, in need of "reinvention," rather than failure, in need of mere "reform."

The almost universally used term "education reform"—besides having a punitive overtone—implies that, at some point in the past, things were okay in schools, and all that is needed to return to this former state is a set of improvements that are relatively minor in nature. Even "school improvement" suggests a need for only modest and incremental change. In reality, aside from the passage of charter school legislation, most of the popular state reform initiatives of the past decade attempt to create more accountability in public education, but they do not directly challenge the basic tenets of what leading, teaching, and learning in schools and districts should look like in the new context of the twenty-first century. The "system," then, is not being asked to function differently than it has in the past; it is only being asked to do better what it has always professed to do.

The basic assumption embedded in this definition of the challenge of change is that we already know how to teach all students new skills, and so the problem is primarily a technical one of improving the performance of the existing system. It is this assumption—this definition of the problem as being minor and technical in nature, with a solution that would leave the system virtually intact—that we question. America's system of public education, especially at the secondary level, was deliberately designed to be a sorting machine. The industrial economy of the twentieth century needed only a very small number of college-educated citizens, such as doctors and lawyers. It wasn't until the 1950s that half of our students received a high school diploma; even through the 1960s, the majority of midlevel managers in businesses did not have college degrees. Throughout the twentieth century, students who dropped out of high school were able to seek and hold good, stable jobs that paid a middle-class wage.

Now, the industrial economy and the kinds of relatively secure, well-paying, blue-collar jobs that it offered in such abundance have all but disappeared. Yet the system that prepares our young people for this very different world remains virtually the same as it was one hundred years ago. In fact, we have never educated all, or even most, students to the standard of "college-ready." It is not as if educators were doing this in earlier decades and then forgot how. The system has not "failed." It was designed perfectly to produce the results it needed, and attained. But if the results no longer meet our needs, it follows that the system does not either. Rather, it has become obsolete—much in the way that one-room schoolhouses became obsolete when we "invented" our current "factory model" schools for a new economic and social era at the turn of the twentieth century.

The problem we face is not just improving the performance of students who are not yet proficient in basic skills. We also do not know how to teach many of the "new skills" outlined by Goleman, Murnane, Carnevale,[18] and others to any of our students—even our "best and brightest." A new public school curriculum, assessments, and teaching methods for developing emotional intelligence and other such "soft" skills simply do not exist. And although one can find "random acts of excellence" in some classrooms and a few public high schools, successful strategies and systems that ensure all students graduate with the skills needed for work, college, and active citizenship remain to be developed and taken to scale.

What we have then is a new challenge—one for which there exists no adequate knowledge base on which school leaders can draw. Nor will there ever be a "base" that can be applied routinely to all situations. We have what Ron Heifetz calls an adaptive challenge.

In his work on public leadership, Heifetz makes a fundamental distinction between technical versus adaptive challenges.[19] A technical challenge is one for which a solution is already known—the knowledge and capacity exist to solve the problem. Meeting such challenges is not necessarily simple. Nor should the results be presumed to be trivial. Learning to remove a person's appendix is a remarkable feat. It may be hard to do, but by now an established and proven procedure exists to gradually teach someone how to do it. An "adaptive" challenge, on the other hand, is one for which the necessary knowledge to solve the problem does not yet exist. It requires creating the knowledge and the tools to solve the problem *in the act of working on it.*

Meeting technical challenges often involves changes within an existing paradigm, whereas meeting adaptive challenges involves reconception of the very paradigm in which one is working. IBM's Selectric typewriter in the 1960s was a dramatic technical improvement over the existing manual keystroke typewriter. But merely improving upon the Selectric typewriter would never have created the IBM personal computer (PC). The PC is much more than a "reformed typewriter." It is a reinvention of what composing in print is all about.

Breakthroughs require the creation of new technologies, which in turn necessitates the creation of new knowledge, all in response to a new context or societal need. Heifetz maintains that this creation requires organizations to look and act very differently. He points out that when individuals and organizations meet adaptive challenges they themselves become something different. It is not merely some new skill or capacity that has been "inputted" into the person or organization. The person or organization grows into a different form: it adapts. Transforming organizations to meet adaptive challenges and become knowledge-generating versus merely knowledge-using organizations—what Peter Senge calls learning organizations[20]—requires very different kinds of leaders—ones who recognize that they, as individuals, may have to change in order to lead the necessary organizational changes.

We believe the national education goal of "leaving no child behind" is a vital one for our country, for both economic and moral reasons. We also believe it is an adaptive challenge of great proportions, not yet well understood. Like Heifetz, we believe the adaptive challenge of reinventing American public schools versus merely trying to reform them has profound implications for those who lead them. This challenge requires all adults to develop new skills—beginning with leaders at all levels—and to work in very different ways. And *there is no school for leaders that will teach them exactly how to make their district into one that will leave no child behind.* Unlike a student pilot learning to land in a stiff crosswind, those who want to transform their schools and districts to meet this new aspiration are launched on an adventure with no flight instructor in the right-hand seat.

---

*There is no school for leaders that will teach them exactly how to make their district into one that will leave no child behind.*

---

As authors, we do not pretend to have all the answers, to be able to counter every crosswind or equipment failure. But through our work in the Change Leadership Group (CLG) with school and district leaders across the United States, we believe we've learned enough to be valued copilots in a common adventure. Our purpose in writing this book—in presenting its concepts and, perhaps more important, the tools and exercises that put those concepts to work—is to help those seeking to improve our schools and districts meet the adaptive challenge before us.

This challenge also suggests that we may need to confront some fundamental assumptions and behaviors about the nature of school, the nature of learning, and the nature of leading. In the remainder of this chapter, we highlight briefly a few of these organizational and individual beliefs before turning in successive chapters to explore them in depth.

## ORGANIZATIONAL BELIEFS AND BEHAVIORS

In our experience, organizations tend to hold a series of beliefs about how to address the need to teach all students new skills. Unfortunately, many of these beliefs can lead to behaviors that actually get in the way of making progress toward that goal. We have selected three such assumptions or beliefs to briefly illustrate this idea; these are covered in more detail in the course of the book.

### Responsiveness

Education systems believe they should respond to the ever changing, rapidly multiplying, and broadly diverse needs and demands of many constituent groups. Many of the best in our profession are quick to drop whatever they are doing whenever a student, parent, administrator, school board member, or local business comes with a request, demand, or suggestion. Traditionally, educators have considered this responsiveness a strength: it characterizes an organization that tries to be all things to all people—the historic mission of public education. But this belief in the value of responsiveness, and the accompanying behaviors it generates, has now become a weakness: it diminishes educators' ability to lead with purpose and focus—an essential requirement for realizing the new mission of all students, new skills.

All too often the work in individual classes, in schools, and in entire districts lacks continuity. Educators often do not have, nor do we push the community to set, real working priorities, to agree on what is most important. Many districts we see have ten (or more) priorities—which means, in fact, they have none. Without determining what is truly important, everything becomes urgent, and, in practice then, nothing is important. Without purpose and focus, how can educators work for the necessary systemic changes in teaching, learning, and leadership? Generate sustained attention on teaching all students new skills? Say "No" to well-meaning distractions that, however urgently advanced, will diminish the ability to deliver on that to which we have said "Yes"?

## Leading and Following

Education organizations value "getting along" in well-defined chains of command and believe leaders should have the answers. We educators are nice people, for the most part, and the majority of us get up in the morning wanting to make a difference in the lives of at least a few children. And, for the most part, we are clear about our roles. Leaders are expected to have answers and to take care of whatever gets in the way of doing what teachers love most—working with kids. Leaders are frequently expected to buffer teachers from any real or perceived meddling from either parents or the community. Teachers want to be asked for input from time to time but often grow weary of long meetings and generally want to focus their attention (and decisions) on what and how to teach. Parents are often a source of complaint and viewed as an excuse for student failure.

Meetings are often perfunctory, with announcements taking up most of the time. Their commitment to getting along means that educators tend to avoid conflict and thus rarely talk about what is required to meet the real challenges of teaching all students new skills. Too rarely do educators identify or solve problems of professional practice together or learn anything new about teaching, learning, and leadership. And too often, what little learning there is comes by listening passively to a one-time presentation on some reform *du jour*. Follow-through is predictably limited.

## Autonomy

Education as a profession has historically promised a relative degree of autonomy, compared with other professions. Indeed, education organizations have been structured to preserve domains of autonomy and individual craft expertise. Many of our best teachers take great pride in the units of study they create and refine by themselves over time—be it a fourth-grade Native American unit, an advanced placement biology class, or an innovative laptop computer program. These successes often become personal—even, perhaps, a source of identity—and it is understandably difficult for educators to open up their practice to scrutiny, share the fruits of their labors with colleagues, or seek constructive criticism from others. For this and other reasons, teachers rarely subscribe to a public, collective knowledge base of professional practice and norms, or engage in collaborative examination of teaching and learning practices.

Leaders, too, can be overly autonomous as each principal tends to his or her own franchise. Those who lead the elementary and middle schools, for example, often overlook what goes on in the high school even when the same students generally matriculate through the whole system. Similarly, high school principals rarely visit their colleagues' buildings. Yet it is often the interchange of these leadership practices that builds the possibility for every student's educational success and graduation.

## INDIVIDUAL BELIEFS AND BEHAVIORS

We have framed some organizational beliefs and behaviors that are traditional and historic to education: a mission that includes trying to please all constituents, a role-bound responsibility of the leader to identify and fix problems by him- or herself, and the right and nearly ubiquitous practice to teach and hone one's craft expertise in isolation, all within a context that values not rocking the boat. It follows, then, that organizations might tend to reward individual behaviors that are consistent with these organizational values and beliefs and sanction those that run contrary. This practice has been both our experience and our observation.

Some of the most highly effective leaders resist these norms by becoming "creative noncompliers." Deborah Meier is such an example. Despite having received international acclaim, including the MacArthur Foundation "genius prize" for her outstanding work in leading highly successful elementary and secondary schools in Harlem, throughout most of her career in the New York City Public Schools this school leader was treated as a pariah. And in Boston Public Schools, where she was a coprincipal, she was supposed to "ask permission" every time she left her building. (She never did.)[21]

### External Risks

The actions taken by education leaders like Meier to achieve success with their schools and districts challenge the status quo of education organizations and risk disturbing the very beliefs on which they were founded and which shape day-to-day behaviors. Their actions first, however, often represent changes in their own beliefs and illustrate the significant transformation required for most leaders and, ultimately, for everyone in the system.

Moving a school or district away from being highly reactive—trying to be all things for all people—and toward greater purpose, focus, and more systemic work to improve teaching and learning requires that a leader take calculated political risks—in effect betting that a certain theory of change and set of aligned strategies will improve student achievement. Leaders who publicly commit their school or district to a course of action with equally public expectations for improvement may provoke disappointment and disapproval of those constituent groups whose interests are no longer front and center. What if the improvements don't come or take longer than expected? Leaders will be held far more accountable than if they'd gone the traditionally safer route, responding to diverse constituents' requests and without short-term accountability measures. Leaders who act publicly and with purpose challenge individual behaviors and beliefs associated with a "responsive" system that continues to remain unfocused and largely unaccountable.

## Internal Risks

Weaning a school or district from collective habits of compliantly "getting along" and moving toward more active engagement in learning and problem solving also requires leaders to give up their role as "experts" who have all the answers. To fashion an organization that can generate the knowledge to teach all students new skills, leaders must confront and support individuals from all levels of the system in ways that enable deep understanding of the reasons for this challenge. Leaders must then find ways for these individuals to coconstruct solutions to their problems of practice.

Unaccustomed to these new roles and expectations, teachers and community members often express a mixture of suspicion and frustration with this new leadership style. Michael Ward, recently retired superintendent of the West Clermont Public School District in Ohio, describes how he began his work by stating at every teacher, parent, and community meeting that being an "average" district was no longer good enough. Over and over, he emphasized that he did not have the answers for the district—they were going to create them together. Finally, a teacher confronted him at a meeting: "Come on, Dr. Ward. We know you have a plan. Just tell us what you want us to do." He did not. Ward was breaking the mold of expected superintendent behaviors by steadfastly insisting that the organization had to meet this new challenge through a more collaborative process of dialogue and inquiry.

## ACCEPTING THE CHALLENGE AND THE RISKS: MOVING TOWARD COMMUNITIES OF PRACTICE VIA COLLABORATIVE LEARNING

As difficult as it is for positional leaders to sufficiently put aside their expertise and become collaborative public learners, we find that the greatest challenge for leaders of schools and districts may be to move their systems away from the highly autonomous work habits that can result only in "random acts of excellence" and toward accountable "communities of practice." Organizations that engage in ongoing dialogue around goals, priorities, and professional standards for individual and group performance intentionally foster the skills and norms that require everyone in the system to work more collaboratively and to be more accountable to one another. Everyone's work becomes more visible—beginning with the leader's. The leader models learning, teamwork, and openness to others' feedback—behaviors very different from those that are traditionally associated with school or district leadership.

When Kennewick, Washington, Superintendent Paul Rosier wanted the district to focus more on continuous improvement of teaching, he committed to spending the equivalent of one day a week in classrooms and actively participated in all teacher and administrator professional development programs. He made it clear that he, too, needed to learn what good instruction looks like and, more important, what the central office had to do to support teachers and principals in this work.

Superintendent Dale Kinsley's leadership of Bellingham, Washington, provides another illuminating example of how leaders can model collaborative learning. When Kinsley set out to create a system where coaching for improvement was the norm at every level, he began by working publicly with coaches himself. These coaches also conducted focus groups with teachers to better understand how he, personally, and the other district leadership could better meet their needs, improve communication, and build trust. Kinsley then met with the faculty at each school to discuss what he'd heard from the focus groups and what he would change. Throughout this process, he talked frankly about what he had learned through his mistakes and publicly acknowledged the value of the coaching he was receiving. Kinsley's behavior publicly challenged the belief that, as a leader, he had all the answers and did not need to improve his own practice. He also set a new communication pattern for the district, breaking as well the perception of an aloof superintendent who rarely interacts with teachers.

The leaders we've mentioned, and others whose stories we tell in the coming pages, are succeeding at improving student achievement in their classrooms, schools, and districts in part because of a personal commitment to become models of the kinds of change they seek for others. Working to change their own individual beliefs and behaviors and modeling these behaviors with their staff, these leaders have taken the first steps toward creating organizational cultures with a laserlike focus on the new challenge of success for all students. These are cultures rooted in new organizational beliefs and behaviors that support and adapt an organization to learn continuously. They are cultures that generate the new knowledge to systematically improve teaching and learning. They are cultures that sanction and support a different way of being to achieve a different end.

But what enabled these leaders to take their first courageous steps? Ward did not simply wake up one morning and decide to dramatically redefine the degree of control he needed to lead an improvement process. He did not just read an inspiring book with suggestions and examples of a new way to operate. Several years into our work together, Ward told us: "We set out to work on our schools and discovered that, in order to really succeed at it, we had to work on ourselves as well."

Ward began by acknowledging that he, as one individual, didn't have all the answers about how to improve learning in every classroom. He realized that if the district was going to meet this new challenge, he would need everyone's best thinking. And so he worked, first, to transform his administration from a group of individuals who were specialists and who rarely collaborated into a problem-solving leadership team. Over time, this group evolved into what we call a leadership practice community—leaders committed to helping one another solve problems of practice related to the district's teaching and learning challenges together.

Soon the leadership team realized the need to transform the ways in which principals worked together as well. First, the meetings with elementary principals, then all the principals, changed from a time for announcements to opportunities to learn together and to create new knowledge about how to improve teaching and instructional leadership. And in time, principals similarly transformed their meetings with teachers, as these new ways of working collaboratively cascaded through the organization. (This transformation progressed through three distinct phases, which we describe in Chapter Eight.) Theirs is a story of both individual and organizational change on behalf of improving all students' learning. You'll hear more of their and others' stories throughout *Change Leadership,* reinforcing the idea that adaptive change—reinvention—requires leaders who look both inward and outward and work on two very different kinds of transformation—their own and their school's or district's. The framework and the tools provided in the following pages will provide you with supports to help you on these two parallel journeys.

In this chapter, we explored some of the broader economic and social changes of the past quarter century and how these help us better understand—and reframe—the nature of the educational challenges we face. We argued that the challenges of transforming American public education are less about failure and reform than about obsolescence and reinvention. We reminded you that America's public schools were never designed to teach all students the new skills required for work, learning, and active citizenship in the new knowledge economy, and we proposed the need to invent a system that can educate all students for success in the twenty-first century. This is an adaptive problem, one in which the necessary knowledge to solve the problem must be created in the act of working on it.

So now it's your turn to focus on your own classroom, school, or district setting. We suggest that you not go on to Chapter Two until you have actively contemplated the questions posed in Exercise 1.1. If you are part of a study group—or a nascent leadership practice community among change leaders coming together to discuss this book—you will want to use the group version of this exercise, found in Appendix A, before reading further in *Change Leadership.*

---

 **Exercise 1.1: Identifying the Problem**

### Step One

Reflect individually on the following questions:

1. From your vantage point in the classroom, school, or district office, what do you see as the greatest challenge you and your colleagues face related to improving your "system" in response to the new challenges we face in education? What is the number one problem you are trying to solve?

2. What are some of the organizational changes required to solve this problem? What practices, structures, or policies may need to change in classrooms, schools, and districts in order to solve this problem?

3. Are there organizational and individual beliefs and behaviors associated with this problem that may need to change, beginning with your own? From what to what?

4. Finally, what might be some of the implications for leadership at your particular level to solve this problem? What might you, as a leader or group of leaders, have to do differently?

## Step Two

Take the time to write down your responses to these questions and to list any additional questions that come to mind. Then put this sheet in a safe place; we will ask you to refer to it later.

## Endnotes

1. Patrick L. Donahue, Mary C. Daane, and Wendy S. Grigg, *The Nation's Report Card 2003: Reading Highlights*. NCES Publication No. 2004-452 (Washington, D.C.: U.S. Department of Education, Institute for Education Sciences, National Center for Education Statistics, 2003). http://nces.ed.gov/nationsreportcard (accessed October 12, 2004).

2. Hillary R. Persky, Mary C. Danne, and Ying Jin, *The Nation's Report Card: Writing 2002*. NCES Publication No. 2003-529 (Washington, D.C.: U.S. Department of Education, Institute for Education Sciences, National Center for Education Statistics, 2003). http://nces.ed.gov/nationsreportcard/writing/results2002/natachieve.asp (accessed October 12, 2004).

3. Jay Greene and Greg Forster, *Public High School Graduation and College Readiness Rates in the United States* (New York: Manhattan Institute for Policy Research, 2003).

4. As quoted in *The Evolution of Physics* (New York: Free Press, 1967), 92.

5. Much of this analysis of "the problem" draws from chapter 1 of Tony Wagner's *Making the Grade: Reinventing America's Schools* (New York: RoutledgeFalmer, 2002).

6. Dennis Doyle and David Kearns, *Winning the Brain Race* (Oakland, Calif.: ICS Press, 1988); Richard J. Murnane and Frank Levy, *Teaching the New Basic Skills: Principles for Educational Change to Thrive in a Changing Economy* (New York: Free Press, 1996); Richard J. Murnane and Frank Levy, *The New Division of Labor: How Computers are Creating the Next Job Market* (Princeton, N.J.: Princeton University Press, 2004).

7. Jamshid Gharajedachi, *Systems Thinking: Managing Chaos and Complexity* (Burlington, Vt.: Butterworth-Heinemann, 1999).

8. Jean Johnson and Ann Duffett, *Reality Check 2002* (New York: Public Agenda Foundation, 2002).

9. Daniel Goleman, *Emotional Intelligence: Why It Can Matter More Than IQ* (New York: Bantam Books, 1997).

10. Anthony P. Carnevale and Donna M. Desrochers, *Standards for What? The Economic Roots of K-16 Reform* (Princeton, N.J.: Educational Testing Service, 2003), 40.

11. Jean Johnson and Ann Duffett with Jackie Vine and Leslie Moye, *Where We Are Now: 12 Things You Need to Know About Public Opinion and Public Schools* (New York: Public Agenda Foundation, 2003).

12. Johnson and others, *Where We Are Now*, 16.

13. Steve Farkas, Jean Johnson, and Ann Duffett with Claire Aulicino and Joanna McHugh, *Playing Their Parts: Parents and Teachers Talk About Parental Involvement in Schools* (New York: Public Agenda Foundation, 1999), 28.

14. Steve Farkas, Jean Johnson, and Ann Duffett with Leslie Wilson and Jackie Vine, *A Lot Easier Said Than Done* (New York: Public Agenda Foundation, 2002).

15. Although 83 percent of all parents state that it is essential their children learn self-control and self-discipline, only a third say they have succeeded in instilling these values, and half of higher-income parents surveyed agreed that giving their children too much was a problem in their family (Farkas and others, *A Lot Easier*, 2002).

16. Johnson and others, *Where We Are Now*.

17. Mihaly Csikszentmihalyi and Reed Larson, *Being Adolescent* (New York: Basic Books, 1984).

18. Goleman, *Emotional Intelligence*; Carnevale and Desrochers, *Standards for What?*; Murnane and Levy, *Teaching the New Basic Skills* and *New Division of Labor*.

19. Ronald Heifetz, *Leadership Without Easy Answers* (Cambridge, Mass.: Harvard University Press, 1994).

20. Peter M. Senge, *The Fifth Discipline* (New York: Currency Doubleday, 1994).

21. Communicated in conversation to Tony Wagner, Cambridge, Mass., October 25, 2003.

**PART ONE**

# Improving
# Instruction

# Creating a Vision of Success

I f the problem you identified at the end of Chapter One was directly related to the *act* of teaching all students new skills—in other words, improving instruction—or leadership on behalf of improved instruction, you may be surprised to learn that you are in the minority. And we're right there with you.

We firmly believe that creating a system focused on the ongoing improvement of instruction must be the central aim of any education improvement effort. It is our "theory of change" that students' achievement will not improve unless and until we create schools and districts where all educators are learning how to significantly improve their skills as teachers and as instructional leaders. In a way, it seems to be a statement of the obvious: our core business is teaching, and our product is student learning. The only way we can improve our product is to get better at our core business.

And yet, having conducted the activity shown in Exercise 1.1 with numerous teams from districts around the country over the past four years, we can say that the challenges participants mention most frequently include:

- Getting "buy-in" from one or more groups—often veteran or high school teachers
- Aligning the curriculum for greater coherence and consistency
- Seeking more family involvement or community support for schools and districts

Efforts to reduce class size, create academic standards, improve curriculum and assessment, increase teacher and community support for reforms, create smaller high schools, and so on are all useful—even necessary. By themselves or in combination, however, they do not lead to improvements in teaching and learning. Unless and until there is a focus on how to develop the teaching skills required to help all students meet more rigorous standards and master the curriculum (and all teachers use assessments to improve instruction), student achievement is unlikely to improve more than marginally. And unless and until there is an understanding of how to organize schools and districts for the continuous improvement of teaching, learning, and instructional leadership, smaller classes and other structural changes will not be enough to ensure that all students learn new skills and graduate from high school college-ready, or are able to take up employment in a twenty-first-century workforce.

## CHALLENGES TO IMPROVING INSTRUCTION

There are a number of historical and cultural reasons why many schools and districts tend to shy away from issues that directly relate to improving classroom instruction. Richard Elmore, who has written extensively about this problem, argues that education administrators' central function has traditionally been seen as "the management of the structures and processes" in schools. Not only have the administrators remained uninvolved in curriculum and instructional matters, they have historically prevented "outsiders" from engaging in the inspection, interference, or disruption of instruction.[1]

Decisions about curriculum and instruction have historically been left to the teachers. In fact, many teachers are attracted to the profession because of the relative "autonomy" it offers. Individual teachers work in isolated rooms all day with groups of children—and largely without any form of supervision. They are not expected to work together to define or discuss what is good instruction and so lack both experience and a common language for this work. The profession therefore lacks processes for creating craft knowledge. This reflects, and tends to perpetuate, a tacit but widely prevailing belief among many educators that teaching *is* more an "art" than a craft, meaning a set of skills that can be learned from others or improved upon with help from the "system." Thus, each teacher is left "to invent his or her knowledge base—unexamined, untested, idiosyncratic, and potentially at odds with the knowledge from which other teachers may be operating."[2]

In the last decade, a number of education critics—especially those advocating a system of educational vouchers or charter schools—have argued that the most significant barriers to educational improvement are political or structural: state laws, union contracts, education bureaucracies. All these, indeed, may represent obstacles, but removing them will not necessarily bring about the results we seek for students. One member of the Change Leadership Group (CLG) had significant experience helping found and lead the board of a well-known urban charter school—a school that was largely freed from state and district mandates and that had neither unions nor bureaucracy. After five years, however, despite the best of intentions and great expenditures of energy and talent, the quality of teaching and student achievement at this school was not significantly better than that seen in the district's conventional public schools. Nationally, there are not yet any undisputed data that make the case that charter schools are getting better results than conventional public schools with comparable populations of students

At the other end of the spectrum, several of the authors have taught in some of the nation's most elite private schools and, in the absence of government or union interference, saw mediocre teaching and no systemic strategies to improve instruction. (Indeed, some researchers are now asking for evidence of "value added" in our most acclaimed independent or suburban public high schools, where students enter already achieving at high levels. When these students leave four years later, there is often little evidence that the teaching has had much, if any, impact on these highly motivated learners.)

---

*Most of us in the profession of education have never been part of a system or community of practice dedicated to continuous improvement.*

---

Teaching and instructional leadership in many schools—both public and private—is often mediocre, and this is the central problem that must be addressed if we are to improve student achievement. We do not believe that those who enter the profession are less skilled or less dedicated than those who choose other professions. Nor do we believe that teaching and instructional leadership are "art" forms that cannot be learned or improved upon. Rather, we observe that most of us in the profession of education have never been part of a system or community of practice dedicated to continuous improvement. Many of us, in fact, have not experienced powerful instruction or effective school leadership in our own school and college years and so have few examples of what "goodness" might look like. Our work conditions often thwart professional learning and reflection.

Imagine that you wanted to improve your skills in playing an individual sport or a musical instrument, but you had never seen any examples of good performance. Imagine further that there was no one you could call to coach you, and so all you did was practice alone all day, every day. Such is the fate of most educators—both teachers and school and district leaders—in America today. How then are we supposed to get better at what we do? As we emphasize throughout this book, we believe both outer and inner work are needed—and we offer steps along the way. First, take a moment to complete Exercise 2.1.

 **Exercise 2.1: Refine Your Problem Statement**

This exercise builds on Exercise 1.1, which you completed at the end of Chapter One.

### Step One

Ask yourself the following questions:

1. How clearly does your problem statement recognize the quality of instruction and its relationship to student learning?
2. What do you think the impact on instruction will be if your problem is solved?

### Step Two

If you have named goals such as curriculum alignment, better communication, and the like (what we believe are peripheral goals), we suggest you name the specific links that connect that goal to the ultimate results you seek in student learning. Improving instruction may turn up somewhere in that chain. Or you may wish to think about another problem or challenge that is more directly related to instruction and then consider, or discuss with your group, what ideas you have about how to improve instruction.

### Step Three

When you have finished, compare your ideas with the overview provided in the section entitled "Seven Disciplines for Strengthening Instruction."[3] This section describes what we think a system focused on continuous improvement of instruction might look like.

## SEVEN DISCIPLINES FOR STRENGTHENING INSTRUCTION

Undeniably, there are great teachers in every school district in America. There are also examples of outstanding individual schools, led by highly effective individuals. Districts as diverse as Lancaster, Pennsylvania, and New York City's Community School District 2 have pioneered a set of practices, implemented in their own unique ways. However, we don't yet have an education system that can produce dependably proficient teaching in every classroom, in every school, day in and day out. And we've not yet seen a K–12 school district where every school is steadily improving student achievement from one year to the next. In other words, we do not know how to bring "to scale" the pockets of excellence (or even dependable competence) that have characterized our education system.

What might a system of schools look like that is focused on developing the skills of all its teachers and leaders? What are the design principles of school networks or districts where all faculty are continuously improving their practice? Since 2000, we have been documenting strategies used to improve teaching in those few districts that have dramatically raised the level of student achievement for all students—including those in the lowest quartile and those from the most at-risk populations.

We have identified seven practices that we believe are central to a successful systemic instructional-improvement effort:

---

The Seven Disciplines for Strengthening Instruction

1. Urgency for instructional improvement using real data
2. Shared vision of good teaching
3. Meetings about the work
4. A shared vision of student results
5. Effective supervision
6. Professional development
7. Diagnostic data with accountable collaboration

---

The Seven Disciplines for Strengthening Instruction should not be interpreted as a blueprint or a checklist. They are, rather, an outline of a *system* of processes and intermediate goals that contribute to the improvement of teaching and instructional leadership and, therefore, student achievement. In the following sections, we discuss each of the seven disciplines in turn; we build on them throughout the book.

## Urgency for Instructional Improvement Using Real Data

As part of this discipline, the district creates an understanding and sense of urgency among teachers and the larger community around the necessity of improving all students' learning, and it regularly reports on progress. Data are disaggregated and are transparent to everyone. Qualitative data (for example, from focus groups and other interviews), as well as quantitative data, are used to understand students' and recent graduates' experiences of school.

This discipline is a stretch for some, because many districts use either the "hide and seek" approach to data or the reverse—flooding people with so much information that they drown in it. By contrast, when Vicki Phillips became the superintendent of Lancaster's schools, she chose a single piece of data to disseminate throughout the community: the number of students who read at grade level by fifth grade. Then she took students to meetings of community and civic groups— the Lions Club, the local chamber of commerce, and so on—all over town to dramatize the data. She explained that only two out of ten students in the district met the reading standard when they left the fourth grade. She requested that eight of the ten students standing on stage with her sit down, asking the audience, "Which eight of our students will we leave behind?" She would then stand by the eight sitting students and ask, "Which of you wants to explain to the parents of these eight kids what has happened to their children and what it will mean for their futures?" Hers was a vivid and powerful, if painful, presentation of data that mobilized the community toward action.

Very often, we find that gathering and sharing qualitative data can create more urgency for change than numbers alone. When we began working with the West Clermont School District, for example, several student focus groups revealed that students longed for teachers who were more respectful of them and who offered more challenging, hands-on learning activities. Mark Peters, principal of one of the high schools at the time, told us the story of his personal conversion to high school "reinvention" during such a focus group, when one of his most at-risk students demanded: "When is it *my* turn to get a good teacher like the honors kids get? One who will answer my questions and care about my learning?"

## Shared Vision of Good Teaching

Achieving a shared vision of what is good instruction is much more difficult than most people imagine. Districts often think there is a common definition of good instruction because all teachers may have attended workshops on particular theories of learning or techniques such as cooperative learning. But there are very few districts in which school and central office administrators, when asked to independently rate a videotaped lesson and provide reasons for their ratings, will find their ratings more or less aligned.

In our work with educators across the country, we use several videotapes of high school English and middle school social studies teachers in action. When we ask participants to grade the same lesson and discuss their criteria, we find that the grades given range as widely as A+ to F. And in the subsequent discussions of the tapes, there is little agreement about the criteria of good teaching. Nor is there a shared vocabulary that would create structure for discussion.

## Meetings About the Work

Ideally, under this discipline, all adult meetings are about instruction and model good teaching. Yet in most school and district meetings, the craft of teaching is rarely a subject of discussion. Regardless of their frequency, meetings most often address announcements and operations—the administration of the work—rather than the work itself—instruction. By contrast, at the San Diego School District's Leadership Academy, meetings conducted at every level of the organization focus on instruction, and often start with school learning walks or demonstration lessons as a prelude to discussions of good teaching and effective teacher supervision. Announcements and the like are usually dealt with through memos. Elaine Fink, who headed the academy until her retirement in 2004, videotaped her meetings with district superintendents (now called instructional leaders) to analyze their content and the extent to which the meetings themselves were models of good teaching.

## Shared Vision of Student Results

With a shared vision, there are well-defined performance standards and assessments for student work at all grade levels. Teachers and students understand what quality work looks like, and there is consistency in standards of assessment. For years, the accepted wisdom was that aligning and improving curricula in districts would improve teaching. Although this work has value, it is less important than discussions that align the standards for student work. It matters less that teachers in a district agree on which books will be covered at different grade levels than that they agree about how students write about what they read and about the expected standards for student work at all grade levels. Student work provides indispensable data for understanding whether these standards have been met and determining the effectiveness of a lesson. A teacher may have taught an apparently coherent and thoughtful lesson, but the real question is what students know and are able to do as a result of the lesson.

---

*A teacher may have taught an apparently coherent and thoughtful lesson, but the real question is what students know and are able to do as a result of the lesson.*

---

### Effective Supervision

Under this discipline, supervision is frequent, rigorous, and entirely focused on the improvement of instruction. It is done by people who know what good instruction looks like. Effective supervision is rare in most districts. Too often, an annual, perfunctory visit by an administrator—who may or may not have clear ideas about what good teaching should look like—is all that passes for supervision. Too often, a major preoccupation of administrators is whether a teacher has "classroom management" skills, as measured by quiet and compliant students. Too few administrators assess the level of rigor in the classroom or whether students are learning what the teacher is trying to teach. Even fewer have learned how to effectively coach teachers for improvement. New York City's District 2, one of thirty-two community school districts in the city, stands in direct contrast.[4] As but one example of effective supervision, when he was superintendent, Anthony Alvarado conducted quarterly school learning walks with every building principal to discuss each individual teacher's work. Principals developed Individual Education Plans for each teacher, and Alvarado expected to see steady improvement from all teachers with each visit.[5]

## Professional Development

Professional development is primarily on-site, intensive, collaborative, and job-embedded, and it is designed and led by educators who model the best teaching and learning practices. During the first five years of Alvarado's superintendency, improving literacy instruction was the only professional development priority in District 2. Alvarado reasoned that if students could not read well, then they were unlikely to succeed in any subject. He and his colleagues had searched the world for the very best literacy teachers to lead these efforts, and imported a group of teachers from New Zealand. With their help, every teacher in the district learned how to teach literacy within his or her respective discipline, and test scores improved across all subjects. As of this writing, District 2 remains one of the very few districts in the country to have significantly raised the achievement levels of nearly every student. When the district then turned its attention to improving math proficiencies, it was able to equal the successes of the literacy work in only two years. How? The capacities and confidence of the system had been fundamentally improved. A key component to the system was the recruitment and training of the best teachers to work part of each school day on instructional improvement with small groups of teachers in their own buildings. Phillips pursued a similar strategy in Lancaster, with equally impressive results.[6]

The successes in District 2 and in Lancaster are in direct contrast to many districts, in which time and money for professional development are used ineffectually and sporadically. It seems clear that professional development activities must be aligned to a few carefully chosen improvement priorities that are informed by and monitored with data.

## Diagnostic Data with Accountable Collaboration

Data are used diagnostically at frequent intervals by teams of teachers, schools, and districts to assess each student's learning and to identify the most effective teaching practices. There is time built into schedules for this shared work. This type and use of data is very different from what is required to create understanding of the need and urgency for change. Highly effective districts administer *diagnostic* assessments four to six times a year at every grade level in reading, writing, and math. The tests are scored internally for quick turnaround, and the results are used to track each student's learning progress so that early interventions can be made. Teams of grade-level teachers, as well as whole school faculties, are then given time to study the data. When one teacher's scores are better than his or her colleagues', the team works to understand which teaching practices may be getting these results, rather than stigmatizing an "underperforming" (or "overperforming") teacher.

## USING THE SEVEN DISCIPLINES

These seven disciplines are not a buffet, where a district can choose one or two for implementation without regard to the others. Rather, they represent an interdependent systems approach to the improvement of instruction. Although one or two may be your most logical entry point, each ultimately affects and supports the others. None can be skipped, and some necessarily come first. For example, few educators may feel the need for (and thus truly engage in) extended discussions of good teaching if the urgency of continuous improvement has not been well established. Definitions of good teaching are incomplete if they do not include data about student work. Effective supervision both requires a shared vision of good teaching and standards for student work and is driven by a variety of diagnostic data. The same data also inform planning for effective professional development and the content of school and district meetings.

*These seven disciplines are not a buffet, where a district can choose one or two for implementation without regard to the others.*

Before you read further, we encourage you to use the diagnostic tool provided in Exercise 2.2 to assess how you think your school or district rates on efforts to implement the Seven Disciplines for Strengthening Instruction. These indicators can serve as powerful discussion prompts and build a shared idea of what is, and what needs to be. The evidence you identify will also help direct your efforts. You can use the diagnostic with different groups—principals, teachers, and central office administrators—to see to what degree views differ and can be usefully explored. And you can periodically reuse the diagnostic as an informal assessment of progress.

## Exercise 2.2: Take Stock: Your Seven Disciplines for Strengthening Instruction

### Overview

This diagnostic tool can help you assess your efforts to implement the seven disciplines. You can also repeat it periodically to assess progress in these areas.

Evaluation:

1. The district or school creates understanding and urgency around improving all students' learning for teachers and community, and it regularly reports on progress.

   - Data are disaggregated and transparent to everyone.
   - Qualitative (focus groups and interviews) as well as quantitative data are used to understand students' and recent graduates' experience of school.

   Not yet started   1   2   3   4   Well established

Evidence:

2. A widely shared vision of what is good teaching is focused on rigorous expectations, relevant curricula, and respectful relationships in the classroom.

   Not yet started   1   2   3   4   Well established

Evidence:

3. All adult meetings are about instruction and are models of good teaching.

   Not yet started   1   2   3   4   Well established

Evidence:

4. There are well-defined standards and performance assessments for student work at all grade levels. Teachers and students understand what quality work looks like, and there is consistency in standards of assessment.

   Not yet started   1   2   3   4   Well established

Evidence:

5. Supervision is frequent, rigorous, and entirely focused on the improvement of instruction. It is done by people who know what good teaching looks like.

   Not yet started   1   2   3   4   Well established

Evidence:

6. Professional development is primarily on-site, intensive, collaborative, and job-embedded and is designed and led by educators who model best teaching and learning practices.

   Not yet started   1   2   3   4   Well established

Evidence:

7. Data are used diagnostically at frequent intervals by teams of teachers to assess each student's learning and to identify the most effective teaching practices. Teams have time built into their schedules for this shared work.

Not yet started    1    2    3    4    Well established

Evidence:

---

Completing the diagnostic provided in Exercise 2.2 on your own should help you clarify some of your own ideas; it may also raise new questions for you. We have found the diagnostic to be even more powerful when individuals share their assessment with others on their team. The valuable conversations that result continue to clarify each individual team member's understanding of the disciplines themselves and lead to group agreement about the most promising areas for further work in your school or district.

## LAUNCHING AN INSTRUCTIONAL IMPROVEMENT SYSTEM: THE CRITICAL FIRST CONVERSATIONS

We have argued that in order to tackle the new education challenge of teaching all students new skills we need to create systems focused on the continuous improvement of teaching, learning, and instructional leadership. At the heart of these new systems are ongoing discussions of instruction—what is good teaching? how do we know it when we see it? and how do we continuously improve the skills of teachers and their supervisors? But, as we have already observed, we lack experience in and a vocabulary for such discussions. If good instruction—in every classroom and for all students—is the goal of systemic change in education, how does one define "goodness"? What constitutes great—or even competent—teaching? Perhaps more important, how do we launch discussions about what is effective instruction? Because this is such an important and thorny question for so many schools and districts, we now turn our attention to a more in-depth discussion of the second discipline goal of "creating a widely shared vision of good teaching" and the issues it raises.

## DEVELOPING A SHARED VISION

Although it is important for educators to understand how researchers have come to define the elements of good instruction, we have found that no robust improvement process can succeed without first respecting the fact that all practitioners in the system have their own beliefs about what constitutes good instruction. How does one begin a constructive conversation among faculty about quality teaching, one that results in an urgency to continue the conversation and a desire to develop a shared understanding? In other words, how might we begin to practice the first two of our seven disciplines, on which all the others depend?

> *How does one begin a constructive conversation among faculty about quality teaching, one that results in an urgency to continue the conversation and a desire to develop a shared understanding?*

As part of a groupwide activity with exactly these aspirations, we had more than one hundred district teams watch fifteen minutes of a tenth-grade English lesson.[7] Although you may eventually want to use a video clip from an actual class in your school or system, we have found that this clip regularly sparks genuine conversation, exposing differences among our ideas of what constitutes quality instruction. These differences are most noticeable when there are many (twenty-five or more) people discussing the same lesson. However, important differences are likely to emerge in much smaller groups as well. To experience this as a *solo reader,* see Exercise 2.3; if you are part of a group, use the group version found in Appendix A.

---

### Exercise 2.3:  Grade the Videotaped Lesson

#### Overview
To "observe" this teaching excerpt taken from a tenth-grade English class, go to our Web site, http://www.gse.harvard.edu/clg/, and view it with Internet video streaming. (Click on "News & Resources" on the main page and then the link for the "Change Leadership Book and Videos.") Our Web site also includes a video of a sixth-grade social science lesson that some readers may want to view instead of or in addition to the first video.

## Step One

Observe the video (up to the place where the teacher says to the students, "Now go to it"). Then, answer the following question:

*If you had to grade the lesson (from F to A, with plusses and minuses allowed), what would that grade be?*

## Step Two

Having made your decision, now think about what criteria you used for the grading. This is "no fault" work—there are no right or wrong answers—you just need to examine what evidence led you to give the lesson the grade you did, whether high or low.

## Step Three

Consider how those criteria might compare with those your colleagues might use. Or how those criteria might have changed for you over the years.

If you can perform this exercise in a group setting, or even with one trusted colleague, the range of responses you will find may surprise you.

---

We have done this exercise with groups of ten and groups of seven hundred (leadership teams from each of a district's K–12 schools and the central office, teams from all the middle and high schools in a state), and we have never found a group without a significant spread. Typically people assign grades as high as A or B+ and as low as F or D. Even when we have a group with the same role (for example, all principals or central office administrators) and who come from the same school or district, we nearly always find widespread differences.

The variation in grades can be the product of any or all of the following:

• People are using different criteria.

• People share similar criteria but weigh their importance differently.

• People have different definitions of what constitutes quality on a given criterion.

Interesting, no doubt. And, as the leaders of one district said to each other, "If we succeed in our efforts at districtwide improvement this picture should change. What if we do it again in a year and see if the spread has shrunk?" We expect that this district's spread will shrink if they regularly observe, assess, and discuss examples of instruction within and without their district. They will have regular experience of the fact that the criteria we prioritize influence our perception and judgment of good teaching.

Consider, for example, the following two responses:

Response #1: "Okay, maybe I overdid it, giving him an A, but I still think he deserves a strong B or B+, just on the grounds of how connected those kids are to that lesson. Sure, he is goofy; his style is not my style, and frankly it gives me the creeps, but those kids are really engaged. He's got their attention. They may be hooting and hollering, but they are hooting and hollering about what is coming up in the lesson. They're not laughing about some kid they are teasing, or what happened in the lunchroom, or something that has nothing to do with the teacher's instructional purposes. They are on task and energetically engaged. I walk through classes every week and I want to tell you, it is a terribly dispiriting experience to see how bored so many of the kids are. So tuned out, zoned out; it's really depressing. Whatever else you want to say, the kids in that classroom are not depressed."

Response #2: "I gave him a D, and I'll tell you why. I agree with whoever said the students are focused, tuned in, and one way or another they are 'with' him. But the more I think about this, I don't even know if I'm responding now as a principal, or just as a mother, or as a person of color, but I just have to say, 'They are focused, but what are they focused on?' This is a tenth-grade class, for crying out loud! He's got them doing work I wouldn't call demanding if it were a seventh-grade class! The actual writing—did you see it? After five passes you still don't have a decent paragraph. Is this high expectations? Is this leaving no child behind? If it were my kid's class I was watching, I'd be terribly disappointed. They're not depressed; I'll give you that. They are happily engaged with him, while *they are being left behind*!"

As these disparate responses (from the same group) indicate, developing shared understandings is a challenging task.

If good instruction—in every classroom and for all students—is the central focus of systemic change in education, then districts and schools need to define "goodness" and come to a shared understanding of what is meant by great, or even competent, teaching. The difficulty of this shouldn't be a surprise. First, our definitions of quality instruction are often tacit and built on assumptions we typically can't name. People tend to feel uncomfortable and awkward in trying to be specific about why they scored this teacher's lesson as they did. Second, even if we are able to articulate our own assumptions, we may still have difficulty communicating with others, who might use the same words to mean different things. Take, for example, the term *engaged*. We often hear someone explain that the videotaped lesson was particularly strong because the teacher "engaged the students." When asked to explain how, we typically hear: "The teacher knew every student's name; he called on almost everyone; and not one kid missed a beat in answering. And every student was involved in the classroom activity." It is also very common for us to hear another respondent stand up and defend a more negative grade, using the word *engaged* in a very different way: "That was a weak lesson because students were not engaged." The respondent will go on to say something like, "When it came to questions that required any real thinking at all, only two students answered. Lots of talking doesn't tell me much. Just because a student talks in class does not mean he or she is learning or even thinking."

Without agreed-upon definitions (or at least a clarification of how a person is using a term) and observable data that support the person's assessment of the lesson, conversations about teaching and learning remain ethereal, reinforcing the teaching profession's weak craft knowledge base, professional language, and standards of practice. We need agreed-upon criteria.

## DEFINING A NEW FRAMEWORK FOR EFFECTIVE INSTRUCTION

In our experience, the unifying criteria most often correspond to three ideal qualities: the rigor of the lesson, its relevance for the students' lives, and the respect evident in the teacher-student relationship. What we call the *New 3 R's*—rigor, relevance, and respectful relationships—provides a useful framework for convening conversations on teaching and learning. The existence of a practical and simple intellectual device such as the 3 R's helps structure and focus our discussions, making it more likely that groups of people can talk with each other across a number of different instructional dimensions instead of past each other. We want to emphasize that we do not see these principles as explicit definitions of good instruction. Rather, they are three broad and abstract concepts that need to be spelled out with much greater specificity if educators are to use them as meaningful terms for evaluating a particular lesson or a teaching method. Our hope is that the framework will provoke ongoing collaborative inquiry and, initially, raise more questions than answers. Eventually, these conversations, when they center on examples of actual classroom practice, can lead to developed, specific, and legitimate definitions of quality instruction.

## Rigor: Mastering Core Competencies

So what, generally, do we mean by *rigor*? In *Teaching What Matters Most,* Strong, Silver, and Perini challenge us with standards for rigor that enable students to understand content that is:

- Organized around complex interrelated concepts
- Concerned with central problems in the discipline that challenge students' previous concepts
- Able to arouse strong feelings
- Focused on symbols and images packed with multiple meanings[8]

Curriculum content is one way to think about rigor. Others view rigor through an instructional lens. Newmann, Bryk, and Nagaoka suggest that rigor refers to the ways that teachers design learning environments so that students construct their own new meanings and understanding in authentic and disciplined ways.[9] Information and ideas can be introduced in a manner that brings forth, challenges, and revises students' preconceptions about a subject. And conversations can be conducted as means for students to explore complex connections and relationships between ideas.

So is rigor about content or about instruction? Or both? Consider these questions about defining rigor as potential starting places for your own reflection and conversation. We certainly see common elements between these approaches in their references to concepts such as complexity, meaning making, connections, and relationships, to name a few. These terms might also echo your own thinking. But these terms are ambiguous at best and leave a great deal of room for interpretation and definition. Our point is that you need to make sense of rigor for yourself and that there are frameworks for thinking about rigor that can guide your inquiry.

We do take a strong stance, however, on what rigor is not: rigor is not simply about students being given more or harder work. Rigor is about what students are able to *do* as a result of a lesson. Rigor implies holding students responsible for meeting certain objective, qualitative standards and measuring progress regularly. Measured how? Many states have a plethora of academic content standards, which often overwhelm teachers because of the sheer volume of what they are expected to cover. When these academic content standards are reflected in high-stakes tests, they obviously require attention. In our view, however, test performance does not often measure students' ability to demonstrate their reasoning and apply their knowledge. In such cases, they cannot usefully serve as meaningful performance standards.

For example, students are required to memorize all ninety-two chemical elements that occur in nature for a statewide fourth-grade science test in Virginia. A better measure of rigorous instruction for fourth-grade science might be an assessment of a student's ability to explain the scientific method and to give an example of an important scientific experiment. The elements can always be looked up, but if students have not learned why the scientific method is important and how it can be used by the time they begin middle and high school, then lab classes will mean very little to them. Similarly, students can memorize certain dates in history, but a more rigorous student performance standard would be an assessment of students' abilities to compare and contrast conflicting accounts of a historical event—such as the Battle of Lexington at the onset of the Revolutionary War—and their skill in writing a well-reasoned analysis of what they thought likely happened, and how that analysis should inform a present-day dilemma.

Another example of rigorous performance standards can be found in the Boy and Girl Scouts' "merit badge" approach to learning. To get an Eagle Scout Merit Badge in Camping, for example, you don't take a multiple-choice test on the parts of a tent and a campfire or merely memorize theories about conservation. You have to pitch real tents, sleep out twenty nights, plan and cook nutritionally balanced meals, and perform an approved conservation project—all rigorous performance standards. In addition, you have to meet certain content standards such as knowledge of first aid.[10]

The requirements we've described concerning scientific method, analysis of historical events, and merit badges allow for and encourage deeper and more complex understanding than rote memorization. In addition to being rigorous, these performance standards are also highly relevant and reflect the interdependence of the 3 R's in defining excellence.

## Relevance: Connecting the Curriculum Through Real-World Applications

The number one question on many high school students' minds is: "What's the point of school—why do I have to know this stuff?" When you ask students why they have to learn the material in any given lesson, most will simply roll their eyes and shrug. Too many students who dare to ask this question aloud receive vague answers such as, "You'll need to know this in college" or, more simply, "Because it's going to be on the test." More often, the question is never asked or answered, either by students or by the teachers themselves. Many teachers are covering material that they have been told they should teach—a textbook or curriculum where little or no effort has been made to explain why something is important to learn or how it prepares the students for adult life. Even less frequently are students helped to pursue their own areas of interest through independent reading or research projects. There's no time; there's too much to cover.

Yet it is increasingly clear that many of today's students do not retain knowledge or master skills that appear to have little or no relevance to their lives. Acculturated as skeptics and experienced consumers, they need reasons to learn, to "buy in" to what's going on in class. We are not suggesting a return to the liberal sixties notion that all learning has to be relevant in a narcissistic sense. Rather, as we discussed in Chapter One, because today's students have less extrinsic motivation to learn, such as fear of authority, their intrinsic motivations to learn must be tapped more than is currently the case in most classrooms.

We need to show students how math concepts apply in the solution of real-world problems and how science is used in workplaces. Students need opportunities to discuss how knowledge of history can deepen their understanding of important current issues. They need to see and understand, through job shadowing and internships, what skills adults need and how they use them in their daily work. Students also need more opportunities throughout their school years to pursue their own individual areas of interest—in part to experience the satisfaction of learning for its own sake, and in part to gain mastery of the skills and discipline needed to be an independent, lifelong learner. These are only a few examples, and what relevance will mean in any particular school or district will naturally vary.

How to draw on students' current experiences and interests and how to help them imagine and be motivated by the futures we desire for them are neither obvious nor easily settled matters. Making these decisions and determining how to recognize and promote the appropriate kinds of relevance in instruction require careful thinking and discussion.

*Relevance*, then, is essential for students to understand the purpose of learning and be motivated to achieve rigor. Students in all ability groups, when asked what changes would help them learn more in school, talk about needing opportunities for hands-on and applied learning. This answer is second only to the issue of teacher-student relationships in their discussions of how schools can be improved.

## Respectful Relationships: Finding the Key to Motivation

This brings us to the third R and the most important element in motivating students to want to achieve at high standards: the quality of *relationships* with their teachers. It has always been true that students tend to learn very little from teachers who they feel are not respectful toward them. They may feel goaded into doing the minimum by a teacher who uses fear and intimidation, but they will never do their best, even in subjects they enjoy. And for today's students, who often have little contact with their parents or other adults, relationships with caring, respectful teachers have become even more important.

As a part of our work with schools and districts we conduct focus groups with students—sometimes in middle schools, but more often in high schools and with recent graduates or dropouts. We ask students to describe their school's strengths, things that need improving, what they might change that would make the greatest difference in their learning, and to define good teaching.

The replies to the last two questions are essentially the same everywhere we go. Students attending urban, suburban, or rural high schools; students who struggle academically; and students who take advanced courses all say the one thing that makes the greatest difference in their learning is the quality of their relationships with their teachers. They want teachers who care about teaching and who are challenging and competent, of course, but what they talk about most often is how they are treated by their teachers. Does the teacher see them as individuals, rather than just faces in the crowd? Does the teacher try to know and understand what students may be dealing with at home or in their neighborhood? To what extent does a teacher go out of his or her way to ensure that all students are learning versus just plowing through the chapters? Or does the teacher only pay attention to the "smart" kids? It is increasingly clear to us that, although many of today's students may have diminished fear and respect for formal authority, they have an increased need to connect with adults who can guide and coach them in school and in life.

Research by the Public Agenda Foundation, the leading public opinion research firm studying Americans' views on complex social issues, confirms our observations. In its study of adolescents' views of school, the foundation reports the most startling finding is the issue of lack of respect in schools, in general, and particularly between teachers and students. Only four in ten public school students thought most of their teachers treated them with respect. And more than two-thirds of the students surveyed said that they learn "a lot more" from a teacher who treats them with respect, explains lessons carefully, and cares personally about them.[11]

Many teachers also want closer relationships with their students. Most feel that they could do a better job with all students if their classes were smaller. A growing number understand that, in fact, they cannot motivate a student whom they do not know, as Ted Sizer, founder of the Coalition of Essential Schools, has often said.[12] Teachers ask: "How can I get to know all of the 130 or more students whom I see in 50 minute classes for a semester or perhaps a year?" The conditions of teaching and learning in most schools—especially secondary schools—make it extremely difficult for teachers to establish the closer relationships with students that many seek. This is a significant problem that we discuss throughout this book.

What constitutes *respect*? How do respectful relationships best promote student achievement? How do we assess whether these relationships exist, and how do we promote them? Addressing questions such as these can lead educators to the clarity they need about what constitutes this aspect of good instruction.

## LINKING THE NEW 3 R'S OF INSTRUCTION

The 3 R's are an attempt to create a systemic framework for discussions of good teaching, and a framework that can produce a more complex, comprehensive understanding of instructional practice. Each concept is dependent on the other two for the entire system to work. Many of us have known rigorous teachers who were so caught up in their material that they were unable either to explain its practical application or to connect personally with most students—and so their lessons left many in the class confused or indifferent. Similarly, there are teachers who excel at making a curriculum more relevant with interesting projects and hands-on work, but the skills students are expected to master may be unclear or well below what they are capable of doing and need to know. Finally, some teachers seek to instill a positive self-image in students through caring relationships, but if they have not taught students real skills, this self-esteem quickly evaporates at the next level of education or the first job interview. Rigor, as a concept, is a starting point for educators to translate the demand for *all* students to master *new* skills into new classroom practices. Relevance and relationships help us begin to understand what is required to motivate all students to want to master these new skills.

There is beauty in the simplicity of the 3 R's as a framework for observing and talking about instructional practice. Yet, as we emphasized earlier, the 3 R's should not be treated as a definition of good instruction, as *the* answer; instead they should be used to provoke good questions:

- Is the instruction we see sufficiently rigorous, relevant, respectful?

- What do we mean by, and take as evidence for, rigor, relevance, and respectful relationships?

- How should we weigh these categories?

- If a lesson is highly relevant, and characterized by good relationships, can we give it a pass even though we agree it is not sufficiently rigorous?

We encourage you to use the 3R framework as a tool for collective and ongoing inquiry. It should be a prime learning objective for any educational organization, at the district or school level, to research, define, and refine robust and clearer definitions of each of these terms—particularly what these definitions might look like in practice. Our discussions should only be your starting point for your own concrete vision of the New 3 R's.

As the literature makes clear (see Appendix B, entitled "Recommended Reading"), these terms can be defined and applied in very different ways. We wouldn't be surprised if you come to share our conclusion that lots of observation, reflection, and conversation are required for any group to agree on its own understanding and application of these key terms.

And finally, as you begin to think about how rigor, relevance, and respectful relationships might frame your thinking about what is good teaching, we suggest that your deliberations be closely connected to decisions about what students need to know and to evidence that they have mastered the material. As we suggested earlier, it is our view that judgments about rigor are neither subjective nor relative; there are, in fact, external validity checks that can be applied to questions about whether a lesson or curriculum is rigorous enough. Ultimately, though, the real test of rigor that all students must pass is whether they graduate college-ready and have mastered the critical competencies required today for college, work, and citizenship. In other words, be sure that your definition of good teaching is yielding the results you seek: all students, new skills. Practical steps you can undertake in defining rigor are set forth in Exercise 2.4.

If you do not have an established norm of "learning walks" (also known as "walk-throughs") in your school or district, we strongly advise you to make an announcement or send a memo to all teachers before undertaking this exercise. You should explain that the purpose of the classroom visits is not teacher evaluation but rather an opportunity for administrators to learn more about quality teaching and learning. You should also seriously consider letting your union leadership know ahead of time what you are doing and why. You might also ask your teachers to suggest one or two indicators of rigor that they would like you to watch for. How do their conceptions of rigor compare with yours? To each other's? Does their input cause you to revise your thinking?

---

## Exercise 2.4:  Define Rigor on a Learning Walk

### Overview

The New 3 R's are best understood as a framework for a conversation about instruction. With that in mind, we encourage you to take the first steps in initiating such a dialogue. We begin with the idea of rigor, which we find to be the most ambiguous and difficult to define.

We want to stress, as we did in the text, that rigor by itself is an insufficient determinant of effective instruction. Its power is in combination with relevance and relationships. We suggest that you eventually determine what all three concepts might actually look like in the classroom at any grade level.

## Step One

Consider the following questions for reflection or discussion:

1. In a (pick a grade level) classroom where "rigorous" instruction is going on, what activities or behaviors would you expect to see? What would the teacher be doing? What would students be doing?

2. In (pick a subject content area and grade level), what might be some of the characteristics of "rigorous" student work?

3. List of some of the most important things that you might now look for related to rigor in classrooms.

## Step Two

Now "benchmark" your definition of rigor by considering to what extent the indicators on your list build the critical competencies needed in a knowledge economy (beyond mastery of the basic skills in reading, writing, and mathematics).

What might you need to revise or reconsider in light of the key competencies, the knowledge economy skills, such as those that Carnevale and Desrochers provided for the Educational Testing Service?

- **Foundation Skills:** Knowing How to Learn
- **Communication Skills:** Listening and Oral Communication
- **Adaptability:** Creative Thinking and Problem Solving
- **Group Effectiveness:** Interpersonal Skills, Negotiation, and Teamwork
- **Influence**: Organizational Effectiveness and Leadership
- **Personal Management:** Self-Esteem and Motivation/Goal Setting
- **Attitude:** Positive Cognitive Style
- **Applied Skills:** Occupational and Professional Competencies

## Step Three

When your "rubric for rigor" is completed to your satisfaction, take the indicators to the classroom, to see what they might really look like in practice and, most important, to foster a conversation that will begin to build a shared and concrete vision of rigor. We suggest you take an hour and a half, and visit ten or so classrooms in a school with your list. Observe each class for perhaps five minutes. If the purpose of the lesson is not clear, ask a student what he or she is doing and why.

How you record your observations is important, as these are the data that will ground your conversation later. Rather than check off the presence of an indicator on your rigor rubric, try to describe, verbatim, what you see that you believe illustrates a particular indicator. Try not to interpret, but instead describe what you actually see so that you can determine if this activity, question, or performance is indeed an indicator of rigor. For example, rather than noting that a teacher's question was complex, record the question itself. Let the decision as to its complexity come later.

## Step Four

When you've finished your learning walk, examine the data you've collected and reflect on what you saw by asking the following questions:

1. Were you able to identify some particular teacher or student behaviors that indicated rigor?

2. Did you see evidence of rigorous content? How did that differ across classrooms, teaching styles, disciplines?

Typically, these observations help educators become clearer about their individual definitions of key concepts such as "rigor." What is much more powerful, we find, is for a team of educators to observe the same lessons and share their responses to these questions. You can imagine how a conversation that addresses the previous questions not only challenges individuals to clarify, rethink, and refine their own definitions but can also allow the whole team to come to powerful, shared understandings.

- Do you agree that what you saw illustrates the rigor indicators on your rubric?
- What areas of commonality can you build on?
- Where do you disagree? What questions do your disagreements raise?
- What else do you need to learn?

---

Performing a learning walk as described in Exercise 2.4 is a step—one that should be informed by an understanding of what constitutes quality instruction. This clarity is key to actually making that instruction happen. We suggest these kinds of observations continue and that, after you have begun to clarify and define what you are looking for, you consider how frequently you are seeing high-quality teaching and learning and what to do as a result of that data. What are some of the most and least frequently observed activities or behaviors? If there are some behaviors or activities that you consider important and that occur quite infrequently, does this suggest a promising area for some focused teacher professional development? As an example, administrators who have done this exercise often tell us they have been struck by the fact that the majority of teachers' questions required mere factual recall and by how infrequently students were asked to offer a reasoned opinion, interpretation, or analysis.

You will need to decide when and how to bring teams of teachers into the conversation, and this exercise can also be used to initiate faculty discussions about effective instruction. For example, Mary Ellen Steele-Pierce, assistant superintendent of the West Clermont School District, initiated instruction improvement efforts with a districtwide discussion of the attributes of good teaching, beginning with a common reading around rigor.[13] Some school principals in West Clermont then launched discussions with their own faculties to jointly develop "attributes of good teaching" rubrics, which administrators used for their "learning walks." Once these walks were completed, they shared their data summary with the full faculty for discussion (without mentioning the names of the teachers whose classrooms were visited) and together reflected on what the data might mean for their professional development priorities as an entire school. These discussions marked a new way of working—together—in West Clermont. Teachers became increasingly organized in communities of practice for shared learning and reflection in each school as the work moved forward over the next several years.

 A few further notes of caution—ones that we will be repeating often throughout this guidebook in different forms. First, our description of how to initiate discussions about rigor and good teaching may sound much easier to initiate than, in reality, they are. We began this chapter with a brief discussion of some of the many factors that discourage educators from scrutinizing and learning about practice—as teachers or instructional leaders. These are significant and longstanding cultural and structural obstacles to the kinds of discussions and classroom observations we've outlined. In practice, developing agreement about what constitutes effective instruction and about how teaching and supervision might best be improved in a school or a district is part of a larger process of changing the culture of our profession and takes years to accomplish. What we suggest are some starting points, not a recipe. Success in this endeavor requires you, as a leader or group of leaders, to undertake an ongoing process of learning and dialogue.

Second, although we have focused the latter part of this chapter on a critical starting point—a shared vision of good teaching—we want to emphasize that though foundational, it is only one of a system of disciplines necessary to bring about instructional improvement. We find all seven disciplines to be essential to the success of a process that results in all students mastering new skills. And as clear as we are about the importance of these disciplines, their manifestation will be different in every system. This work is messy and requires continuous inquiry, dialogue and reflection, trial and error, revision and refinement. That is what adaptive change is all about.

Contrary to the messages of some political and educational leaders in the past, and perhaps even to our own secret wishes, there is no single solution, quick fix, or silver bullet that will magically enable all students to succeed. We have to remember that teaching all students new skills is a new aspiration—like landing astronauts on Mars—and achieving this goal will require not only fundamental systemic and structural changes and the creation of new knowledge, but also changes in our shared and individual beliefs and behaviors. It is this inner work that we address in Chapter Three.

## Endnotes

1. Richard Elmore, *Building a New Structure for School Leadership* (Washington, D.C.: Albert Shanker Institute, 2000).
2. Deanna Burney, "Craft Knowledge: The Road to Transforming Schools," *Phi Delta Kappan* 85, no. 7 (March 2004): 3.
3. The Seven Disciplines for Strengthening Instruction was first published by Tony Wagner in "'Beyond Testing': The Seven Disciplines for Strengthening Instruction," *Education Week* (November 11, 2003), Commentary.
4. For further information, we recommend the following: R. F. Elmore and D. Burney, *Continuous Improvement in Community District #2, New York City* (University of Pittsburgh, HPLC Project, Learning Research and Development Center, August 1997); E. Fink and L. B. Resnick, *Developing Principles as Instructional Leaders* (University of Pittsburgh, HPLC Project, Learning Research and Development Center, 1999); L. B. Resnick and M. Harwell, *High Performance Learning Communities District #2 Achievement* (University of Pittsburgh, HPLC Project, Learning Research and Development Center, 1998); K. Maloy, *Building a Learning Community: The Story of New York City Community District #2* (University of Pittsburgh, HPLC Project, Learning Research and Development Center, 1998).
5. Richard F. Elmore with Deanna Burney, *Investing in Teacher Learning: Staff Development and Instructional Improvement in Community School District #2, New York City* (Philadelphia: University of Pennsylvania, Consortium for Policy Research in Education, 1997).

6. Elmore and Burney, *Staff Development.*

7. This clip comes from Episode 29 in the Association for Supervision and Curriculum Development (ASCD) series, *Video Library of Teaching Episodes.* The clip of the sixth-grade class is Episode 15, from 1989, in the same series (Alexandria, Va.: ASCD, 1991).

8. Richard W. Strong, Harvey F. Silver, and Matthew J. Perini, *Teaching What Matters Most: Standards and Strategies for Raising Student Achievement* (Alexandria, Va.: Association for Supervision and Curriculum Development, 2001).

9. Fred M. Newmann, Anthony S. Bryk, and Jenny K. Nagoaka, *Authentic Intellectual Work and Standardized Tests* (Chicago: Consortium on Chicago School Research, January 2001).

10. U.S. Scouting Service Project, "Camping Merit Badge Requirements." http://www.usscouts.org/usscouts/mb/framesindex.html (accessed September 29, 2004).

11. Jean Johnson and Steve Farkas, *Getting By: What American Teenagers Really Think About Their Schools* (New York: Public Agenda Foundation, 1997).

12. See Theodore Sizer, *Horace's Compromise: The Dilemma of the American High School* (Boston: Houghton Mifflin, 1985).

13. West Clermont used the Strong, Silver, and Perini framework from *Teaching What Matters Most*—see note 8—to orient their discussions.

# Committing Ourselves to the Challenge

As we indicated in the Preface, to succeed in the work of reinventing education, change leaders must cultivate a new kind of attention, a dual attention. We need to sharpen our vision *outward*, seeing more deeply into the organizations we are trying to improve. We also need to sharpen our vision *inward*, seeing more deeply into ourselves, and the way we must change, as well. Tough as it is, to bring about important changes in the organizations we lead, we must consider the need for our own change. Indeed most leaders will subscribe to the belief that, as leaders, we should not ask others to do what we would not ask of ourselves.

As educational leaders engaged in this journey, just what it is we each have to change will take some time to answer. Throughout *Change Leadership*, we provide tools that are designed precisely to help you think about what might be getting in your way, to see things in your own beliefs and behaviors that normally are hidden from view.

## IDENTIFYING YOUR COMMITMENT

As educators and as authors, we assume your wholehearted commitment to improvement and concern that the focus of this improvement be instruction. We now give you the opportunity to apply this commitment to your role as a leader in your school district. Use Exercise 3.1 to zero in on yourself *as an individual* in helping move this work forward. What aspects of your individual role (whether superintendent, principal, teacher, department head, curriculum coordinator, or some other role or combination) are most relevant to and important for improving instruction in your district?

 ## Exercise 3.1: Make the Commitment

What one or two aspects of your own role, if you were to dedicate yourself to them, would make the biggest contribution toward improving instruction in your district?

What is the most important thing that you need to get better at, or should change, in order to make progress toward this goal?

Now that you've identified this focus, frame your response as a kind of "commitment." You don't need to know how you actually *would* get better at this. You don't even need to have confidence that you *could* get better at it. You just need to be willing to try to work on it, and to let that be a part of your learning activity.

To help you frame this most important improvement goal as a commitment we have provided the beginning sentence stem for your response:

*I am committed to the value or importance of . . .*

---

One assistant superintendent who answered the questions raised in Exercise 3.1 identified her leadership of the monthly principals' meetings as the aspect of her work where she could make the biggest contribution toward improving instruction in her district. Intrigued by the idea that all adult meetings should be about instruction and should be models of good teaching (the third of the Seven Disciplines for Strengthening Instruction), she decided that she could work to focus more of her meetings with principals on better support for classroom instruction. She stated her commitment as:

*I am committed to the value or importance of making sure every monthly principal meeting focuses on instruction.*

Other commitments that educational leaders have made that are clearly tied to the improvement of instruction include:

*I am committed to the value or importance of becoming a principal who is mainly an instructional leader rather than a building manager.*

*I am committed to the value or importance of working with the other teachers in my department to identify our "best practices."*

*I am committed to the value or importance of giving every special needs child the opportunity to succeed.*

---

*Be sure that the commitment you have chosen is one that feels powerful and is likely to yield rich learning and progress.*

---

In the remainder of this chapter and throughout this book, we'll be asking you to refer to the commitment you developed in Exercise 3.1 and to keep working with it in different ways as you reflect on, plan for, and act for change.[1] Be sure that the commitment you have chosen is one that feels powerful and is likely to yield rich learning and progress. We suggest that your commitment meet the following criteria:

- It should feel as if it is genuinely true for you (not just something you are supposed to believe or do).
- It should be clear how this commitment relates directly to improved instruction.
- It should not yet be fully realized, meaning that there is plenty of room for improvement and future growth.
- It should implicate *you*. It should be clear how the realization of the commitment depends on changes that you make to the way you work. This is a crucial criterion and an easy one to slip out of. Check to make sure that the commitment is not really about other people shaping up rather than you changing in some important way. For example, does "I am committed to the importance of accountability" really mean "I think it would be great if others would follow through on what they say they'll do"? Check to make sure it is not so vague that your role in better meeting the commitment can easily disappear.
- It should feel quite important to you, so that you imagine its realization, if you could achieve it, as personally valuable and powerful.

If the commitment you have identified does not meet one or more of these criteria, we suggest that you revise it or choose another before going any further. At the very least, if you are working through this book in the context of a team, each individual should make his or her commitment known to the other team members. If you have any doubts that you have identified the most juicy, potentially powerful commitment for yourself, you might also consider taking one or both of the following steps:

1. Make the case to yourself that working on this aspect would yield high-value improvements in instruction. You should be able to:

   a. Provide persuasive reasoning and evidence around how progress in this area will improve instruction.

   b. Include a solid research base that supports your reasoning about how this will improve instruction.

   c. Consult with colleagues to see if your reasoning makes sense to them.

2. Request honest and well-intended feedback from colleagues about which aspect of your work, if improved, would most contribute to improved instruction.

## SPOTTING YOUR OBSTACLES THROUGH SELF-REFLECTION

Anyone who has tried to plan for and implement change understands the need to spend some time identifying and clarifying goals and commitments. There is much internal work that needs to be done between the time that leaders first embrace the commitment to improve instruction and their first, even modest, visible steps forward. One step is to devise a plan or process for achieving these goals, trying to anticipate the obstacles that are likely to cross our paths as we try to realize our aspirations.

Drafting a convincing and thorough list of obstacles may not require too much thought. Any of us might name the veteran teachers, or the new teachers, or the high rates of teacher turnover, or the teachers' union, or the poor communication among central office administrators. We could easily name the unplanned for but predictable distractions that arise in any given academic year: individual crises involving students, families, or teachers; criticisms; and fads emerging and demanding attention in the larger community and public arena. We cited many of these issues as typical first-draft problem statements at the beginning of

Chapter Two. These and other obstacles are all too familiar to anyone in public education.

We certainly agree these obstacles exist and that the skilled leader needs to chart the course of change carefully, to anticipate, evade, and counter the difficulties that litter the path. But in this book, we invite you into a very different process of planning for and implementing change. One of the hardest aspects of charting the change course, and one often left out of the planning and implementation process, is identifying the ways that we might also create obstacles that get in the way of *our own* plans. This idea might initially seem a bit strange. Could it really be that we, the leaders, the ones focusing so much of our energy and effort on leading the charge, might actually be acting in ways that frustrate our commitments, hamper our progress, foil our plans? It is our experience that this is often the case.

---

*One of the hardest aspects of charting the change course . . . is identifying the ways that we might also create obstacles that get in the way of our own plans.*
*Or,*
*Could it really be that we . . . might actually be acting in ways that frustrate our commitments, hamper our progress, foil our plans?*

---

Take the example of Arthur, a respected and well-liked superintendent with whom we have worked, who was leading the process of instructional improvement in his district. He framed his own improvement goal as, "I am committed to moving my district from 'good' to 'great' by creating a common vision of rigorous instruction." Arthur worked closely with his leadership team to develop agreement around this goal and to create a shared vision of good instruction. The leadership team then brought this vision to the principals in the district, generating discussions and making revisions until there was widespread agreement around the final document. Arthur knew that a key next step in the improvement process would be to begin holding the principals and other key administrators accountable for implementing this vision in their schools. He needed to provide them with clear direction about how they should act. And yet, when he took an honest inventory of all his actions, he found that he was stalling.

Arthur first took more time to double-check that everyone was actually in agreement about the vision, that all the details had been ironed out, all "i's" were dotted and "t's" crossed. He also delayed discussions with his leadership team about specific actions to take next—discussions about how they and the principals would be able to determine if teaching was aligned with the vision they had worked so hard to create. He continued to wait, to test the waters, to stall, and in doing so, he recognized that he was actually allowing the momentum for change to slow. He was hindering the progress of his own plans.

Arthur's story might initially seem to indicate that he was not really willing to take the hard steps necessary to improve instruction. But the reverse may actually be more accurate. First, we believe that Arthur's reluctance to act did *not* indicate that he lacked a sincere and passionate commitment to creating a common vision of rigorous instruction. Nor do we think that Arthur was the primary obstacle to creating this common vision. In fact, we could easily have told a very different story, describing all the things that Arthur *was* doing on behalf of realizing his plans, commitments, and goals, even while he continued to hesitate.

What, specifically, Arthur realized he was doing, or not doing, is not nearly as important as the fact that he included his own actions (or lack of action) among his list of the obstacles to change. This self-reflection and recognition—this inner work—is, we believe, the hardest and most powerful step in accepting one's responsibilities as a leader. In taking this honest look at himself and his behavior, Arthur allowed himself the opportunity to see his own actions in a new light, an essential view if he is to reconsider those actions. If we accept the learning that can come from such self-examination, we actually take on a new kind of responsibility for observing and monitoring our behavior in ways that can lead to our own greater productivity.

*This self-reflection and recognition . . . is, we believe,*
*the hardest and most powerful step in accepting*
*one's responsibilities as a leader.*

Arthur is far from unique in being an obstacle to the very progress he hopes to make. In fact, we believe that when we examine our own roles in taking on any of the truly difficult challenges we face, we are likely to find myriad and important ways that we frustrate our progress and complicate the challenges, whether through action or avoidance. For example, a former principal who was fairly new to her job as a central office administrator readily admitted that she was having a difficult time working with the principals in her district to improve instruction. She acknowledged that she was spending her time and energy assigning blame for the lack of progress instead of creating opportunities for open and honest dialogue about the situation. She recognized that she was making assumptions and jumping to conclusions about why progress was slow and who was at fault without first examining the relevant data or understanding why others were acting as they did. In accepting responsibility for these obstacles, she was able to see her own role in the situation more clearly.

Similarly, a principal dedicated to becoming an instructional leader described the ways that his own actions interfered with his commitment to improving teaching in his own building. He vowed to spend more time visiting classrooms in order to observe and better supervise teachers. However, he admitted that he was unable to find the time to visit classrooms because he continued to engage in some of the noninstructional activities that he loved, such as eating with kids in the lunch room, meeting with individual parents on a regular basis, and taking phone calls from concerned community members. Identifying and listing these behaviors enabled him to see that continuing all these activities with the same attention and intensity would effectively prevent him from ever getting into classrooms.

Identifying the ways we are undermining our commitments is a key step necessary for the much deeper learning we'll be undertaking in later chapters. So now it's your turn. As you reflect on the commitment you have named in Exercise 3.1, consider and respond to the question posed in Exercise 3.2.

---

### Exercise 3.2: Recognize Counterproductive Behaviors

What are you doing, or not doing, that is keeping your commitment from being more fully realized? As you begin your list, use the following guidelines:

- Keep your list to specific behaviors—things you do or don't do. For example, if you are about to write something that is not a behavior (such as "too many distractions"), reword it to focus on a behavior (such as "I initiate conversations about more trivial matters when I should be addressing high-priority items").

- Refrain from listing your reasoning about why you engage in these behaviors, or what you should do about your behaviors.
- List only those behaviors (or things you are not doing) that undermine or work against your commitment.

1.

2.

3.

4.

5.

---

Once you've completed the exercise, what next? For now, just making the list and reflecting on it is sufficient. Your personal learning is a journey that will continue throughout the book. Completing the exercises is a first step and provides the foundation for additional work in later chapters. It is not necessary to share this list at this time, although later we will encourage you to discuss more of what you're learning with your colleagues.

You may now feel a strong inclination to attack the behaviors you've identified in an effort to whittle down and then eliminate every item from the inventory you just created. That urge is understandable, especially given the time and care we have asked you to take in developing a powerful and personal commitment toward improving instruction. Even though it reflects your interest to be more effective on behalf of your goals, we suggest you don't attack these behaviors. Yet. As we've learned, people *may not* become more effective by going directly at their counterproductive behaviors. Instead, and in the spirit of the deep, rigorous learning we seek for students, we may be better served by first investigating and understanding more about the purpose and value of these counterproductive behaviors. So hold off on the direct attack and follow our thinking for a few more chapters. At that point, you will be able to mine your inventory for even deeper learning, yielding the genuinely effective productivity you seek.

### Endnote
1. These activities draw on the work of R. Kegan and L. L. Lahey, *How the Way We Talk Can Change the Way We Work* (San Francisco: Jossey-Bass, 2001).

# Reflections

In Chapter Two, we developed the idea that improving student achievement is, first and foremost, a task that requires improving instruction and instructional leadership. We suggested historical and cultural reasons why individuals and the organizations that employ them have been and continue to be reticent to tackle issues related to instructional improvement. We saw ways in which work conditions actually thwart professional learning and reflection.

We then outlined what a *system* focused on continuous improvement of instruction might look like. The Seven Disciplines for Strengthening Instruction—urgency for instructional improvement using real data, shared vision of good teaching, meetings about the work, shared vision of student results, effective supervision, professional development, and diagnostic data with accountable collaboration—provide a framework for a system that can contribute to the improvement of teaching, instructional leadership, and student achievement.

We also described the New 3 R's—rigor, relevance, and respectful relationships—as a framework to discuss teaching and the changes needed to prepare all students for the new future. These 3 R's are vital to defining a framework for effective instruction for today's students and the world in which they find themselves. Rethinking rigor is a critical first step for *adults* who are committed to teaching all students the new skills needed in today's world. Adults must also recognize that *students* put respectful relationships and more relevant lessons first as essential for their being more motivated to succeed in school.

In the last two chapters, we've elaborated on some of the individual and organizational behaviors and beliefs that may need to change in order for us to transform our schools and districts. We've seen examples of success stories: leaders who have taken steps to realize their commitment to improving instruction. Many of these steps required first shining light into the corners of both the system and the psyche: discovering what has been getting in the way of improvement. We've seen the hard work, both inner and outer, that is required along the way.

In the next chapters, we explore the need to generate energy for change and ways in which we can overcome natural, and sometimes buried, immunities to change.

**PART TWO**

# Why Is This
# So Hard?

# Generating Momentum for Change

Transforming America's public schools to teach all students the new skills required for success in the twenty-first century is a monumental educational challenge. It's also an adaptive problem, one for which the necessary knowledge to solve the problem must be created in the act of working on it. In the preceding chapters we elaborated on some of the individual and organizational behaviors and beliefs that may need to change in order for us to transform our schools and districts. Now in this chapter we explore how individuals and organizations can either frustrate or generate greater momentum for the kinds of focused change that are needed for improved teaching and learning.

Most public education leaders believe that time and money are the resources that will most effectively move improvements forward. There is, of course, a fundamental truth to this answer. Many districts struggle with overcrowded classes and have little or no time for professional development or even teacher planning meetings. Better funding might go a long way toward solving these problems. In our experience, however, it's not that simple: teaching and student achievement don't necessarily improve in districts that are well funded and have extensive professional development programs. The reality is that a system focused on the continuous improvement of learning, teaching, and leadership requires more than time and money.

A short example illustrates the point. One member of the Change Leadership Group (CLG) studied a school district that had received a major grant for professional development. This district had also implemented school improvement teams, ninth-grade teacher teams, common planning times, and smaller classes. The district leadership had great intentions, and the strategies appeared promising. However, the professional development programs had a different theme or topic each month (such as Cooperative Learning, Cognitive Coaching, and so on). The biweekly meetings of the school improvement teams were without agendas, and the topics that wound up being discussed were not clearly connected to student learning. For example, one school team spent two meetings discussing whether chocolate milk should be available at lunch—only to decide after hours of deliberation that it ought to be the school committee's decision. The ninth-grade teacher planning meetings also had no agendas and were spent discussing details of upcoming field trips or individual students' behavior problems, generally without resolution. After more than a year of implementing a variety of professional development programs and having ineffectual meetings at every level, there had been no discernable improvement in any observed classroom teaching. What was going on? To answer that, we look at the bigger picture.

## OBSTACLES TO IMPROVEMENT VERSUS MOMENTUM FOR IMPROVEMENT

We have identified three categories of organizational tendencies—reaction, compliance, and isolation—that drain momentum away from change. Separately and together, these tendencies sap the momentum that is vital for improvement. They developed over time as an understandable, and even appropriate, response to the educational aims and social norms of the past. Now, in a different era, they represent barriers to improvement, barriers to the adaptive work that is needed. Overcoming these tendencies and replacing them with their positive counterparts—purpose and focus, engagement, and collaboration—releases momentum for systemic and sustainable change.

In the following sections, we discuss and contrast each of the obstacles to improvement with their opposite momentum generators. Each section also includes an exercise for characterizing where an organization is on each continuum.

## Reaction Transforms to Purpose and Focus

Education is, of course, a "helping" profession. Our ability to respond to children's needs is an indicator of our success and a source of pride. American public education is also a "local" enterprise, held closely by and accountable to the community it serves. As a result, teachers and administrators are generally very responsive to the needs, concerns, and priorities of parents and school board members. And because education is also a profession that has historically lacked a tradition of clearly developed "craft knowledge" and strong professional associations (as noted in Chapter Two), it is particularly vulnerable to political whims and trends.

Although this culture of responsiveness may have served us well in the past, the pressures on schools to react to new societal demands have increased exponentially in the past several decades. We are asked to work with a rapidly growing population of children who often have special needs, disabilities, and limited English proficiency. Society also expects schools to take on new challenges such as sex education, drug education, and character education. With these come escalating demands for accountability and the accompanying barrage of testing and data collection. American public education is also highly politicized and becoming more so, with constituencies making demands on the politicians or school board members they elect. Their various agendas get translated into new and unrelated priorities and programs to be enacted by the school or district.

These conditions have caused many educators to move beyond appropriate responsiveness to a position of reaction. School and district administrators feel compelled to react even more quickly to urgent problems that arise in daily administration. Disruptive students, angry parents, concerned board members, and demands to attend hastily called meetings at the central office can all serve to distract and dilute the focus of leaders. Many of these demands and the reactions they provoke have no relationship to instructional improvement.

Ask almost any public school administrator or teacher to name the top priority in his or her district and the likely answer will be improving test scores. This response is itself a reaction to external accountability and not necessarily about improving student learning. If you then follow up by asking which two or three strategies are being used to achieve this result, you are likely to get a puzzled look or a list of twenty discrete programs or activities.

Simply put, the individual teacher, school, or district with ten priorities has none. And without a well-defined and integrated set of strategies for improving learning, teaching, and leadership—in short, a *system*—it is hard to imagine how leaders can be anything but reactive. Without defined and focused priorities, directly connected to improving instruction, we see little likelihood of raising student achievement.

---

*Simply put, the individual teacher, school,*
*or district with ten priorities has none.*

---

A clear purpose and focused efforts are indispensable to a successful change process in any organization. Many districts claim that the improvement of instruction and instructional leadership is their purpose or mission, but an examination of human and fiscal resource allocation often shows little alignment between the professed focus and how time and money are spent.

In contrast, the political will and courage to coalesce and align an organization around its purpose is illustrated by the actions of Alvarado and Fink in District 2. Once they declared literacy to be their sole focus, all their actions in the first five years of the work were directed toward reinforcing this commitment and making it a reality. Results of the alignment included:

- All principal meetings and all professional development programs were required to serve the goal of developing and implementing a shared vision of powerful literacy instruction in all grades and in every subject.
- Every teacher learned to be a literacy teacher.
- All principals learned how to help teachers become experts in teaching literacy.
- A steadily increasing percentage of the district's resources were allocated to this one priority—professional development around literacy instruction.

All adults employed by District 2 knew and understood this focus, its key improvement strategies, their particular role in implementing these strategies, and how these strategies helped them achieve their goals. After five years of this sustained focus on improving literacy instruction, all of the district's test scores showed a significant increase. They then had the capacity to transfer their improvement strategies to math, and took only two years to achieve comparable results. Laying the groundwork for adult learning and continuous improvement broke the pattern of reaction and allowed them to move forward.[1]

---

## Exercise 4.1: Reaction Versus Purpose and Focus Diagnostic

*Purpose and focus* refers to whether you have a goal that is clearly focused and understood. Note that it is not about how well you are doing in relation to your goal. General questions to consider include:

1. Is there a clear district or school focus?
2. Is this focus widely known throughout the system?
3. Are we able to resist certain pulls and tugs because they are peripheral to our purpose?

Some indicators of what a system at either end of the spectrum might look like follow. Use these to rate your school or district on the continuum.

| *Reaction* | *Purpose and Focus* |
|---|---|
| • Insufficient attention to instructional improvement. | • Clear focus on instructional improvement. |
| • Absence of well-defined strategies for improving learning, teaching, and leadership. | • Well-defined strategies for improving teaching and learning. |
| • Highly responsive to external agendas. | • External pressures are assessed and filtered based on their relation to the focus on and strategies for instructional improvement. |
| • Many priorities—no sense of what is most important. | • All adults in system know and understand the key improvement strategy(ies), what they need to do, and how it is going to get them to the organization's goals. |
| • Multiple discrete strategies that are not aligned or connected. | • Strategies, time, money, and professional development are aligned in service of improving teaching and learning. |

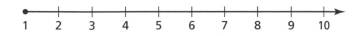

1  2  3  4  5  6  7  8  9  10

As you review Exercise 4.1, what examples come to mind that indicate the purpose and focus within your school or district? Once you have rated your district or school on the continuum provided, we invite you to turn to Appendix A and use the group version of this exercise with others in your district or school. We have found that the greatest potential in these exercises lies in the discourse that emerges when individuals share their ratings, their perspectives, and their reasoning.

## Compliance Transforms to Engagement

Coupled closely with a tendency to be reactive is an attitude of *compliance* in a bureaucratic culture. Again, the reasons for this tendency are historic and understandable, beginning with the trend over the past century in American public education to consolidate small schools and districts into larger and larger administrative units. The resulting organizational structure is fairly hierarchical, with teachers reporting to principals who report to the superintendent. Education has, in fact, been more rule and procedure oriented than most white-collar work cultures and, in many ways, is run more like a factory than a corporation. As recently as the 1970s, many districts had time clocks and punch cards to record teachers' daily attendance. In some public schools, educators are still required to sign in and out every day, and in some districts, principals must obtain permission to leave their buildings. Overall, bureaucratic and compliance-driven responsiveness has increased under the weight of new reporting and accountability mandates.[2]

By temperament, many educators value "getting along." Challenging the system, or even encouraging critical thinking, has never been a hallmark of public education. Indeed, with most faculty and administrative meetings taken up with announcements and other "administrivia," there is little or no time set aside in school or district schedules for discussion and debate of professional matters. To the contrary, new initiatives, programs, or strategies for school or district improvement are usually presented to principals and faculty with the expectation that they will just "go along" in return for some say in curriculum decisions and a high degree of autonomy in the classroom.

This culture of compliance may promote a degree of managerial efficiency, but it does not enable the kind of intellectual inquiry and engagement required for authentic and sustainable improvement. In a highly bureaucratized culture that values buy-in rather than ongoing debate and discussion, teachers and principals may appear to "go along," while instead harboring a great deal of skepticism or even cynicism about the new project or program they've been told to use. So they may do the minimum or adopt a "wait and see" attitude. Veteran educators, who have seen too many reforms come and go, frequently sit silently in meetings, saying to themselves, "This, too, shall pass."

When Vicki Phillips became superintendent in Lancaster in 1998, she found herself in meetings where no one spoke. We can imagine the body language she must have seen—polite expressions, hands folded neatly, arms crossed—a posture at once alert and reclined. Even when asked for their opinions, principals and teachers did not become more engaged, which Phillips concluded represented a pervasive sense of fear and mistrust throughout the district. They were waiting for the new superintendent to tell them what to do, fearing she would play "gotcha" if they offered her the wrong answer. Their prior experiences had created these very logical assumptions.

Believing that everyone's opinion and best thinking were needed to solve the district's chronic achievement gap, Phillips worked hard to create a climate of intellectual engagement where questioning, dialogue, and respectful debate became the norm in all meetings. She recognized the critical nature of her own actions in these meetings and deliberately set out to establish an environment of safe participation for learning by issuing credible invitations to speak, stressing why practitioner input was so important, and diminishing the status differences during such conversations.

Indeed, research on team learning by Amy Edmonson of the Harvard Business School stresses that the strongest predictor of real engagement is the level of psychological safety (or trust) that exists within a group. Edmonson found that group members tacitly assess the interpersonal risk associated with behaviors necessary for learning (such as asking questions or publicly learning from mistakes) and adjust their actions in meetings accordingly.[3] Anthony Bryk and Barbara Schneider's research on trust in school improvement work is consistent with Edmonson's findings.[4] Phillips' role in asking for input, creating a level playing field for conversation, and modeling her own desire to learn was instrumental in breaking the norms of the past.

This is not to suggest that Phillips didn't make any decisions on her own. Indeed, she introduced an initiative to transition half-day "play" kindergartens into a full-day, academically oriented instructional program for all children throughout the district. In making her decision public, she outlined the rationale for her decision, citing twenty years of research as a key influence. Convinced that the change was necessary, she did not allow dissenting voices to dissuade her. In fact, she proudly tells the story of a veteran kindergarten teacher who rose in a meeting to publicly disagree with Phillips' decision but then agreed to give it a try, despite her reservations. Six months later, the teacher came to tell Phillips what she'd learned about how much kindergarteners can do if given the opportunity and how she wanted to help train other teachers. Although the decision was Phillips', being free to disagree may have enabled this teacher skeptic to give the new program her best effort, rather than the lethargic inertia that often accompanies a compliant decision to "get along."

Engagement, then, does not necessarily imply total agreement. Rather, it means creating a culture where working together to address problems becomes the norm at every level in the organization. Engagement in educational improvement efforts means faculty meetings where educators think through and discuss various instructional strategies. At the district level, it means principals' meetings with authentic professional challenges and problems of practice to discuss and learn about together. Engagement requires leaders to model learning and actively express differences in views, drawing on those differences as resources for learning. It asks people to openly share what is and isn't working in their classrooms and schools. It therefore requires the presence of social norms that create the psychological safety for people to make suggestions, offer challenges, and try on new ideas. These kinds of actions result in a culture of highly engaged individuals, characterized by a strong sense of personal and shared responsibility for the district's (or school's) goals and strategies for the collective enterprise of teaching and leading.

See Exercise 4.2 to determine where your school or district falls on this continuum. We invite you to consider examples and to share this information as a group by using the group version of this exercise provided in Appendix A.

 **Exercise 4.2: Compliance Versus Engagement Diagnostic**

As you assess the level of *engagement* in your school or district, here are some general questions to get you started:

1. How much ownership is there among all adults in the system and how do you know?
2. Is there ownership just at the top, or do people throughout the system feel genuinely committed to the instructional improvement goals?

3. How much does it seem people are working to meet someone else's goal versus meeting a goal they own or co-own?

4. Are people participating productively during meetings?

Here, also, are some specific indicators of both ends of the continuum.

| *Compliance* | *Engagement* |
|---|---|
| • Teachers and principals are expected to "go along" with mandates; no procedures exist for generating conversation and collaborative decision making. | • Productive dialogue and debate regarding organizational strategies and goals are nurtured. |
| • Communication tends to be one-way. | • Communication is multidirectional. |
| • Culture tends to be rule and procedure driven. | • Culture is characterized by strong sense of personal and shared responsibility for the strategies and goals of the district. |
| • Teachers and principals do not take risks and do not investigate successes and failures. | • Professional discourse is focused on learning from professional challenges. |

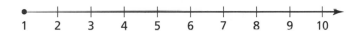

## Isolation Transforms to Collaboration

American public and private school educators generally work alone. In fact, one of the attractions of the profession traditionally has been the high degree of autonomy afforded classroom teachers with respect to decisions about teaching methods and curriculum. School principals, too, have traditionally enjoyed a measure of latitude in how they run their buildings. So long as educators appear to go along with current leaders' initiatives, they can make a number of decisions about how they run their classrooms or schools. In many respects, the ways in which educators' work is organized has not changed significantly during the last century. One-room schools have simply been consolidated under one roof, and although teachers no longer teach all subjects to every grade, they often still spend their entire day with children and have very few opportunities or demands to work with

gues. Building and central office administrators may be required to attend
meetings, yet these gatherings are usually concerned with the administra-
the organization—rather than with the problems and opportunities associated with teaching and instructional leadership.

---

*Indeed, virtually every other profession in modern
life has transitioned to various forms of teamwork,
yet most educators still work alone.*

---

This isolation of adults at all levels in the education system actively discourages
their learning and capacity to improve their practice. Indeed, virtually every other
profession in modern life has transitioned to various forms of teamwork, yet most
educators still work alone. Even in the popular media, 1960s "lone ranger" images
such as lawyer Perry Mason and physician Marcus Welby have transitioned to
images of teams solving problems together—such as the physicians of the TV show
*ER* or the detectives of the *CSI* series. This transition has not been reflected in
education. Like Jaime Escalante, played by Edward James Olmos in *Stand and Deliver,* and the character of John Keating, played by Robin Williams in *Dead Poets
Society,* teachers tend to work all alone.

Yet we are seeing that improving adult performance at every level in schools and
districts requires teamwork and *collaboration* that produces new learning and solves
the inevitable problems of practice that emerge during adaptive work. The idea of
"professional competence" suggests not that educators must be completely knowledgeable, right, and in control but instead that we are sufficiently knowledgeable
and aware of what we do and do not know (and thus need to learn). Collaborative
professionals are able to ask questions, request help, share their practice, and receive
input from colleagues. (See Exercise 4.3.) They are able, where appropriate, to put
aside their expertise so that they can be open to new thinking, potentially disrupting their own previously held and perhaps cherished assumptions. Collaborative
professionals do this with a belief that their questions serve a larger good and, ultimately, are part of what enables the district to succeed in reaching all students. A
basic assumption is that all adults become responsible for all kids. None of the problems we experience are ours alone. A fellow fourth-grade teacher likely struggles

with some of the same issues as his or her colleagues. How the fourth-grade teachers effectively address these matters will have implications for the fifth-grade teachers the following year. And so on, up through the grades.

---

## Exercise 4.3: Isolation Versus Collaboration Diagnostic

Here are some general questions about collaboration to consider:

1. Are meetings focused on learning, teaching, and leading?
2. Do organizational members possess and use the skills of dialogue and inquiry?
3. Do people share problems of practice at meetings?

Some indicators of what a system at either end of the spectrum might look like follow:

*Isolation*
- Teachers and administrators work in *isolation*.

- There is no opportunity or urgency for collective problem solving.

- Good leading and teaching exist as random acts of excellence in the system; there is little dissemination of best practice.

- There are few expectations for collaborative work among adults.

*Collaboration*
- The work of teachers and administrators is a public enterprise within the school.

- Educators collectively solve problems that inhibit effective teaching and learning.

- Standards of practice for teaching and leading exist, and are shared and specific.

- There are clear and shared expectations around the nature and ends of *collaboration*.

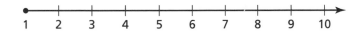

1   2   3   4   5   6   7   8   9   10

---

Adults need to work together to solve core problems of practice so that they can develop, or at least contribute to, standards of practice and an authentic knowledge base. Sharing problems of practice helps provide the means of identifying and exploring standards of practice, which can then be adapted to the particular situation of a particular classroom or a particular student. The capacity to address problems of practice assures that individuals are not left to struggle with problems on their own. Instead, collaboration ensures that professionals can share in the trials and successes of teachers' daily interaction with students.

Before we describe a new way of organizing work that structures opportunities for increased focus, engagement, and collaboration, review the diagnostic exercises we've provided on each of the continua (Exercises 4.1, 4.2, and 4.3). Use them to better understand the dimensions for momentum and to locate your school or district along the continua from momentum drain to momentum generation. Think of your own examples and evidence and consider what it would take to move forward in the area most in need of attention.

## GENERATING THE MOMENTUM FOR SYSTEMIC CHANGE

Generating the knowledge to teach all students new skills while working to educate the students presently in our care is incredibly demanding. And the tendencies of reaction, compliance, and isolation reinforce each other and create a *system* of barriers to adaptive change. If vague or excessive priorities diffuse and fragment the work of an organization, the isolation already inherent in the profession is exacerbated. Without clear priorities and focus, schools and districts cannot collectively learn and solve problems. Compliance inhibits the momentum required by adults to own and lead the work of improving teaching and learning; work or learning that is without purpose rarely gathers much steam.

In contrast, the opposites of these characteristics point to practices and behaviors that create the momentum for adaptive capacity. Very effective schools and districts consistently have high degrees of purpose and focus, engagement, and collaboration, particularly around learning, teaching, and instructional leadership.

## COMMUNITIES OF PRACTICE AS A STRATEGY

It is relatively easy to describe the ideal attributes of purpose and focus, engagement, and collaboration. It is also comparatively easy to describe how these attributes help build a school or district that has greater adaptive capacity. Putting these attributes into practice is much more difficult. The default cultures of our schools tend to work against these attributes. As a result, infusing a system with purpose and focus, engagement, and collaboration challenges individual and organizational beliefs and behaviors.

This task of transforming the culture of schools and the way we orient the work of schooling cannot be accomplished by dictum; more than charismatic leadership is required to set these changes into motion and to sustain the momentum "rightward." One means of introducing the attributes of purpose and focus, engagement, and collaboration into systems of schools is for educators to adopt an organizational form that is increasingly being used in a variety of professions. This form, which Wenger and Snyder describe as communities of practice, consists of networks of professionals that exist to develop members' capacities, to build and exchange knowledge, to transfer best practices, and to solve "problems of practice."[5] Establishing role-alike communities of practice, where teachers, administrators, and change leaders meet in their respective groups to discuss their practice could help promote purpose and focus among all participants.

Communities of practice are characterized by a shared passion, commitment, and identification with a group's purpose. They promote engagement by providing forums for professionals to learn, grow, and become more effective at their craft. Being part of a community with standards of practice and working collectively to solve authentic problems of practice can also help provide a greater sense of efficacy, a factor correlated with job satisfaction and increased student learning.[6] Moreover, communities of practice fundamentally disrupt the extreme isolation among educators in American schools, promoting collaboration anchored directly in our professional practice.

## Communities of Practice for Teachers

Many national leaders and organizations promote the concept of teacher collaboration as a key strategy for improvement. Rick DuFour, Ann Lieberman, and others describe "professional learning communities" as a way for teachers to come together to share ideas and to learn.[7] The Coalition of Essential Schools, the National School Reform Faculty, and Harvard's Project Zero created a structure known as Critical Friends Groups to help volunteer groups of teachers discuss their work.[8]

Perhaps the most fully developed model of teacher collaboration to improve practice is the lesson study process described by James Stigler and James Hiebert in *The Teaching Gap*.[9] In a manner similar to the Total Quality Management philosophy that W. Edwards Deming pioneered in Japan in the 1960s as a strategy for improving the quality of products and services, Japan now assigns primary responsibility for improving practice to its teachers. Organized by grade level or subject content area, teams of teachers meet regularly to discuss the learning challenges of their students and collaboratively develop lessons that more effectively meet their students' needs. Teachers take turns teaching these model lessons, observing each other and reflecting together. They continue to refine each lesson until they get the learning they expect from students. Only then do they share them more widely with colleagues and go on to a new problem of practice.

The lesson study process, which Stigler and Hiebert suggest goes a long way toward explaining why the level of instruction in most Japanese classrooms appears consistently higher than that of other countries, creates the opportunity for collections of teachers to develop new knowledge about their craft and to develop standards of teaching practice. This school-based professional development is considered part of a teacher's job and is reported to be highly valued by Japanese teachers. If a lesson study process were linked to the focus of schools and districts, say literacy, then communities of practice could help uphold and promote purpose and focus.

There are lessons for us here that may parallel those of Total Quality Management. The Japanese were quick to adopt Deming's strategies for improving the quality of products back in the 1960s. It was not until U.S. corporations found themselves losing market share to the Japanese in the 1980s that they embraced Deming's secret of employee involvement. In a knowledge economy, businesses find that more active engagement of their employees in improving their service or product also improves morale, quality, and productivity. In the same way, school-based professional development holds enormous promise for teachers, schools, and the children they serve.

For these teacher communities of practice to be effective, they must have real student data to inform the conversation. Data should be disaggregated by teacher, not to expose those who may be getting poor results, but rather to identify and learn from those teachers who are getting results far above average with comparable groups of students. Take, for example, two earth science teachers in a school we recently visited. With comparable groupings of students, one achieved a 92 percent pass rate on the state test with her students, whereas just 49 percent of the other teacher's students passed the test. Why did these teachers get such different results? How can we possibly know that "effective practice" is truly effective unless we examine what learning occurs as a result? As painful as this might be, we cannot improve until we know the effects of our efforts.

## Leadership Practice Communities

Although teachers' communities of practice are becoming increasingly common, communities of practice for school and district leaders—what we call leadership practice communities (or LPCs)—are still very rare. Leaders need their own LPCs for several reasons. First, few school principals or district personnel have received training in how to be instructional leaders—or even how to do effective supervision. LPCs provide principals with opportunities to present and discuss problems of practice related to supervising teachers, and they also provide central office staff opportunities to discuss principal supervision.

Leadership practice communities are also a strategy for moving beyond "pockets of excellence" within districts to creating greater alignment and consistency of performance standards throughout the system. In opening up their own practice for ongoing discussion, leaders model the behaviors that are expected in teacher communities of practice throughout the system. And when leaders routinely have opportunities to present case studies related to whole school improvement—and can discuss and agree on what are the most effective strategies across the system— the entire system becomes more focused and coherent. LPCs, then, are a strategy both for developing individual leaders' capacities and for generating consistently higher performance throughout the system.

*Leadership Practice Communities are a strategy both for developing individual leaders' capacities and for generating consistently higher performance throughout the system.*

Grand Rapids School District in Michigan provides a case in point. As a central component of the district's improvement strategy, talented central office personnel with school leadership experience were given an important new role, that of "coach." Each of these individuals was responsible for providing support and building the capacity of principals and their respective schools to improve dramatically. In the beginning, there was great enthusiasm for this new role and for the potential impact this new cadre of coaches could have for "driving improvement through the system." Over time, though, coaches readily admitted frustration and confusion concerning their role and their effectiveness. Coaches were working independently from each other, struggling in isolation to solve the new problems of practice they faced.

As a result of this growing frustration and confusion, the group of coaches worked collectively to build a written framework that could guide and inform their work. Moreover, they began to anchor their biweekly conversations and professional development in concrete problems of practice such as how to provide difficult feedback to a school improvement team about its school plan; how to identify and tap into existing district resources to build school-level capacity; and how to generate greater understanding, ownership, and urgency among school personnel for the improvement work. Using a protocol (see Box 4.1 on Step Back Consulting), individuals shared their dilemmas and this "community of coaching practice" discussed and wrestled with identifying effective solutions. This group admits they have much more work before them as they develop each other's skills and begin to generate and codify standards of coaching practice. They have begun by anchoring their collaborative conversations in particular dilemmas they face that are tied to the priorities of the district improvement goal. A result is newfound momentum and engagement among the coaches to succeed in their challenging and sometimes frustrating new role.

---

## Box 4.1:  Step Back Consulting: A Protocol for Building Communities of Practice

Step Back Consulting is based on a number of learning principles:

- For powerful small-group learning to occur, all members must have a role that matters to them and keeps them active.
- Groups are helped by a sense of urgency and momentum, a feeling that there is something important to do and hardly enough time in which to do it.
- The less the consultee talks, the greater the chance for the consultee to learn.

Here, briefly, is how it works. The times given are based on a typical one-hour session.

**Step One.** The consultee presents the issue, problem, goal, or project. (10 minutes)

**Step Two.**  The consultee answers clarifying questions from the group. (5 minutes)

---

**Step Three.** The consultee "steps back" and becomes a silent observer. The consultee's job is to remain silent and oversee actively, perhaps by keeping notes of ideas and internal reactions. The group takes on the project as if it were theirs, pondering questions such as:

- What would they think to do?
- What would they avoid doing?
- How do they find themselves reconceiving the project? (35–40 minutes)

**Step Four.** The consultee rejoins the conversation and describes how he or she experienced the process, what it was like to sit back and watch as others temporarily took on the project, what he or she thought, and what he or she learned. (5–10 minutes)

**Step Five.** Finally, the group collectively reflects on the implications of the discussion, identifying any principles of practice that were brought to light.

In our experience, consultees are often surprised to discover how challenging just sitting back turns out to be. Often this is a lesson in how difficult it is to reconstruct our experience or change our minds. We may be overinvested in our constructions, have a hard time keeping an open mind, or simply not give new ideas a fair hearing.

The dynamics of Step Back Consulting lead to a high-energy, high-involvement group process on behalf of the consultee. Most people find the experience novel, rewarding, and transportable: something they'd undertake again, even in different settings. The power of this experience is due in part to the fact that the collaborative conversations are anchored in discrete and meaningful dilemmas that individuals experience in their professional practice. These dilemmas become case studies in progress, creating opportunities to investigate, reflect, listen, and learn.

Regular use of a teaching tool, the case study, which is common to law, medicine, and business, can be invaluable for promoting learning in administrators' LPCs. For example, we have observed groups of principals discussing case studies of individual teachers they are supervising. These case studies offer a learning opportunity for their colleagues, at the same time supporting the principal and the teacher being studied. Sometimes, the principals even role-play difficult supervision conferences with each other to increase their skill in communicating difficult information clearly and effectively. Assistant superintendents and other central office supervisors can also present case studies of principals and schools with whom they are working. The work of the Connecticut Center for School Change and Washington grantees of the Bill & Melinda Gates Foundation has shown that superintendents also benefit from ongoing communities of practice where they walk through classrooms together, present case studies about their districts' work to one another, and discuss the challenges of leading this work.

Unlike the ways they often function in other professions, education leaders' communities of practice ultimately cannot be left only to those who "volunteer"; they must become the way we all do our work in schools and districts, even if volunteerism is an initial strategy for implementation. School and district administrators therefore need to think creatively about how to promote communities of practice without inadvertently reinforcing education's norm of compliance. Our experiences show that the first step in this process is not to mandate these practices unilaterally but for leaders to model them in a public commitment to their own learning. Over time, participation in communities of practice will change the culture of reaction, compliance, and isolation so prevalent in education.

In this chapter, we investigated the dynamics of purpose and focus, engagement, and collaboration and their role in a system that improves instruction in our schools. We presented snapshots of these dynamics in action to paint a more vivid picture of the right side of the continuum. But the road to the "right side" is not without challenges. The bumps in the road that we have shared mostly involved challenges found in an organization as a whole. In Chapter Five, we take a closer look at the *individual* implications for this work, the inner work that is required. Although change leaders must pay attention to the larger, systemic functions of the organization, it is also important for them to keep an eye inward, on how they are making sense of the improvement process and on their own contributions to its pace and success.

### Endnotes

1. Richard F. Elmore with Deanna Burney, *Investing in Teacher Learning: Staff Development and Instructional Improvement in Community School District #2, New York City* (Philadelphia: University of Pennsylvania, Consortium for Policy Research in Education, 1997).

2. See F. Hess, *Spinning Wheels: The Politics of Urban School Reform* (Washington, D.C.: Brookings Institution Press, 1998).

3. For more information, see Amy C. Edmonson, "The Local and Variegated Nature of Learning in Organizations: A Group-Level Perspective," *Organization Science* 13, no. 2 (March-April 2002): 128–146.

4. Anthony S. Bryk and Barbara L. Schneider, *Trust in Schools: A Core Resource for Improvement* (New York: Russell Sage Foundation, 2002).

5. From E. Wenger and W. M. Snyder, "Communities of Practice: The Organizational Frontier," *Harvard Business Review* 78, no. 1 (January 2000).

6. D. Armor, P. Conroy-Oseguera, M. Cox, N. King, L. McDonnell, A. Pascal, E. Pauly, and G. Zellman, *Analysis of the School Preferred Reading Programs in Selected Los Angeles Minority Schools*, Report No. R-2007-LAUSD (Santa Monica, Calif.: RAND, 1976). ERIC Document Reproduction Service No. 130 243.

7. Richard Dufour and Robert E. Baker, *Professional Learning Communities at Work: Best Practices for Enhancing Student Achievement* (Bloomington, Ind.: National Educational Service, 1998); Ann Lieberman, "Practices That Support Teacher Development: Transforming Conceptions of Professional Learning," *Phi Delta Kappan* 76, no. 8 (April 1995).

8. Faith Dunne, Bill Nave, and Anne Lewis, "Critical Friends Groups: Teachers Helping Teachers to Improve Student Learning," *Phi Delta Kappa Center for Evaluation, Development, and Research Bulletin*, no. 28 (December 2000); Tina Blythe, David Allen, and Barbara Powell, *Looking Together at Student Work: A Companion Guide to Assessing Student Learning* (New York: Teachers College Press, 1999).

9. James W. Stigler and James Hiebert, *The Teaching Gap: Best Ideas from the World's Teachers for Improving Education in the Classroom* (New York: Free Press, 1999).

# Exploring Individual Immunities to Change

I n Chapter Four, we investigated the dynamics of purpose and focus, engagement, and collaboration and their role in a system that improves instruction in our schools. We were focusing solely on the *organization* and its cultural attributes. We now want to weave leadership into the system—specifically *you* as a leader—as the biggest resource for change. Although change leaders must pay attention to the larger systemic functions of the organization, it is also important for them to keep an eye inward, on how they are making sense of the improvement process and their own contributions to its pace and success.

## ATTENDING TO COUNTERING BEHAVIORS

In Chapter Three, Exercise 3.1, we asked you to name a personal commitment on behalf of improving instruction. We also asked that you check your commitment against certain criteria that would increase the likelihood of it being a powerful goal. Once you had that goal in mind, you took the brave next step of generating a list of all your behaviors that counter that very commitment (Exercise 3.2). We realize that this might have been a difficult list to create. Now it's time to bring that commitment and those behaviors to the front of your mind so that we can help you move one step deeper in your personal and professional reflection. As you do this, we'll also show you how one high school principal worked through the process (see the text boxes in the following pages).

## Sherry's Story

We worked with a principal of a high school, Sherry, who identified a strong commitment to engaging the teachers in her school building in honest and supportive dialogues around their teaching practices. As Sherry envisioned what this commitment would look like, it was evident that the success of these dialogues would depend heavily on a school culture characterized by purpose and focus, engagement, and collaboration.

Looking at her behavioral inventory, however, Sherry could see how she was unintentionally enabling the school to stay firmly planted on the left side of these continua. For example, she:

- Proposed a new curriculum without accompanying support for teachers to learn that curriculum and make it their own.
- Let other responsibilities interrupt the instructional focus of staff meetings, thereby inhibiting a powerful and commonly held sense of their focus and purpose.
- Did not stop negative and backhanded comments about colleagues' practices when she overheard them in the teachers' lunchroom, even though she saw how these comments could undermine staff members' trust in collaboration.

The first thing that you may notice as you review your list of countering behaviors is how some of them might keep you (and your schools or districts) on the left side of the continua, closer to reaction, for example, than purpose and change. As you look at your list of countering behaviors, what impact might they be having on your organization's culture? How can you relate these to the three continua? We now ask that you complete Exercise 5.1 and rate your commitment and behaviors on a scale of 1–10.

### Exercise 5.1: Evaluate Your Commitment and Behaviors

#### Your Commitment

To what extent would the realization of your commitment represent (or lead to? or produce?) a school culture of greater focus and purpose, engagement, and collaboration? Rate each on a scale of 1 to 10, with 1 being the left side and 10 being the right side.

| Reaction | 1 2 3 4 5 6 7 8 9 10 | Purpose and Focus |
| Compliance | 1 2 3 4 5 6 7 8 9 10 | Engagement |
| Isolation | 1 2 3 4 5 6 7 8 9 10 | Collaboration |

## Your Behaviors

To what extent do the behaviors you listed in Exercise 3.2 undermine movement toward purpose and focus, engagement, and collaboration? Rate your behaviors on the following scale.

| Reaction | 1 2 3 4 5 6 7 8 9 10 | Purpose and Focus |
| Compliance | 1 2 3 4 5 6 7 8 9 10 | Engagement |
| Isolation | 1 2 3 4 5 6 7 8 9 10 | Collaboration |

If your commitment shows potential to move your school or district rightward on the continua but your behaviors keep you to the left, it might be very tempting to want to tackle those behaviors so that you can make progress on your noble goal. However, as we mentioned earlier, changing these behaviors temporarily without getting at their source almost guarantees short-lived successes. Counterintuitive though this might seem, we ask that you hold off for a bit before taking new action.

> . . . Changing these behaviors temporarily without getting at their source almost guarantees short-lived successes.

## A DEEPER LOOK

As you read this book, you will be using this commitment and your list of behaviors to generate a deeper look at your personal beliefs and behaviors. Exercise 5.2 is provided to help you keep track. The first stages of completing this exercise are easy: simply copy your commitment (from Exercise 3.1) into the first column and list your behaviors (from Exercise 3.2) in the second column.

Now on to the third-column entry. Look at the list of the behaviors you generated in the second column and try to imagine what it would be like to do the exact opposite of them. As you imagine trying to do the opposite of your second-column

### Exercise 5.2: Look Inward: Your Four-Column Immunity Map

| 1 | 2 | 3 | 4 |
|---|---|---|---|
| Commitment | Doing/Not Doing | Hidden/Competing Commitment | Big Assumption |
| | | | |

behaviors, do any even remotely uncomfortable feelings emerge for you? Use the third column to list some of those discomforts or fears. Do you feel uneasy if you imagine yourself not doing the things you *are* doing? If so, you are beginning to sense a crucial feeling that connects you to the powerful energy keeping you from actually doing those things you listed in column 2. It is in this place of discomfort, or what psychologists and philosophers call disequilibrium, that you can begin to sense the nascent possibilities of personal, *individual* change.

---

### Sherry's Story, Third Column

Sherry tried to imagine what it would be like for her to:

- Provide teachers with adequate support and professional development in the new curriculum.
- Say "no" to responsibilities that interfered with staff meetings about instruction.
- Speak directly to teachers about their lunchroom conversations and peer relations.

When contemplating these actions, all kinds of uncomfortable feelings began to arise for her. For example, when Sherry imagined what it would look like if she were to provide teachers with adequate support and training in the new curriculum, she realized she held fears that she, too, would be held accountable for their successes and failures as teachers. She wrote:

*I fear that I would be held accountable for the success and failures of the teachers as instructional leaders.*

---

## FINDING THE COMPETING COMMITMENT

The next step is a conceptual move that is a bit trickier. In our practice, we find that these fears or discomforts can be so powerful that they actually lend themselves to another kind of commitment, one that competes with the first-column commitment. A word of caution: this *competing commitment* will not be what you would normally think of as a commitment; in fact, you might not even be aware of it. In contrast to the first-column commitment, which is the sort of commitment we "have," the competing commitment is the sort of commitment that "has us." It is not the sort of commitment that you will want to shout from the rooftops, as you might the first-column commitment. It probably feels less noble and more self-revealing. So, to help you make this move, first draw a line underneath the fears or discomforts that you just generated in that third column. Below that line, write this introductory phrase:

*I am also committed to . . .*

Now consider how you might put words to a commitment that protects you from having to face those fears and discomforts. For example, if I feared others might lower their opinion of me, I might consider that I have a commitment "not to run the risk that others will think less of me." No one wants to picture these competing commitments emblazoned on a plaque, but recognizing their existence is an important step.

---

*No one wants to picture these competing commitments emblazoned on a plaque, but recognizing their existence is an important step.*

---

### Sherry's Story, Competing Commitment

In her third column, underneath her stated fear, Sherry wrote

*I am committed to not being held responsible for the improvement of the teachers' instructional practices in my building.*

Stating a competing commitment may sound counterproductive to you at first, but understanding the rationale behind this self-preservation can in fact be very—even critically—productive. Because it is in direct conflict with your first-column commitment, it may also be the very reason it is difficult for you to gain any traction on that commitment. Why would you want to change those second-column behaviors if you were fearful of the consequences? And yet, why would you expect to make progress on your first-column commitment if you continue those second-column behaviors? And how do we imagine we can so easily alter these behaviors now that we see they are not merely ineffective—relative to our first-column commitments—but highly effective, even brilliant, behaviors—relative to our third-column commitments!? Seeing our first- and third-column commitments together creates a picture of a system that we call an immunity to change, because, like biological immunities, it protects us from doing things that might (or so it seems) put us at risk or compromise our well-being.[1]

---

*These behaviors . . . [are actually] highly effective,*
*even brilliant, behaviors relative to our*
*third-column commitments!?*

---

Be sure that your third-column commitment helps create a powerful map of your emotional immune system. Not only should you feel a kind of tightening in your stomach as you reread this commitment, but it should also be clear how this commitment is self-protecting and how your countering behaviors make complete sense.

---

*Partnering with another person will help you*
*progress through what is admittedly difficult work.*

---

Once you have checked your entry against these criteria, we encourage you to share your completed Exercise 5.2 with a trusted colleague—ideally someone who has also worked through columns 1–3. In asking you to share this with another person (see Box 5.1 for guidelines), it is not our intent to put you in a vulnerable position. Rather, we believe that partnering with another person will help you progress through what is admittedly difficult work. In addition, working in tandem often encourages a form of mutual accountability that keeps each of you focused and moving forward through the process.

---

## Box 5.1: Sharing Your Competing Commitment

Before sharing your third-column commitment with a colleague, please make sure that the two of you have agreed on the following norms:

- This partner should not be someone who supervises you or whom you supervise, because we do not want you to risk a potentially evaluative relationship.
- It is not the role or responsibility of the other person to point out all the other hidden commitments or fears that you may not have considered.
- It is also not the role or responsibility of your partner to liken what you wrote to his or her own experiences.

However, it is the responsibility of your partner (or you) to:

- Listen attentively to what the other person says.
- Help you hone your entry so that it meets the criteria listed earlier (that is, does it sound self-protecting as opposed to noble? Does it counter the first-column commitment? Do the behaviors in the second column now make all the sense in the world?).

---

Why are we encouraging you to write these competing commitments at all? And then share them? Why put yourself in that potentially awkward position? We truly believe (and our experiences confirm) that *if you can see how and why you are preventing yourself from changing, you will have a better chance to change.* And we believe that making your work more public—albeit safely—increases the likelihood that you will continue this work. How exactly to continue the work is discussed in Chapter Six. In this chapter, all we are trying to accomplish is a deeper view of the problem by understanding how your internal immune system holds it in place. As Einstein put it: "The formulation of the problem is often more important than the solution."[2] Of course, we ultimately want to help you "solve the problem," but if you start out with only a partial view of the problem (in this instance, tackling the second-column behaviors) then the progress of your goal will be hindered.

-----

*. . . If you can see how and why you are preventing yourself from changing, you will have a better chance to change.*

-----

## TAKING THE NEXT STEP

For now, let's revisit Arthur. As you may remember, Arthur was committed to moving his district from "good" to "great" by creating a common vision of rigorous instruction. Although he successfully collaborated with others to craft this common vision, he was less successful in his individual efforts to carry out the next step in the process: holding others accountable for the actions their particular roles suggested. He examined his own behaviors and saw how he was impeding his own good intentions by putting off critical meetings with those responsible for moving the work forward, and by overscrutinizing the description of instruction for any possible ambiguities before taking it to the field.

As a reflective person, Arthur agreed to consider any discomforts or fears that might emerge if he were to stop waylaying the change process and start holding others accountable for this vision that was shared in his district. In turning toward these discomforts, Arthur recognized the uncharted nature of this journey and, potentially, the personal and political risk in moving ahead. Did he really want to lead the school district in this direction when he was unsure of the results? What if all the people with whom he worked found out that there were times when he felt very uncertain about what he was doing? What if there were negative consequences? The school district had never taken on such a unified effort. Not only would it be an enormous amount of work but there was the possibility it would not go as planned. He would be leading the organization into an expensive, time-consuming, and uncomfortable change process that might not amount to any significant improvement. Recognition of these fears told Arthur that he was, in fact, also committed to not risk being seen as a failure. His map, with the third column completed, is shown in Exhibit 5.1.

# Exhibit 5.1:
# Arthur's Four-Column Immunity Map

| 1 | 2 | 3 | 4 |
|---|---|---|---|
| Commitment | Doing/Not Doing | Hidden/Competing Commitment | Big Assumption |
| I am committed to moving my district from "good" to "great" by creating a common vision of rigorous instruction. | I am not holding others accountable.<br><br>I am procrastinating critical meetings.<br><br>I am scrutinizing the description of instruction rather than helping others to shape it. | (I fear that others would find out that I do not know what I am doing. I fear that I would lead the organization down the wrong path. I fear that this effort would not go as planned.)<br><br>I am committed to not having others discover I am uncertain about how we will accomplish our goals.<br><br>I am committed to keeping others from finding out that I'm not always sure of the next step.<br><br>I am committed to not moving the district one step further until I can be absolutely sure I know how to successfully complete the journey. | |

Arthur could easily see how his third-column commitment competed with his first-column commitment. If he was committed to not taking one step further until he was absolutely sure of how to complete the journey successfully, then there was no way he would be able to take the risks necessary to move his district from good to great. And Arthur could see how his second-column behaviors made all the sense in the world given his third-column commitment. If he was committed to not taking one step further until he was absolutely sure, then of course he would not hold others accountable for implementing changes, would not schedule meetings to discuss next steps, and would continue to delay implementing the new description of good instruction! In the traditional style of school leadership, Arthur's need to be the sole leader of the organization and to not include others in the adaptive change process would have been a noble attribute. However, these same actions countered a new style of leadership—one that furthered collaborative efforts toward purpose and focus and engagement. Although Arthur had every intention of moving his district closer to collaboration, purpose and focus, and engagement, he recognized that his third-column entries demanded deeper reflection before he could tackle the countering behaviors. That reflection made all the difference.

### Endnotes

1. R. Kegan and L. Lahey, *How the Way We Talk Can Change the Way We Work* (San Francisco: Jossey-Bass, 2001).
2. As quoted in *The Evolution of Physics* (New York: Free Press, 1967), 92.

# Reflections

O ur goal in the preceding two chapters has been to help you understand and overcome common organizational and individual tendencies that inhibit adaptive change. We explored ways that organizations can help create and release momentum for change, ways in which they can move from reaction to purpose and focus, from compliance to engagement, and from isolation to collaboration. Communities of practice—networks through which people can develop their capacities, build and exchange knowledge, transfer best practices, and solve problems of practice—offer practical knowledge and support where it is most needed. Because there is also internal work that must be done, we described how you can identify and name the tensions that hold you immune to change and growth.

In the next two chapters, we turn to examine *organizations* and *individuals* as systems, and the multiple dimensions that must be understood and addressed to be successful in this work.

**PART THREE**

# Thinking Systemically

# Relating the Parts to the Whole

In the preceding chapters, we have used the word *system* as a way of illustrating the interrelated nature of the elements that make up an organization or a change effort. This way of thinking, first introduced in the late 1950s by MIT professor Jay Forrester, became popular in 1990 when the now classic work *The Fifth Discipline* was first published. In it, Peter Senge proposes a systems thinking framework as the foundation of what he terms a learning organization. As a result of this pioneering work, systems thinking is now understood and practiced in many professions. It has been less commonly used in the field of education.

A system is a "perceived whole whose elements 'hang together' because they continually affect each other over time and operate toward a common purpose."[1] Systems thinking is about trying to keep that "whole" in mind, even while working on the various parts. More "ecological" than logical, it recognizes that simple, linear cause-and-effect explanations sometimes miss the fact that today's effect may in turn be tomorrow's cause, influencing some other part of the system. This shift in thinking, and the need to understand the interrelationships among the various components of the work, presents an enormous learning challenge for change leaders. It requires addressing a number of questions:

- How can change leaders form a more holistic picture of change processes that makes sense to themselves and to others?

- How can change leaders learn to identify the contributors to an identified problem?
- Where do change leaders look to find these contributors?
- How does a leader build a shared vision of success that is coherent and is truly owned and inspiring to others?

---

*More "ecological" than logical, it recognizes that simple, linear cause-and-effect explanations sometimes miss the fact that today's effect may in turn be tomorrow's cause, influencing some other part of the system.*

---

These are difficult questions to answer individually, and rarely do leaders have the data needed to answer them all at once. Yet it is very difficult to develop a thoughtful strategy for change without some clear answers—or at least some thoughtful hypotheses. What is needed is an analytic framework for understanding the interrelated parts or elements of the change process in schools and districts. This chapter explores a means for leaders to develop and practice new ways of seeing the "whole."

## ARENAS OF CHANGE

We offer an approach to thinking systemically about the challenges and goals of change in schools and districts, which we call the *4 C's*—competency, conditions, culture, and context.[2] As we walk you through each of these components, we encourage you to become familiar with the ideas represented by each and with the relationships you see among them. We start with competencies because development of adults' skills is the most obvious and familiar realm of the change work. From here, we move to the other arenas of change and some strategies for improvement that may be progressively less familiar to the reader.

The goal of change we proposed in Chapter Two—improving teaching and learning—remains at the center of the work. As we discuss the 4 C's, we ask, what do leaders need to think about to achieve this goal throughout their school or district?

## Competencies

Most efforts to improve education have at their core a focus on professional development as a way to build competency. In this context of school transformation, we define *competencies* as *the repertoire of skills and knowledge that influences student learning.* Skillful, competent adults are a foundation of this work. Teachers and administrators at every level of the system need to develop their competencies regularly through ongoing development opportunities. This is not a terribly new idea. But we have come to understand the limits of competency building as a stand-alone strategy for change. Even with a focus on improving instruction, developing educators' competencies is necessary but insufficient for reinventing schools. Competencies are most effectively built when professional development is focused, job-embedded, continuous, constructed, and collaborative. But—and here's where the system comes into play—implementing this type of professional development necessarily implicates many parts of the system.

To illustrate, we'd like to introduce you to Luis and Althea, whose stories illustrate the systemic nature of schools and districts. Luis is a ninth-grade English teacher at "Franklin High School" in a district where student literacy rates are uniformly low and where teachers have had little training in how to teach literacy at the secondary level. After much research and discussion, district leaders have decided to focus change efforts on improving students' literacy skills through the teaching of writing. His district sends all its English teachers for training in "writers' workshop," a comprehensive strategy for teaching writing that has been in use for more than thirty years. Luis and his colleagues learn about the importance of having students write frequently and the value of live, one-on-one conferencing with students instead of just filling papers with red ink. They learn how to increase motivation with relevant writing topics and authentic audiences outside of school.

Luis comes back from this training with very mixed feelings. On the one hand, he is excited to try these new approaches to teaching writing. They make sense to him. But almost immediately he is overwhelmed by the reality of what it would take to put these new ideas into practice. Luis has 130 students. How many sets of 130 papers can he grade in a month? The same goes for conferencing. Luis tries a few one-on-one conferences and begins to understand how valuable they are—both as a way to teach writing and as a means to better know students in order to learn what writing topics might motivate them. But each takes more than fifteen minutes. How many can he do in his one planning period per day? When will he prepare his lessons, if all his time is taken up with student conferences? Finally, he begins to have students read their work aloud in small groups so they can get feedback from peers, but here too, Luis quickly becomes discouraged. The students enjoy reading their work aloud, but it takes time for every student to have a turn. With all the required material that he must cover, time is a precious commodity in Luis' classes.

Althea is Luis' principal at Franklin High. Their district has come to understand the need to teach principals how to supervise for instructional improvement. In addition to working with English teachers on writing, it is developing the competencies of its principals as instructional leaders. Althea and all the principals in her district have received training in how to do school learning walks. The principals have also been examining and discussing videotapes of teaching, and for the first time Althea feels more confident about going into classrooms and determining what might be most important to teachers' practice. She is learning the skills of powerful supervision that far surpass her earlier training in the bureaucratic details of how to fill out an evaluation form. She sees how her time in the classrooms can enhance the opportunities for students through better support for her teachers. She is excited to think of herself as a leader of instruction who might effectively practice these new competencies.

When Althea thinks about scheduling some classroom visits, she immediately realizes there are problems. The district leadership places a premium on answering parent and central office phone calls and e-mails promptly. Furthermore, the district's test scores have plateaued in recent years, so Althea has been expected to spend her time ensuring that all teachers are covering the required state standards. The district is also stressing the importance of improving the daily attendance rate in its high schools and wants school administrators to spend more time tracking down truants and "in-school" dropouts—students who come to school to see friends but who rarely attend classes. Althea knows that if she is to expand her role in supervising individual teachers, phone calls and e-mails won't get answered promptly, and daily student attendance numbers won't go up. She also knows that the skills of the few teachers with whom she can work in a month may improve at the expense of the school's test scores in all classes. When she is not busy doing hall sweeps for kids out of class, should she rush to the office to answer phone calls and e-mails? Ride herd on her assistant principals and department heads to make sure everything in the curriculum gets covered? Or can she afford the luxury of spending more time in classes trying to give in-depth help to a few teachers? She can't do it all. She begins to wonder how she might become clearer about her highest priorities and what other conditions in her work environment might be changed in ways that would enable her to focus on what's most important.

## Conditions

For both Luis and Althea, opportunities to further develop and effectively use the new competencies they've acquired are seriously undermined by the conditions of work imposed on them. We define *conditions* as *the external architecture surrounding student learning, the tangible arrangements of time, space, and resources.* Some examples include:

- Time spent with and for kids, with colleagues, with parents, with the community
- Explicit expectations around roles and responsibilities, student outcomes tied to assessments, laws and policies, contracts
- Scale and structure, including size of physical plant, organization of physical plant, teacher-student ratio, transitions between grade levels

Luis' instructional goals ran into several challenges associated with time—time for reading student papers, time for students to "workshop" their writing with each other, and time for him to confer with students individually. For Luis to use his new competencies to improve his teaching, one condition that might need to change is the number of students for whom he is responsible. But the district office, although eager to improve students' writing and support the investment it has already made in the writers' workshop, is also wrestling with recent budget cutbacks and is not in a position to allocate resources for smaller class sizes.

Let's assume that the district comes to appreciate the time barriers that frustrate the implementation of writers' workshop. It decides to tackle this condition of teaching and learning and reduces the number of students Luis sees by combining English and history into a double block. Now Luis sees 65 students a day for ninety minutes instead of 130 students for forty-five minutes. The district then takes the additional step of "looping" ninth- and tenth-grade classes, so that Luis now teaches the same group of students for two years. Suddenly, without spending additional money, Luis' two-year overall student load drops from 260 students to 65 students! Luis is ecstatic. For the first time in his professional career, the conditions of teaching and learning in his school allow him to know all his students well. Now Luis can begin to try out the new competencies he has learned to teach writing. He feels more successful with more of his students than ever before.

Meanwhile, the district also acts to improve the conditions that enable Althea to use her newly developed competencies related to improving instruction. First, and perhaps most important, the superintendent receives the school board's approval to clarify expectations about principals' roles and responsibilities. The central office has stated that improving instruction is the priority. The district leadership supports the principals in this instructional leadership role by encouraging principals to delegate more of their managerial responsibilities to other administrators so that they can spend more of their time in classrooms. They even designated an ombudsman position for each school and trained individuals in these roles to handle complaints and minor disciplinary cases. With these clarifications and supports, the conditions of Althea's job have changed fundamentally; she is no longer expected to have an open office door and deal with every crisis the minute it comes up. Instead, she has authorization to block two hours in her calendar every day to be in classrooms to exercise her new competencies for improving instruction.

Conditions represent the visible arrangements and allocations of time, space, and money. In contrast, culture, which we take up in the next section, refers to the invisible but powerful meanings and mindsets that are held individually and collectively throughout the system.

## Culture

We define *culture* as *the shared values, beliefs, assumptions, expectations, and behaviors related to students and learning, teachers and teaching, instructional leadership, and the quality of relationships within and beyond the school.* Culture refers to the invisible but powerful meanings and mindsets held individually and collectively throughout the system. The current culture has impeded Althea and Luis' ability to deepen the understanding and application of their learning; they encounter new difficulties as they attempt to use their newfound competencies and changed conditions to positively influence student learning.

Luis is anxious to compare notes about his students' work with other humanities teachers, and he thinks that perhaps they ought to be developing some common standards for grading students' writing. But despite the fact that teachers see their departmental meetings as a waste of time, past attempts to make these meetings more substantive have met with covert, and sometimes overt, resistance. Luis also observes that many of his colleagues appear distrustful of the administration and even of one another. In the staff lounge, a few veteran faculty are always heard complaining about the principal, or they're griping about the parents, or the kids' poor behavior. Increasingly, Luis feels disheartened by the culture of isolation and lack of respect in his building, which undermines any attempts at collaboration. He knows his principal, Althea, is well meaning but wonders if she's intimidated by those veteran faculty. It appears to be a vicious cycle, and Luis wonders how it will ever get broken. So he retreats to his classroom—the one place where he can create a culture of mutual respect and shared accountability.

Althea also wonders how she is going to influence some of her veteran teachers' beliefs and behaviors and the culture of the building. Additionally, she has been spending a good deal of her time in classrooms now, and the more she observes, the more questions she has about how to effectively move teachers to higher levels of competency. What are the best ways to conference with teachers? Which teaching skills are most important to emphasize first? These topics weren't covered in the principals' two-day training, and even if they had been, Althea would probably not have been able to take in the information back then. But now that she's ready to try new approaches, she remains silent rather than ask for the help she feels her colleagues could provide. In her district, principals don't ask for help or even acknowledge that they have questions about their roles as leaders. Not only is there very little real communication among the principals, but many see one another as rivals for the attention of the superintendent, the highest test scores, the prestige of new programs, or extra discretionary resources that the district sometimes doles out to the "favored ones." The culture of the district, Althea begins to realize, is one of isolation and competition, where principals are rewarded for having all the answers. As she sits, frustrated, in yet another district administrators' meeting where announcements take up most of the time, it suddenly occurs to her that she has unwittingly replicated the same culture in her school. She resolves to work with Luis and her other teacher leaders to, at the least, transform her school's culture into one that is more collaborative and values the process of inquiry and adult learning.

Althea knows that to succeed with her most challenged kids, creating a more collegial adult learning culture at Franklin High isn't enough. She knows that she needs more collaborative relationships with parents, for example. And she and her teachers need to become clearer about the skills the school's graduates will need—two elements of what we call the "context" of teaching and learning. Nevertheless, Althea leaves the meeting excited about the idea of working to improve the culture of her building. She knows that's where she must start.

## Context

A fourth influence on Luis and Althea's work, and the work of all of us in schools and districts, is the social, historical, and economic context in which all these efforts take place. By *context* we are especially referring to "*skill demands" all students must meet to succeed as providers, learners, and citizens and the particular aspirations, needs, and concerns of the families and community that the school or district serves.* As we discussed in Chapter One, the world of the 2020s, the knowledge economy of the future, for which our students are preparing, will be very different from the world of the 1970s—and even from what we experience today. Understanding context means knowing more about the worlds from which students come and those for which they must be prepared.

Context also refers to the larger organizational systems within which we work, and their demands and expectations, formal and informal. For a school this might be the district; for the district it might be the state; the state exists within the context of the federal government. We need to understand *all* this contextual information to help inform and shape the work we do to transform the culture, conditions, and competencies of our schools and districts. And we may, in turn, need to influence elements of the context in which we work, as well. Figure 6.1 illustrates the interdependencies of the 4 C's.

As Althea works to build a more collaborative culture in her school, focusing particularly on creating communities of practice that will replace or transform those departmental meetings, Luis and his colleagues are working to set common standards for students' writing. They have begun to question whether their standards are high enough and wonder what level of writing proficiency colleges now expect. The community college across town has long complained that nearly half of the district's graduates have needed some form of remediation in writing, so Luis seeks permission from Althea for a team from his Humanities Department to spend the day visiting classes and talking with the professors there. The team members are surprised to learn that students require help with much more than just the mechanics of good writing; many come to the college not knowing how to organize their thinking or to express their reasoning clearly in essays. The college teachers are also concerned about students' lack of research and study skills. These insights lead Luis and his colleagues to begin talking about how they can strengthen students' analytic skills and build more independent research projects into the curriculum. It further sharpens their focus on the competencies they need to continue to develop to be effective literacy and writing teachers.

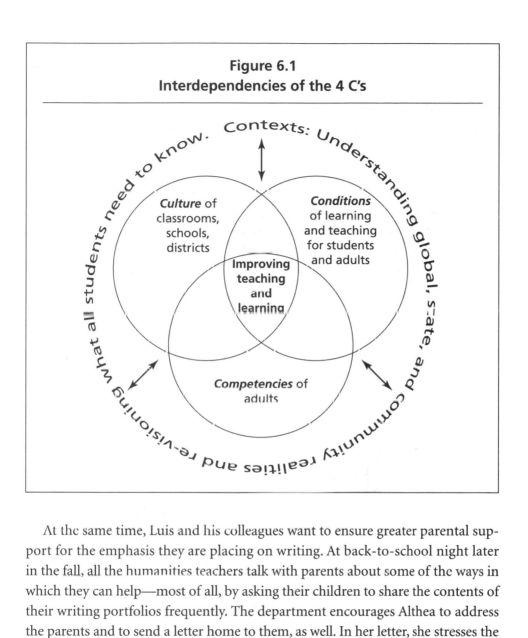

**Figure 6.1**
**Interdependencies of the 4 C's**

Contexts: Understanding global, state, and community realities and re-visioning what all students need to know.

Culture of classrooms, schools, districts

Conditions of learning and teaching for students and adults

Improving teaching and learning

Competencies of adults

At the same time, Luis and his colleagues want to ensure greater parental support for the emphasis they are placing on writing. At back-to-school night later in the fall, all the humanities teachers talk with parents about some of the ways in which they can help—most of all, by asking their children to share the contents of their writing portfolios frequently. The department encourages Althea to address the parents and to send a letter home to them, as well. In her letter, she stresses the importance of all students having the right conditions for learning at home—a supervised two-hour quiet time in the evenings for schoolwork. And she gives parents her e-mail address, encouraging them to contact her with any questions or concerns they might have. She also launches an advisory committee to help the school create a culture that is more responsive to the needs and concerns of all parents, not just the ones who are vocal.

By reaching out in these ways, Luis and Althea are acknowledging the importance of the contexts within which they work. Through conversations with the college teachers, Luis comes to better understand the skills his students most need—*the world for which they must be prepared.* And by listening to and working more proactively with parents, Althea and her teachers are attempting to better understand and even perhaps to positively influence *the world from which their students come.*

We have captured some of Luis and Althea's baseline challenges in competencies, conditions, culture, and context in a graphic organizer (see Figure 6.2). Although their journey has just begun, they have set some crucial changes in motion. Just as important, they have begun to recognize how one element of their work affects another; this insight reflects the core of systems thinking.

*Your system—any system—is perfectly designed to produce the results you're getting.*

Another dimension to systems thinking is that a system runs on its own momentum and all its parts work together to keep it going. The interactions of these parts naturally create some kind of product or result. In fact, your system—any system—is perfectly designed to produce the results you're getting. In our illustrative story, the result Luis and Althea wanted was improved student learning. To change even one feature of that—students' writing—the *system* had to change, and, as Luis and Althea discovered, all parts of the system had to be addressed. The challenge in systems work, we find, is that because the system flows so effortlessly (before you begin to change it), it is hard to see the parts that are interacting and how they work together to hold the results in place.

With a beginning understanding of the 4 C's and how these interrelated elements affect the task of improving learning, teaching, and leading in place, we now invite you as an individual (or your community of practice) to use this systems thinking tool as a way to better identify and diagnose some of the factors that influence the problem you've been working on throughout this book. (See Exercise 6.1 and Figure 6.3.)

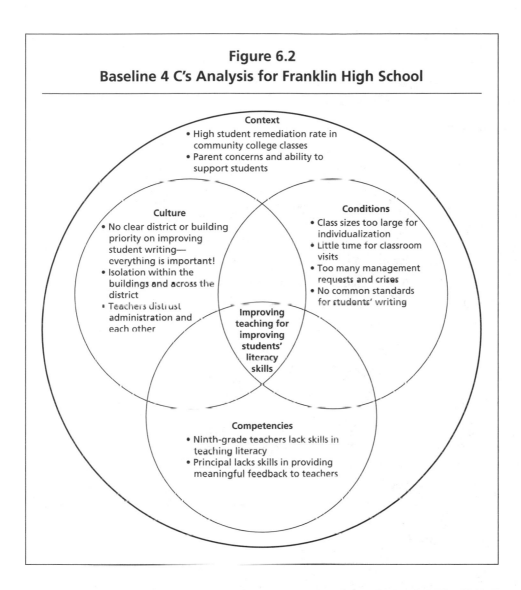

## Figure 6.2
## Baseline 4 C's Analysis for Franklin High School

**Context**
- High student remediation rate in community college classes
- Parent concerns and ability to support students

**Culture**
- No clear district or building priority on improving student writing—everything is important!
- Isolation within the buildings and across the district
- Teachers distrust administration and each other

**Conditions**
- Class sizes too large for individualization
- Little time for classroom visits
- Too many management requests and crises
- No common standards for students' writing

**Improving teaching for improving students' literacy skills**

**Competencies**
- Ninth-grade teachers lack skills in teaching literacy
- Principal lacks skills in providing meaningful feedback to teachers

---

## Exercise 6.1:  4 C's Diagnostic Tool—As Is

### Step One
Using a blank version of the 4 C's chart provided, put the problem statement you refined in Chapter Two (see Exercise 2.1) in the center of the overlapping circles.

### Step Two
Now take some time to reflect on the contributors to your current system as they relate to the problem you've identified. The following questions can get you started.

## Competencies

*How well do we:*

- Think strategically?
- Identify student learning needs?
- Gather and interpret data?
- Collaborate?
- Give and receive critiques?
- Productively disagree?
- Reflect and make midcourse corrections?

## Conditions

*How well do we create and maintain:*

- Time for problem solving, for learning, for talking about challenges?
- Relevant and user-friendly student data?
- Agreed upon performance standards?
- Clear priorities and focus for each person's work?
- District- and building-level support?

## Culture

*How would we characterize:*

- Our level of expectations for all students' learning? (Consistently high? Medium? Low? Or a mix of these depending on which students?)
- Our school's agenda? (Multiple and unrelated? Frequent changes? Steady, consistent focus? Related initiatives that build on each other?)
- The communications between district and school leadership to teachers? (Directive? Compliance oriented? Engaged in building cosponsorship and ownership?)
- Adult relationships with each other? (Lacking trust? Trusting?)
- Adult views of responsibility for all students' learning? (Blames others? Sees various contributors, including oneself?)

## Context

*How well do we:*

- Understand and work with students' families?
- See clearly the core competencies students will need for work, citizenship, and continuous learning?

## Step Three

Now add brief, bulleted descriptions of the strengths or assets your school or district has—as they relate to the problem you're trying to solve—to the appropriate circles or the overlaps between the circles. We encourage you to go back to the seven disciplines diagnostic (Chapter Two, Exercise 2.2) and the three continua diagnostics you completed in Chapter Four (Exercises 4.1, 4.2, and 4.3) and consider your responses as current contributors to your system.

## Step Four

Using a different color, insert bulleted descriptions into the appropriate circles, listing the weaknesses or challenges that will need to be overcome in order to solve your problem.

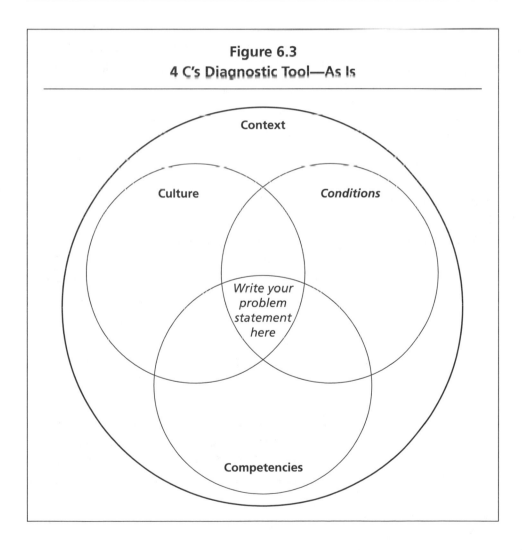

**Figure 6.3**
**4 C's Diagnostic Tool—As Is**

Context

Culture

Conditions

Write your
problem
statement
here

Competencies

This exercise can be a great help in beginning planning. For example, Luis and Althea's baseline analysis (shown in Figure 6.2) was an important early step in their school improvement work. Once you've completed this exercise, we encourage you take time to consider any new insights or questions that arise from your diagnostic work. For example:

- Does your understanding of the problem change in any way?

- Do you see new or different ways of going at the problem?

- Does your diagnosis begin to suggest some work that needs to be done before other work can be undertaken?

Do you feel ready to answer these questions? If not, what more would you need to know? Are there specific data you need to collect in order to develop a robust picture of the various contributions of the 4 C's? How might you collect these data? What is your next step? A real-world example may help as you tackle these questions.

## TOWARD TRANSFORMATION: USING THE 4 C'S

In Chapters Two and Four, we briefly mentioned the work of Superintendent Tony Alvarado and his deputy superintendent (later his successor) Elaine Fink. We now explore some of their work in greater depth as a way of illustrating how change leaders have used systemic thinking to guide an improvement process.

Community District 2 was one of thirty-two community school districts in New York City until a citywide reorganization in 2003. It included about 22,000 students from exceptionally diverse backgrounds: 29 percent white, 14 percent African American, 22 percent Hispanic, 34 percent Asian, and less than 1 percent Native American. English was a second language for about 20 percent of the students, and nearly half came from economically disadvantaged families.[3]

Beginning in the late 1980s, District 2 began a long-term, systemwide instructional improvement effort. Over the next ten years, District 2 demonstrated dramatic results, moving from sixteenth out of thirty-two in test results across New York to second (just behind a predominantly white, middle-class district).

What accounts for such dramatic results? The answer to that question is a rich and important story, one documented more fully by various researchers.[4] The abridged answer is that District 2 adopted a tenacious focus on the improvement of literacy instruction, and kept this its sole focus for the next five years. District leaders reallocated resources from the central office, freeing up funds to funnel into the improvement of literacy instruction. Leaders began to promote and model a strong normative culture of respect, trust, and accountability for learning. Furthermore, the district developed an intensive infrastructure for job-embedded professional development—for administrators and teachers—focused on literacy instruction.

> *Leaders began to promote and model a strong normative culture of respect, trust, and accountability for learning.*

The story of PS 198, an elementary school within District 2, provides a view into how Alvarado, Fink, and the school principal worked systemically to turn that school around.[5] It also can help expand understanding of the interrelationship of the 4 C's.

## Working Within the Context

In the 1990s, a large majority of families served by PS 198 lived in poverty. More than 90 percent of its students were eligible for free or reduced-fee lunch (a nationally used indicator of poverty in schools). It consistently ranked last on reading scores in the district. Superintendent Tony Alvarado hired a new principal, Gloria Buckerey, in 1996. Buckerey worked hard to weed out incompetent teachers, brought in several staff developers, and hired new young teachers. Few of them lasted more than a year. The job seemed overwhelming, and after three years nothing had changed. Only about 25 percent of the fourth graders were reading at or above grade level on the comparatively easy standardized tests that were then in use. The problem of poor student achievement and high staff turnover became so severe that the State of New York put PS 198 on its list of "Schools Under Review" in 1998. If things didn't change quickly, the state would close the school. Alvarado and Fink decided new strategies were needed to turn the situation around, and Fink began visiting the school monthly. Over a period of about six months, she developed an action plan for change focused on literacy.

Fink's decision to begin their improvement work with literacy was not unexpected. As we mentioned, the sole focus of District 2's school improvement efforts—in staff development, in conversations with principals—was how to improve teaching and learning for literacy. District leadership reasoned that if students could not read, comprehend, and write well, then they certainly were not going to be able to decode math or science texts. Fink also knew that trying to attend to science, social studies, and math skills all at once would not provide the focus—and the opportunity for success—that teachers and students needed.

### Changing the Conditions of Teaching and Learning

One clear way to improve students' literacy skills is to simply have them spend more of their day reading and writing. Therefore, the first thing that Fink did as she began to work with Buckerey and her PS 198 faculty was to examine the school schedule. She did not try to impose a new schedule. She simply posed a problem for Buckerey and the faculty to solve: How are we going to find more time in the day for literacy instruction and for adult learning? Together, they created a new schedule that allowed for three-hour literacy blocks in the school day and devoted significantly more time for teachers to talk together about their work. The faculty also decided that the "specialist" teachers—those who taught art, science, music, and so on—would learn how to teach literacy and be an additional resource in the classroom for those literacy blocks. Fink allocated extra resources to the school for two additional reading specialists.

The immediate result of these changes was that every reading group could now work intensely with a teacher every day rather than once a week. Fink and Alvarado also established a summer program for all the students in PS 198 to give them more time for learning. In the second year, they added another program to better prepare incoming kindergartners for the start of school. These programs were so successful that they were subsequently adopted throughout the district in those schools serving the most at-risk students.

### Developing the Competencies of Teachers and Principals

When Fink began analyzing the school's reading test data, she quickly realized that three-fourths of the fourth graders had spent their entire school careers with beginning teachers! These inexperienced teachers didn't know how to teach the balanced literacy program supported by District 2. And because the turnover rate was so high, there were no teachers in the building with the skills to help their less experienced colleagues. Fink approached the union and suggested that they create a new Distinguished Teacher position—with extra duties and a higher salary.

Two distinguished teachers, the best literacy educators in the district, came to the school and worked alongside regular classroom teachers, modeling how to teach literacy and coaching their peers. These distinguished teachers also worked with all the staff during the time available for whole school professional development.

Although literacy was a nonnegotiable focus in District 2, Alvarado and Fink did not believe that all schools and all students would best learn from one curriculum. As Fink said in a conversation with one of us, "You don't stand in front of your principals and say 'all schools should. . . .' Each school, like each child, has its own unique learning challenges. This is about kids' learning; it's not about philosophy. All kids need rigor, but they learn in different ways, need different things."[6] Fink worked with Buckerey, the visiting distinguished teachers, and the faculty to adapt the district's balanced literacy program to the particular needs of the students in PS 198. All teachers now spent one half hour each day on word study (phonics), in addition to all the other elements of the literacy program. Gradually, and with support from internal and external experts, they all learned how to strengthen their ability to teach the balanced literacy curriculum.

As fruitful as this was, Fink and Buckerey realized that the competencies teachers were developing could be considered successful only if there was evidence that students were now learning more. Using the same "graded" reading texts with all students, the faculty developed common indicators of progress and prepared charts for each student that showed exactly what reading level each had attained. Fink visited every classroom in the school and discussed *each* student's chart with Buckerey *monthly*. They also reviewed each teacher's individual learning plan and made changes, as needed, according to the students' reading progress. (These practices, pioneered in PS 198, eventually became widespread in the district.)

Finally, the two worked closely to develop Buckerey's abilities to coach her teachers and run effective staff meetings. Fink told all her principals, "I have failed you if I can't teach you how to teach your teachers." She provided time for Buckerey to be in study groups with other principals, make school visitations, and work with another principal in the district who was assigned to be her "buddy."

## Transforming the District Culture

As Fink's earlier comment implied, the district had an explicit understanding that any one school's problem was everyone's problem. Its motto was, "isolation is the enemy of improvement." Alvarado and Fink helped other principals understand that PS 198's struggle was shared by all of them—and that its students depended on the cooperation of the entire system. Principals of other schools knew that a disproportionate share of the financial resources was going to PS 198, and they supported that decision, as did the board. They worked collaboratively to investigate and develop new leadership and supervision skills. Monthly principals' meetings were focused solely on discussions related to improving instruction, and many began with school learning walks. Alvarado and Fink emphasized that the culture of the district had to connect adults' learning explicitly to the improvement of instruction and to students' learning.[7] Their other motto was, "if it's not about teaching and learning, then it's not about anything."[8] In effect, their entire district was made up of nested communities of practice related to the continuous improvement of instruction.

*Their entire district was made up of nested communities of practice related to the continuous improvement of instruction.*

What were the results of their efforts? They were more successful than they ever thought possible. Two years after PS 198 was put under review by the state, it was taken off the list. By the end of year three, 55 percent of the students scored in the top half of a newer and much more difficult literacy test. Their scores were in the middle range of a district whose test scores were the second highest in the region and whose literacy scores continue to improve every year. In 2000, Gloria Buckerey was honored by the state as the principal who had made the most progress of any principal leading a School Under Review. And two of Buckerey's teachers had themselves become distinguished teachers in District 2.

What Alvarado and Fink accomplished as educational leaders in District 2 remains one of the few successful examples of systemic districtwide change. Over a period of years, they created an engaged, knowledge-generating culture with a clear focus and widely shared commitment to provide a quality education for all students, where teachers had a shared vision of good teaching, and where there were powerful collaborative relationships based on trust and respect. This cultural shift created the impetus to change the conditions of teaching and learning and sustainable development of educator competencies at every level. Teachers in District 2 sometimes complained about how hard the work was. They also said they had never been in a place where there was more collaboration, collegiality, and opportunity for professional growth.

We have several purposes in telling this remarkable story of school and district transformation. We want you to see that this work can be done. We certainly want you to feel the pull of success as you read about their accomplishments. We also want you to begin to understand their transformation from the systems perspective and how the larger system of the district became an important context and facilitator of the school's successful efforts, each with distinct and explicit roles focused on the same goal.

We also have another purpose. We want to prepare you to do some further analysis of your own school or district so that you can move from the problem you identified (what we call your *As Is* state, your current reality) to thinking about how your system might look if it is producing the results you need—all students, new skills (your *To Be* picture). What is important is that both your *As Is* and your *To Be* pictures capture the contributors to the results you have, as well as those that would need to be in place to get the results you want. We also encourage you to begin thinking about how to get from "here" to "there." To help you do this, we'll map out the 4 C's of PS 198's journey.

The left side of Exhibit 6.1 should look familiar to you. It is similar to the systems view you completed for your own school or district's problem. (Again, we want to stress how much more you will get out of this book if you are using this information for your own setting!) You should recognize the contributors—such as inexperienced teachers teaching students in the early grades and a static curriculum delivery orientation—to PS 198's low literacy achievement from their story. It represents a snapshot of their system at the beginning of our story.

The right side of Exhibit 6.1 is a snapshot of PS 198's system at the end of our story and shows the contributions to a system that is yielding different results—high literacy achievement. We call this their *To Be* picture; it represents the view we believe they would have drawn had they used this framework to guide their planning. We have laid both diagrams out side by side to illustrate the difference in the two systems and how each component needed to be different in order to bring about different results.

The change from the *As Is* to the *To Be* side, the strategies that PS 198 used, are briefly summarized here. These strategies represent the thinking that guided the results identified in the *To Be* picture. They are the key efforts that moved PS 198 from low to high levels of literacy and the actions taken to carry them out. We include a synopsis of those actions, as illustrative examples, pulled from our story.

# Exhibit 6.1:
## PS 198, New York City's District 2 (Full Systems Analysis with Strategies for Transformation)

**As Is** →          **Strategies**          **To Be** →

### As Is

**Context**
- Economically diverse
- Large majority of students in poverty
- Racially diverse
- Lowest reading scores in district
- High staff turnover
- Under state review
- District focus on literacy

**Conditions**
- Insufficient time in schedule for literacy instruction and adult learning
- Insufficient number of adults to teach literacy
- High number of inexperienced teachers in early elementary classes

**Culture**
- Insufficient focus on core problem of literacy
- Adults don't see themselves as learners
- Curriculum delivery orientation
- Adults work in isolation

**Low literacy achievement**

**Competencies**
- Minimal teacher knowledge of how to teach children literacy
- Insufficient principal knowledge of how to help teachers effectively teach literacy

### To Be

**Context**
- Economically diverse
- Large majority of students in poverty
- Racially diverse
- Highest reading scores in district
- Low staff turnover
- Off state review
- District focus on literacy

**Conditions**
- Schedule that allows for literacy work with specialists and adult learning time
- Enough teachers for daily work on literacy with students
- Targeted and effective professional development

**Culture**
- Clear and laser focus on literacy
- Shared understanding and ownership of student achievement problem—no blame
- Shared vision throughout the school and central office re: good teaching
- Learning orientation
- Collaborative problem solving based on trust and respect

**High literacy achievement**

**Competencies**
- All teachers develop and continue to deepen literacy expertise
- Principal continuously learns how to support teacher effectiveness and run effective staff meetings

As we've seen, the 4 C's diagnostic generates a rich *As Is* picture, a dynamic snapshot of current assets and challenges in relation to one another and to the identified problem. As PS 198's strategies make clear, the construction of this *As Is* picture is only a first step.

We now invite you into some forward thinking about your future and what you are doing and will do to get there. Use Exercise 6.2 and Figure 6.4 to begin the movement toward your goal.

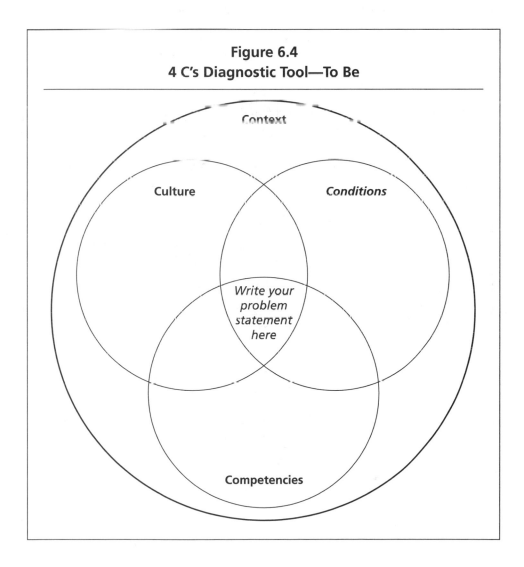

**Figure 6.4**
**4 C's Diagnostic Tool—To Be**

Context

Culture     Conditions

Write your
problem
statement
here

Competencies

| Strategy | Action |
|---|---|
| Focus only on improving literacy teaching. | Give school explicit permission to focus only on literacy:<br><br>• Allocate resources.<br><br>• Focus professional development only on literacy. |
| Develop principals as instructional leaders. | Deputy superintendent makes monthly visits to teach principal how to use student reading data to work with teachers and their individualized learning plans:<br><br>• Connect principal to study groups with other principals.<br><br>• Lead school learning walks.<br><br>• Lead monthly principal meetings.<br><br>• Assign "buddy" to principal. |
| Increase time for students' literacy learning. | Establish summer opportunities for all students to begin (kindergartners) or continue working on literacy:<br><br>• Give responsibility to school to revise schedule for increased time on literacy with students, and for adult learning around effective literacy instruction. |
| Reallocate resources. | • Work with other schools and school board to send needed finances to PS 198.<br><br>• Provide two reading specialists.<br><br>• Work with union to develop Distinguished Teacher position. |
| Make data-based decisions. | Analyze student and teacher data for which students, with which teachers, with what outcomes:<br><br>• Develop "graded" reading texts and chart student progress to inform teacher strategies. |
| Develop collaborative relationships among adults. | • Work collaboratively with the school to adapt balanced literacy program to meet its needs. |

## Exercise 6.2: Moving Toward the Goal, via the 4 C's

### Step One: Create a Picture of Success

Earlier in this chapter, in Exercise 6.1, you used the 4 C's to develop a more systemic understanding of the problem your school or district is tackling. Now it's time to review your completed version of the 4 C's diagnostic tool.

What would success look like if the problem you identified (in the middle of your *As Is* picture) were solved? In other words, what results do you want your new system to create? Be as precise and specific as possible. Write a description of this picture of success into the middle of the 4 C's visual provided.

---

*What would success look like if the problem
you identified (in the middle of your As Is picture)
were solved?*

---

### Step Two: Build the *To Be* Picture

Complete the figure by identifying all the changes within each of the four arenas of change—competencies, conditions, culture, and context—that are necessary if you are to realize your picture of success. You may wish to revisit the questions we suggested in Exercise 6.1, to prompt future-state thinking, such as: *How should we be able to characterize . . . ? How will we be able to . . . ? What will we have in place for . . . ?*

Map these changes onto the visual within the most appropriate circle. Some changes you identify may not fit neatly within a single circle; place these in the appropriate overlapping spaces of the diagram. We encourage you, in completing this visual, to be exhaustive in your thinking—list every change you imagine will be necessary to solve your problem. Think, in true systemic fashion, of the relationships between the change arenas. What relationships will exist, and what shifts will they cause in other arenas? What might need to be intentionally engineered in one arena to provoke change in another?

This completed visual represents your *To Be* picture, a systemic and dynamic vision of the future to which you aspire. This visual should help identify the landscape of work that is necessary in order to make progress on the problem in your *As Is* picture.

Your two visuals now help present a picture of the distance between where you are and where you want to go. We encourage you to consider any observations or questions that emerge, such as:

- *What insights about the problem and the potential solution(s) do these visuals offer?*
- *Are there any standouts or surprises?*

### Step Three: Identify Current Strategies

Identify any existing strategies that are in place (or are being implemented) that are intended to help you solve the problem and realize your *To Be* picture. In other words, identify what you and others are doing to move from where your school or district currently is to where you would like it to be as you've captured it in your *To Be* picture. Before engaging in this exercise, you may find it helpful to revisit the strategies and actions that District 2 undertook with its work in PS 198.

### Step Four: Consider the Current Strategies

With respect to the strategies you've identified, consider the following questions:

1. Consider the degree to which each strategy fully addresses a systemic understanding of the problem or solution. Do the strategies address the main contributors to the problem or the main changes necessary to realize your goal?

2. If there are multiple strategies, consider the degree to which they, as a whole, address a systemic understanding of the problem or the main challenges necessary to realize your goal.

3. What blind spots, if any, can you identify in the current work?

4. In what ways do your strategies recognize and seek to affect the relationships between the contributors you identified?

5. What additional strategies might be necessary in light of your *As Is* and *To Be* pictures? Your thoughts will be an important backdrop when we take up the question of how to work more strategically.

---

## ANOTHER USE FOR THE 4 C'S

The *As Is–To Be* diagnostic tools can also be used to create a greater understanding of the need for fundamental change—reinvention versus reform—as you realize what a shared vision of success might actually look like. For example, Grand Rapids Public Schools used the *As Is–To Be* tool in an ambitious redesign of its comprehensive high schools. District leaders wanted a way to engage shareholder groups (students, parents, teachers, higher-education leaders, and business partners). They used the tool in mixed-group conversations to facilitate an understanding of why Grand Rapids needed to dramatically redesign its high schools. This process enabled individuals to share and hear perspectives of the dilemmas of high schools and what would be required to truly transform them into schools that can nurture, support, and educate all high school students. The result? They achieved a deeper sense of focus and purpose, more engagement among various shareholders who felt a sense of genuine ownership of both the problem and the solution, and greater collaboration in the effort to transform the high schools.

We discuss the phasing and staging of a change process in more depth in Chapter Eight. But first, it's time to consider systemic thinking from another angle, this time looking inward to personal, individual learning and growth.

## Endnotes

1. Peter M. Senge, *The Fifth Discipline Fieldbook* (New York: Currency Doubleday, 1994), 90.
2. A description of the 4 C's was first published by Tony Wagner in *Making the Grade: Reinventing America's Schools* (New York: RoutledgeFalmer, 2002), 134–146.
3. These data are from Richard F. Elmore and Deanna Burney's *The Challenge of School Variability: Improving Instruction in New York City's Community District #2* (Philadelphia: University of Pennsylvania, Consortium for Policy Research in Education, 1998).
4. For further information, we recommend the following: R. F. Elmore and D. Burney, *Continuous Improvement in Community District #2, New York City* (University of Pittsburgh, HPLC Project, Learning Research and Development Center, 1998); E. Fink and L. B. Resnick, *Developing Principals as Instructional Leaders* (University of Pittsburgh, HPLC Project, Learning Research and Development Center, 1999); L. B. Resnick and M. Harwell, *High Performance Learning Communities District #2 Achievement* (University of Pittsburgh, HPLC Project, Learning Research and Development Center, 1998); K. Maloy, *Building a Learning Community: The Story of New York City Community District #2* (University of Pittsburgh, HPLC Project, Learning Research and Development Center, 1998).
5. This account is based on a presentation by Anthony Alvarado and Elaine Fink at the Grantmakers for Education conference (Boston, Mass., November 7, 2000) and subsequent conversations with both Alvarado and Fink. Anthony Alvarado served as superintendent in New York City's Community District 2 from 1987 until 1998 and was succeeded by his colleague Fink. A slightly different version of this story was first published in Wagner's *Making the Grade* (note 2).
6. In discussion with Tony Wagner after the Grantmakers presentation (note 4).

7. For a more complete description of District 2's "Theory of Action" and strategies for professional development, see Elaine Fink and Lauren B. Resnick, "Developing Principals as Instructional Leaders," *Phi Delta Kappan* 82, no. 8 (April 2001): 598–606.

8. The culture of District 2 in the late 1980s and 1990s bore a close resemblance to the culture of collaborative problem solving and teacher teamwork that has been the primary strategy used in Japan to improve public education. *The Teaching Gap* by James Stigler and James Hiebert, which we mentioned earlier as an example of a teacher-driven community of practice, describes what the Japanese call the lesson study process, where groups of teachers work together to identify a common learning problem of students and then create a model lesson to solve the problem. Lessons are refined collaboratively and then, when proven successful, are widely disseminated.

# The Individual as a Complex System

**W**e hope that the 4 C's have provided you a way to think about the multiple dimensions of your district that you'll need to attend to in the change process. One reason we like the 4 C's framework is that it reminds us to think about districts as systems, complex wholes in which many interrelated features together produce whatever results you're getting. As we noted in our cautions and reminders, it is easy to get drawn to just one or a few of those features, or to focus on a process goal—such as better relationships—and lose sight of the results that are supposed to come from those relationships. It is also typical to view the contributors as a list of things to take care of and miss the critical dynamics of how they interact and reinforce each other. Seeing organizations as systems is, for most of us, new.[1]

What we propose in this chapter is also new and therefore unfamiliar. The tendency we have to see only parts of organizations applies to us as individuals, too. As individuals, we can also be inclined to pay attention to particular parts of ourselves more than others. For example, back in Chapter One we asked you to identify a first-column commitment. You may have thought about how difficult it is to move your district toward a goal of improved instruction. In doing this, you tapped into your frustrations and your complaints. And, in considering how to articulate a goal that would feel powerful and important, you surfaced your own strongly held wishes, hopes, and beliefs for yourself and for your district. In doing this reflecting, you were largely listening to parts of yourself that, for most people, are relatively easy to attend to. Most of us are used to reflecting on these familiar parts of ourselves.

We have been also asking you to develop a larger interior "problem space" related to your commitment by reflecting on other parts of yourself—you can apply systemic thinking here, too. What you did in diagnosing and planning for your school or district you could do for yourself as an individual. When you recorded your behaviors that undermined your first-column commitment, identified fears that would arise if you were to behave differently, and named a third-column commitment that competes with the first, you needed to pay attention to other, perhaps less familiar, parts of yourself. You made your problem space larger. Our four-column immunity map helps us see that these less familiar parts of ourselves are closely related to and just as powerful as the parts we typically exercise. In other words, just as Althea realized that she was creating a school culture that was reproducing the basic aspects of the district culture, there are sometimes tacit parts of our individual systems that affect the ability of other parts to be successful in our more conscious efforts.

## HIDDEN COMMITMENTS AND PERSONAL IMMUNITIES

In the same way that the 4 C's chart helps us diagnose the problems of our organizations by understanding them as complex systems, the four-column immunity map helps us diagnose our personal immunities to change by understanding *ourselves* as complex systems. To illustrate this point, it is useful to draw two arrows that connect the first and third columns. These commitments often cancel each other out, as you can see by revisiting Arthur's four-column commitment map in Exhibit 7.1 (first presented in Chapter Five, Exhibit 5.1). We'll show you what we mean by adding arrows to Arthur's chart:

*The four-column immunity map
helps us diagnose our personal immunities
to change by understanding
ourselves as complex systems.*

# Exhibit 7.1:
## Arthur's Four-Column Immunity Map, Revisited

| 1 | 2 | 3 | 4 |
|---|---|---|---|
| Commitment | Doing/Not Doing | Hidden/Competing Commitments | Big Assumption |
| I am committed to moving my district from "good" to "great" by creating a common vision of rigorous instruction. | I am not holding others accountable.<br><br>I am procrastinating critical meetings.<br><br>I am scrutinizing the description of instruction rather than helping others to shape it. | (I fear that others would find out that I do not know what I am doing. I fear that I would lead the organization down the wrong path. I fear that this effort would not go as planned.)<br><br>I am committed to not having others discover I am uncertain about how we will accomplish our goals.<br><br>I am committed to keeping others from finding out that I'm not always sure of the next step.<br><br>I am committed to not moving the district one step further until I can be absolutely sure I know how to successfully complete the journey. | |

Viewed as a complex system of interrelated parts, Arthur's four-column immunity map makes a different kind of sense than it initially did. We see how his strongly held commitment to creating a common vision of rigorous instruction would require him to take some big risks. So that commitment is counterbalanced by his also powerful and usually hidden commitment to appearing as if he always knows what the next step is and how the district will accomplish its goals. The commitments compete with each other, effectively canceling each other out, so that Arthur makes little or no progress toward his first-column commitment.

Understanding Arthur as a complex system also allows us to see that the presence of his competing commitments does not lessen the sincerity of his first-column commitment. We believe that he, like many leaders, is quite genuinely dedicated to making the progress he has identified as necessary for his district to improve. What we see is that he must acknowledge his hidden commitments—which are also powerful and genuine—in order to understand fully what is at stake for him in undertaking the difficult work of change.

We hope that as you reconsider Arthur's map, you can more easily see these complex dynamics at work in your own life and work. Creating this way of seeing the bigger problem may not initially seem like much of an accomplishment. In fact, it may seem rather negative to you. What might have appeared as a fairly simple weed to pull from your life has now grown into a whole system of tangled roots and vines! But establishing this awareness of your own system of immunities actually represents great progress. In our view, just being able to see your immune system and keep it in mind means that you are now able, for perhaps the first time, to dig deeply enough to alter that system. Digging deeply can unsettle the balance of your competing commitments and enable you to make progress toward fulfilling your first-column commitment.

---

*Just being able to see your immune system and keep it in mind means that you are now able, for perhaps the first time, to dig deeply enough to alter that system.*

---

As we show you how to create the digging tool, you'll enter your version of it in the fourth column of your own immunities map that you began back in Chapter Five (see Exercise 5.2: Look Inward: Your Four-Column Immunity Map). Picture the arrows from Arthur's revised map transposed on top of yours (or, better yet, draw the arrows in) and you'll also see that by linking columns 1 and 3, this map can illustrate how your commitments compete and counterbalance each other.

## BIG ASSUMPTIONS AND IMMUNITIES

The fourth-column heading—"The Big Assumption"—is the key ingredient that actively holds your internal immune system in place. By "assumption" we mean something you have constructed as a way of understanding and making sense of your world. It is a kind of rule or prediction about what will happen if you act or appear in particular ways. As is often the case with rules, there are many times when they make good sense and should be applied to the situation at hand. But we can run into problems if we are so obedient to these rules that we follow them even when they don't apply very well to other situations. And sometimes we are just plain wrong! We call our fourth-column assumptions "big" because, as we've said, they "have us" more than we "have them." Potent as they are, we generally don't even recognize their existence or that we may have a choice about whether we should trust them and follow them—or change them.

To identify the Big Assumption keeping his immune system in place, Arthur took the inverse of what he had written in his third column, and replaced the words "I am committed to" with the words "I assume that if. . . ." By doing this, Arthur converted each of his third-column commitments into sentence stems, as follows:

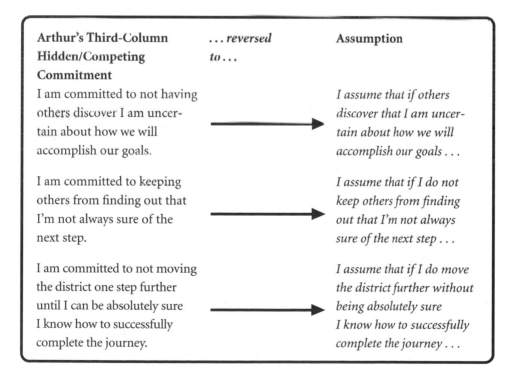

| Arthur's Third-Column Hidden/Competing Commitment | . . . reversed to . . . | Assumption |
|---|---|---|
| I am committed to not having others discover I am uncertain about how we will accomplish our goals. | | *I assume that if others discover that I am uncertain about how we will accomplish our goals . . .* |
| I am committed to keeping others from finding out that I'm not always sure of the next step. | | *I assume that if I do not keep others from finding out that I'm not always sure of the next step . . .* |
| I am committed to not moving the district one step further until I can be absolutely sure I know how to successfully complete the journey. | | *I assume that if I do move the district further without being absolutely sure I know how to successfully complete the journey . . .* |

Then, having entered his "reversed" commitments into his fourth column, he completed the sentence by adding a "then" and his conclusion. Arthur wrote:

*I assume that if others recognize that I am not exactly clear about every step of the way, or see that I am at all uncertain,* **then they will lose confidence in me as a leader, see me as an ineffective leader, and I will be a failure.**

Identifying his Big Assumption was a moving experience for Arthur. As he looked at what he had written, he recognized how forcefully it had been governing his life. In part, he experienced something of the dread and anxiety that arose within him whenever he thought about tackling some of his second-column behaviors. He also was immediately reminded of his first days as superintendent of the district, when he had taken stock of all that was expected of him and all that he wanted to accomplish. Despite his sincere eagerness for change and willingness to work long and hard hours, his job seemed overwhelmingly complicated. Driving home from work in the evenings, he was often flooded by doubts about whether he had "the right stuff" for this job. He grew accustomed to pushing those thoughts away whenever they arose. And yet, here they were again, along with a knot in his stomach.

At the same time, though, Arthur felt a rush of something like relief going through him. These thoughts and fears were now words on the page, and even though he knew they represented a powerful force in his life, he could already begin to see that they weren't necessarily "*the way things are.*" They were limiting, but not permanent, just "*the way I have been living my life.*" He could even begin to imagine, in a dim but hopeful way, that he might not always have to live his life and do his work according to the rule of his Big Assumption.

Assumptions limited Arthur's views of himself and his world. How will it be with your own Big Assumption? Take a minute now and record your own Big Assumption in your working version of Exercise 5.2.

---

*If your Big Assumption has [a] stomach-tightening effect . . . , chances are you have identified a very juicy and robust one. That's a good sign!*

---

If your Big Assumption has the stomach-tightening effect that Arthur's did, chances are you have identified a very juicy and robust one. That's a good sign! If it does not, we suggest that you check it against the following criteria to come up with something more compelling for you. The Big Assumption should:

- Show why your third-column commitment feels absolutely necessary. ("If I take my Big Assumption as unquestionably true, then my third-column commitment naturally follows.")

- End calamitously. (The conclusion should feel like a disastrous consequence, perhaps like your very own personal version of hell.)

- Display a constricted world. ("My Big Assumption shows me a larger world I could live in theoretically—for example, a world in which I let people see I am not always sure I know what to do—but my Big Assumption tells me *I must not go there! Danger is waiting there!* So I must live in a more confined space.")

If your Big Assumption does not meet all these criteria, take some time to try to revise it. Sometimes, you just need to experiment a bit with the wording to find something that really resonates. To take it to the next level, find a time when you and a partner can share your Big Assumptions with each other.

---

*Even small modifications to the Big Assumption can have considerable impact on a person's behavior and performance.*

---

Congratulations! You are now ready to reconsider your relationship to your Big Assumption, which we will take up in Chapter Nine. By that, we don't mean that we want you to completely give it up. There may be many circumstances under which it is a very reliable and useful guide for your life. But its role in preventing you from realizing the deeply held commitment in your first column suggests that you may want to learn where it may be overgeneralized, unnecessarily rigid, or a bit exaggerated. In our experience, even small modifications to the Big Assumption can have considerable impact on a person's behavior and performance. This personal reflection and reframing of our individual assumptions mirrors the processes required for the adaptive organizational work so critical to real transformation.

## Endnote

1. Peter M. Senge, *The Fifth Discipline* (New York: Currency Doubleday, 1994).

# Reflections

In Chapter Six, we examined the systemic nature of organizations and individuals. We offered a framework—the 4 C's—for understanding the competencies, conditions, culture, and context necessary for achieving your district or school improvement goals. This framework can help build a greater understanding of the need for fundamental change. In addition, the 4 C's can support the process of reinvention versus reform.

In Chapter Seven, we addressed hidden commitments and immunities, digging deeper to discover personal learning challenges. We showed you how the four-column immunity map provides a framework for understanding the complex systems within individuals, focusing particularly on how a systems perspective can illuminate a powerful lever for transformation.

Although we have indicated that these new skills will be useful as you undertake rather monumental changes, we've not yet helped you to think about how to make these changes, how to phase and stage a change process that can bring about and sustain your *To Be* picture. That is the subject of Chapter Eight.

In Chapter Nine, we describe a variety of ways that individuals can work strategically to alter their Big Assumptions, and so release themselves from their own immunity to change. Because that work can feel a bit scary, we provide some solid handholds to help you work strategically and regulate the pace of your own transformation.

**PART FOUR**

# Working Strategically

# The Ecology of Change

What does it mean to work more strategically? How do districts and schools move from the current reality, their present conditions, to the future—the future as they want it to be? How do they strategically use data, accountability, and relationships to overcome the organizational resistors to change and generate engagement and collaborative practice that is purposeful and focused? What are the phases of a successful and sustainable change process for continuous improvement of learning, teaching, and leadership? What comes first, and what needs to wait? What does it all look like?

By attending to the phases of a change process, leaders can lay the groundwork for movement along the continua toward the greater purpose and focus, engagement, and collaboration that are vital to successful change efforts.

## PHASES OF WHOLE-SYSTEM CHANGE

There are three phases in our ecology of change framework: preparing, envisioning, and enacting. The first of our Seven Disciplines for Strengthening Instruction—which is about using data to create understanding of the problem and urgency for change—is an essential element of the first two phases, preparing for and envisioning success. The other six disciplines are the outcomes, the goals, for the third phase, that of enacting change.

    **1.** In the preparing phase, leaders of a reinvention process plan for the changes ahead. They develop a shared and informed understanding of

- the need and urgency for undertaking change,

- the changing world and how all educators in the system will need to take responsibility for preparing students to succeed in it, and

- the ways that educators will need to work differently with each other to fulfill these responsibilities.

2. As the envisioning phase begins, understanding and urgency for change expand into the greater school or district community. This expansion involves community shareholders accepting greater responsibility clarifying how they must adapt their roles to support their students effectively. Trust among shareholders deepens and respect increases.

3. In the enacting phase, improving instruction is the primary and overriding priority. Change efforts focus on which instructional practices work and what needs improvement. All educators provide and receive regular information about how each one's work needs to and can better achieve instructional goals. This communication among educators depends on and allows for the development of even greater degrees of collaboration, professional respect, and mutual trust.

These three phases are also distinguished from each other in the ways that they each involve three critical spheres of work—what we call the change levers—for school and district reinventions.

## CHANGE LEVERS: DATA, ACCOUNTABILITY, AND RELATIONSHIPS

Each of the change levers—data, accountability, and relationships—plays a pivotal role in successful implementation of all three phases. *Data* refers to all the quantitative and qualitative information we have or can gather that is related, directly or indirectly, to student success and well-being in schools. This is not simply information about student learning, achievement, and performance, though that is central; we are also referring to information that pertains to adults and the organizations within which they work. Statistics can convey important information and have a kind of "numbers don't lie" ability to convince. But often we have found that qualitative data (such as that generated from interviewing students and adults in focus groups about their experiences with school) are particularly powerful in illuminating and communicating key insights. Seeing the faces, and hearing the stories, hopes, and opinions of those in our own community moves us emotionally, reminds us of the moral imperative behind our work, and enables us to see the information as living in three dimensions instead of in just one. The stories, the faces, and the voices remain with us with an insistency that numbers can rarely inspire. Above all, more and better data can help us define the various challenges related to improving students' learning, and track the vitality of our change effort.

---

*The stories, the faces, and the voices remain with us with an insistency that numbers can rarely inspire.*

---

*Accountability* denotes a set of mutual understandings that define what people in schools and districts are held accountable for, and to whom. These are the collective expectations people have for others in the system and delineate what people can be counted on to do to help all students learn new skills. *Vertical accountability* is top-down and usually describes how leaders hold subordinates responsible for work. Compliance, rather than discussion, is often the expectation. A good vertical accountability system is essential for school systems to function. However, by itself, vertical accountability rarely generates new professional knowledge or significant performance gains. *Horizontal accountability* is quite different. It is more reciprocal and relational because it is grounded in mutuality—individuals and groups know what they can count on one another for. Horizontal accountability is fueled by shared commitments and sense of purpose in the work and by collegial respect. There is therefore less need to establish and enforce formal rules and lines of authority. Horizontal accountability often arises through the kinds of ongoing discussion and problem solving that characterize communities of practice. Developing a system of who is accountable to whom and for what—and having a means to track progress—are critical elements of improving any system's performance.[1]

Finally, *relationships* refers to the quality of attitudes, feelings, and behaviors of various individuals and groups toward one another as they engage in the work of helping all students learn. Respectful and trusting relationships are essential if educators are expected to take the risks involved in change, to learn from each other, to remain deeply committed to their students and their community, and to share responsibility. In their book, *Trust in Schools,* Bryk and Schneider illustrate the critical role trust plays in enabling successful school improvement. The four elements of what Bryk and Schneider call "relational trust" include respect, competence, personal regard for others, and integrity. Their research shows that the presence of relational trust in schools correlates more highly with improved student achievement than any other single factor.[2]

The levers of data, accountability, and relationships come into play and serve different purposes within each phase. For instance, according to our framework, the purview of data collection and interpretation begins with change leadership and then widens to include the larger community. Forms of accountability are initially more vertical but evolve to emphasize horizontal accountability. Trust and respect deepen, strengthening relationships and enabling new forms of communication and professional learning. By the enacting phase, a laserlike focus on improving instruction becomes evident in all three change levers. Finally, movement through the three phases corresponds with rightward movement on the three continua.

Individuals engaged in systemic change often find it difficult to draw clear distinctions among the phases of their work. The phases describe the stages of a long-term, cyclical process of continuous improvement—stages that often overlap or recur. We therefore don't expect that you will be able to pinpoint all your work as characteristic of any particular phase. The distinctions should become more apparent, though, when you step back to view the larger patterns and processes of change.

It is also common for people to discover that they have tried to start their change work in the enacting phase. Perhaps you are well down the road in your school or district change efforts and have already done some of what we consider essential in laying the foundations, but other aspects of the work may have had less attention. For most of you, we assume our descriptions of the elements of the work may lead to some kind of *midcourse correction,* rather than a total restart.

Finally, we are not suggesting that the first two phases of preparing and envisioning require you to sit on your hands, unable to take action or begin interventions. In fact, pilot programs designed to experiment with particular kinds of change initiatives and leadership strategies often yield valuable learning for how reinvention should best be planned and undertaken. Again, we emphasize that this work is of a very iterative, cyclical nature. Some readers may find the following graphic useful in marking their progress, but realize that the edges blur: in practice, phases often seem to overlap and intertwine. We encourage you to explore the relationships between phases and between the levers.

| Progress Through the Phases and Levers | | | |
|---|---|---|---|
| | Phase | | |
| **Lever** | **Preparing** | **Envisioning** | **Enacting** |
| **Data** | | | |
| **Accountability** | | | |
| **Relationships** | | | |

## STRATEGIC CHANGE IN ACTION

The three phases of reinvention are a framework to understand and bring about critical staging and sequencing for success. As we describe each phase, we explore the particular work and strategies of that phase in the context of data, accountability, and relationships. We provide a diagnostic for each phase to help you identify where your school or district is within the phases of change. Note that the indicators we include in the diagnostic are illustrative, not complete.

To help bring the somewhat abstract concepts of the three phases of reinvention to life, we tell and compare the stories of two of the districts with which we have had the privilege to work: Corning-Painted Post, New York, and Grand Rapids, Michigan. Corning is a suburban district with an enrollment of 6,000, and Grand Rapids is a larger urban district serving over 24,000 students. Both stories span a two-and-a-half-year period, during which time each district developed its own unique strategies for gathering and using data in sophisticated ways, strengthening accountability for instructional improvement, and building trusting relationships as a foundation for communities of practice at all levels. We take the time to tell these two stories for several reasons. First, we want to show how the change process has certain similarities, no matter where the district is located or its size. But we also want to highlight some differences in the public engagement challenges in "good" suburban districts versus those districts where the problem of poor student performance is already widely recognized.

## Preparing for Whole-System Change

The work of reinventing schools and districts is not technical work that can be controlled by fiat from the top of the organization.[3] Instead, it is adaptive work that requires changes in people's heads, hearts, and actions. It requires all individuals in schools and districts to stay purposefully focused on the same work, be engaged in a thoughtful and deliberate manner, and work collaboratively toward common ends (the right side of the three continua). Getting schools, districts, and the individuals within them to begin working in these new ways requires that leaders prepare the community and educators for the transformations and hard work ahead. To generate the much needed momentum and urgency for change, people need to fully understand the *why* behind the journey they are beginning. This understanding can also reinvigorate people who entered schools and districts with the most ideal of intentions but who, over the years, have gradually become skeptical, resigned, or lethargic.

*To generate the much needed momentum and urgency for change, people need to fully understand the* why *behind the journey they are beginning.*

Preparing for change also entails identifying a group of leaders to own and continuously oversee the change efforts. Reinventing schools and districts is awkward, hard, and messy work. Because there are no road maps, this work requires tolerance for ambiguity. Working as a team, leaders must coordinate their diverse perspectives and see the big picture of the change process.

Although there are no checklists that leaders can simply "mark off" as they move through this phase of a change process, there are identifiable outcomes for successful completion of this phase, including:

- Leaders who articulate a deep understanding and urgency related to both the need for improving learning and teaching for all students and the development of a systemic approach to the improvement process
- Leaders with a plan for generating a greater sense of urgency, understanding, and ownership among teachers, parents, and the community to improve learning and teaching

- A representative steering committee in place that meets regularly to help guide the change process

Because the change levers—data, accountability, and relationships—all play particular and important roles in the preparing phase, we discuss each in more depth.

**Data for Leadership Understanding and Urgency.** Within the preparing phase, data are used to capture the hearts and minds of individuals to understand the problem and to cultivate urgency for the hard work ahead. To these ends, data must be persuasive on logical and emotional levels, touching individuals about the humanity of the effort so as to create and sustain energy.[4]

As mentioned in Chapter Two, many schools and districts typically have either a "hide and seek" or a "fire hydrant" approach to data. There may be too little data about how students are doing, or the data are not widely known or understood by teachers, parents, and the community. Alternatively, when too much data is released, people are overwhelmed and confused about what it means and what's most important. Our experience has shown us that tracking and publicizing a few key data points is an effective first step in establishing greater understanding and urgency for change. Identifying which data points are key depends on the unique circumstances within each school and district.

For example, when Corning-Painted Post School District began its districtwide improvement initiative in 2002, there was widespread belief in the district and across the community that theirs was a "good" suburban district, known for its innovative education practices. Teachers knew in general how the district and their individual schools performed on state-mandated tests. But almost no one in the district was aware of some critical data indicating that one in five high school students dropped out between ninth and twelfth grade. Even fewer knew that only about 60 percent of the seniors were meeting the requirements for a Regents Diploma, which in two and a half years was scheduled to become the new state standard all students would have to meet in order to graduate. And so, to help people better understand what was and wasn't working in the district, these and other key data points (including some surprising data about the elementary and middle school test results) needed to be shared and discussed.

With clear definition of the results they needed (and were not realizing), district leaders then discussed the need to create a system focused on continuous improvement of instruction as the overarching strategy that was most likely to improve student learning and graduation results. To generate *As Is* data about this strategy, the Administrative Council (which consisted of all the central office and building administrators in the district) filled out and discussed the group version of the Seven Disciplines Diagnostic exercise (see Chapter Two, Exercise 2.2, and Appendix A).

Grand Rapids began its districtwide improvement that same summer with the arrival of a new superintendent, Bert Bleke. One of his first steps was to familiarize himself with the district's student performance data, which looked quite different than Corning's data. State test scores were dismal, especially in reading, and high school dropout rates were alarmingly high. There was already awareness among Grand Rapids educators that they faced complex problems, and this awareness was the main reason why Bleke was brought in. But this awareness was never discussed formally and publicly. Furthermore, although each school knew its data in a general way, few fully understood the depth of the problem throughout the district or the full implications of the data. The ways that Bleke used data to create understanding and urgency for change therefore took a very different form than it did in Corning (and required less time and fewer resources). Bleke decided that, for the first time, he would hold public discussions about Grand Rapids' student achievement data. And he decided that their work should begin with the improvement of literacy, which determined the *kind* of data he would share with others. Acknowledging the harsh reality that the community faced quickly resulted in the systemwide urgency he needed. By bringing people together around very specific data, he was able to rally the energy needed for a new improvement effort focused on literacy and reading.

**Shared Accountability for Solving a Common Problem.** In the preparing phase, change leaders also begin to institute new forms of accountability that require collective ownership of and responsibility for the system's problem. Effort is made to disrupt the commonly held view that insufficient student learning is "someone else's fault." As long as everyone focuses on others' faults, finding a scapegoat for the problems they all share, no one meaningfully changes his or her beliefs or behaviors. No one takes responsibility. In contrast, when leaders begin owning these problems and taking responsibility for student achievement, they model a different and more productive way of approaching problems. The collective mindset shifts to a deeper level of engagement, bringing about a new sense of purpose, mission, and commitment to change.

*When leaders begin owning these problems
and taking responsibility for student achievement,
they model a different and more productive
way of approaching problems.*

Corning leadership made this shift. Rather than resorting to faultfinding, Corning leadership framed their problem—the need to improve student performance—as a consequence of a rapidly changing society where students who dropped out of high school were no longer able to get decent jobs that paid a middle-class wage. Donald Trombley, then superintendent, talked about obsolete systems that needed reinventing from beginning to end, K–12. It was, he said, "a new challenge that was everyone's responsibility and no one's fault." He made it clear that it wasn't just the teachers who were the problem and who alone were expected to change. His public stance was that everyone in the system, including the central office, now shared accountability for the problem and the solution. He and others in the district used a phrase we often use in our seminars for leadership teams: "no shame, no blame, no excuses." He also suggested that educators could not expect to motivate all students to want to succeed without active parent and community support.

The shift looked similar in Grand Rapids. In fact, Superintendent Bleke also framed the challenge of improving student reading capacity as one with "no shame, no blame, and no excuses." Whenever he shared student performance data, he made a point of illustrating how the world had changed, and consequently, why all students now need literacy skills to survive. Bleke also formed a District Leadership Team that would spearhead and own the improvement work. As the team entered into their first discussions of the changes they hoped to bring about, they began to accept that they were all responsible for the problem, that they could not accept the results any longer, that the district could succeed in this ambitious endeavor, that it had what it took to tackle the problem, and that it was their responsibility to drive this message and the improvement work throughout the district.

**Establishing the Foundation for Trusting Relationships.** During the preparing phase, leaders must begin to forge relationships that afford new ways of working and talking with one another. Many individuals and groups within a system may have little experience working productively together and must learn to collaborate. In certain settings, there may be a history of dysfunctional relationships that have created distrust and suspicion. Establishing trust and respect are necessary conditions to collaborative work toward a common end and are critical variables in school and district success.

The leadership of what came to be known as the Quantum Leap Project in Corning knew that they needed to actively cultivate trust if they wanted everyone's engagement in the change process. They designed a collaborative and transparent approach to planning and implementing a multiyear initiative to systemically improve teaching and learning. They recognized the need for new strategies to generate stronger parent and community partnerships to improve student learning and increase the community's trust in the educators. Early in the project, the district established a steering committee composed of key central office administrators, several principals, the chair of the school board, and the director of the Corning Corporate Foundation (the benefactor of this initiative). With the support of several consultants, this team met every few weeks to plan their strategy and to assess progress during the first year of the project. Meetings were open to anyone in the community, and minutes were published as public records. Conversations in the meetings were intended as much for participants' learning as for decision making, and the group developed a high degree of openness, trust, and mutual respect as they worked together. Decisions were generally made by consensus after a good deal of discussion, drawing on substantive information and varied perspectives. Individual committee members also took responsibility to meet with key constituent groups not represented on the Steering Committee (such as teachers' association building representatives, community leaders, and the media) to discuss the need for the Quantum Leap Project and to answer questions.

In Grand Rapids, when Bleke first interviewed for the superintendency, he was struck by the palpable lack of trust and hope in the district. He knew that he must mend relationships—especially involving the schools and the district office—with the union, and build stronger relationships among educators if their work ahead was to succeed. As he drew attention to literacy, he emphasized that the district would need to work in a new way. He specifically talked about the need for trust, respect, and openness if they were to deliver on the best interests of the children. He repeated this message at every opportunity and, most important, his actions matched his words. For example, he learned each principal's name and was present at all districtwide principals' meetings. He sent bus drivers coffee and donuts on the first day of school and he visited every school building. Throughout, he encouraged discussion and invited people to ask him tough questions, to which he responded respectfully. And he demonstrated the critical importance of every staff member in educating Grand Rapids students—not just classroom teachers, but kitchen staff, athletics teachers, bus drivers, and the union head, as examples. These actions, combined with his message of "no shame, no blame, no excuses," were critical to building trust throughout the district.

In the preparing phase, a small group of leaders works to understand the nature of the current problem and then comes to take responsibility for and guide the change process. Once this foundation has been laid, change leaders move to the next phase, to bring a larger group of educators and community members into the process of understanding the context of the twenty-first century. In the process, they provide greater pressure for change and begin building a collective sense of where these efforts will lead.

To take stock of where you see your school or district on this journey of preparing for change, see Exercise 8.1.

## Exercise 8.1: Change Phase Diagnostic: Preparing

Use the indicators below each continuum to help in your assessment of where you believe your school or district falls in respect to the change levers in the preparing phase. The indicators are illustrative, not complete.

### Preparing Phase
DATA FOR LEADERSHIP UNDERSTANDING AND URGENCY

| 1 | 2 | 3 | 4 |
|---|---|---|---|
| Not present | Emerging | Developing | Well underway |

**Indicators of Data in Preparing Phase:**

- Leadership has created compelling data sets that have the potential to create urgency (they can mobilize the intellect and passion of people to alter the status quo and their individual behavior).
- Current qualitative and quantitative data have been gathered and then formatted in a way to generate urgency to change or address a specific problem or challenge.
- Leadership has developed an understanding of the gap between the current reality of the schools and the demands the twenty-first century puts on high school graduates.

- Leadership has developed a clear plan for how to educate the community about the specific challenge(s) using compelling data sets.
- Leadership oversees a general inventory of data systems to understand how useable and useful the current data are to the necessary consumers of it [for example, How accessible is data throughout the system? What form(s) is collected and disseminated? Do the people who need to use the data have the necessary skills to use it effectively?]

ACCOUNTABILITY FOR SOLVING A COMMON PROBLEM

| 1 | 2 | 3 | 4 |
|---|---|---|---|
| Not present | Emerging | Developing | Well underway |

**Indicators of Accountability in Preparing Phase:**

- The current state of schooling is openly examined in the context of a dramatically changing economy and society, reducing any sense of blame or victimization among educators throughout schools and districts.
- Educators throughout the system begin to understand that the challenge of educating students for the twenty-first century is everyone's responsibility, one where administrators and teachers share accountability for the problem and the solution.
- A leadership team is created or rechartered for the purpose of overseeing, guiding, and nurturing the overall reinvention process.
- Leadership understands the need for and agrees to next steps for engaging a critical mass of shareholders (inside the schools and among community members) in understanding the problem.
- Leadership gains a shared understanding of what graduating students need to know and be able to do, and this understanding begins to inform next steps.

BUILDING TRUSTING **RELATIONSHIPS** WITH COLLEAGUES AND COMMUNITY

| 1 | 2 | 3 | 4 |
|---|---|---|---|
| Not present | Emerging | Developing | Well underway |

**Indicators of Relationships in Preparing Phase:**

- Leadership team has a shared understanding of the cultural dimensions of a successful change process (that is, collaboration, commitment, and proactivity/redesign as cornerstones of an effective culture, and that norms of no shame, no blame, and no excuses enable these cornerstones to take hold).

- Leadership applies these values to how they work together as a team.
- Leadership works to surface and address dysfunctional relationships throughout the system so as to enable new forms of collaboration.
- Leadership creates new constructive relationships with and cosponsorship of the change efforts with necessary leaders among shareholders (for example, teachers associations, parent groups, community members, businesses).

## Envisioning Whole-System Change

In the envisioning phase, leaders help educators and community members understand the need and urgency for change. These shareholders begin to focus on how they need to adapt their roles to enable their students to succeed in the twenty-first century. They begin to see the need to work together in new ways, especially more collaboratively. Change leaders form communities of practice for themselves, where their work increasingly focuses on the continuous improvement of teaching and learning. They intentionally model this different way of working, with its clear focus, to leaders and teachers throughout the schools and district.

Identifiable outcomes for successful completion of this phase include:

- A critical mass of teachers, parents, and community members who understand the need to improve all students' learning and who are engaged in a process of envisioning solutions. This includes a deeper understanding of what all high school graduates need to know for work, learning, and active citizenship in the twenty-first century.

- Educators who understand the importance of developing all teachers' skills, as well as the skills of administrators as instructional leaders. There is an emerging and concrete vision of good instruction.

- Establishment of a few clear districtwide goals and strategies, focusing on improving teaching and learning.

- A growing awareness of the need to work more collaboratively at all levels, with recognition of the need for trust and respect to support new, more vital forms of collaboration.

**Data for Community-Wide Understanding and Urgency.**   In the envisioning phase, change leaders strive to communicate their understanding and urgency to the wider community. As a result, all educators develop deeper understandings of the current problem; ideally this generates the desire and the energy to sustain the change efforts over time. Data are employed creatively, compellingly, and strategically to focus the community's attention on the children who are the heart of the work. Within schools and districts, educators collect data to assess the degree to which they share common professional standards that drive collective practice and define excellence in all classrooms.

---

*Data are employed creatively, compellingly, and strategically to focus the community's attention on the children who are the heart of the work.*

---

One of the first tasks of Corning's Quantum Leap Steering Committee was to create a concise one-page fact sheet on student achievement in the district, highlighting the key gaps and challenges at all levels of the school system. But the group knew that more was needed to create a deeper and broader sense of urgency for change. Having presented the high school data to his administrators, Trombley now had to take the risky step of publicizing this information and other key data with his teachers and the community—most of whom thought things were fine in their public schools. Borrowing the idea of a "living bar graph" (as Superintendent Vicki Phillips used in Lancaster), Trombley went in front of his entire staff and board early in the first year of the project. He lined ten students up on the stage, explained the 20 percent dropout rate, and asked two students to sit down. He told the audience that, of the eight remaining, only five students were currently meeting the soon-to-be required state graduation standard, and asked three more to sit down. Then he turned to the crowd and said, "We're on track to leave half of our students behind—whose children will they be?"

Trombley's living bar graph drew on people's reason and their emotions to dramatically enhance their shared understanding, and underscored the urgency of the need for change. The next step went even further. The Steering Committee gathered qualitative data from student focus groups and showed edited videotapes to faculty, parents, and the community of high school students discussing their school experiences. Teachers and parents alike were moved by students' pleadings for more personal connections with teachers and more hands-on, active learning experiences in their classes. The combination of quantitative and qualitative data created a much clearer and more compelling picture of why systemic change was needed in the district.

Toward the end of the first year, Corning's Administrative Council also began to gather data to see how consistently they defined good teaching. Each council member graded the tenth-grade English lesson discussed in Chapter Two. The range of grades in the council was virtually the same as that of every other group: A through D. This fact convinced council members to begin the work of creating a shared vision of quality instruction.

In Grand Rapids, the clarity developed in the preparing phase about students' low literacy scores helped jump-start the improvement work and establish literacy as a district priority. Some District Leadership Team members then began to study their student data and current teaching practices throughout their K–8 schools. From both these data sources they developed a deeper understanding of their problem (a characteristic of how data are used in this phase). They concluded that teachers faced unprecedented student literacy challenges and, consequently, needed new teaching methods.

A literacy committee, which included teachers and administrators, was formed to research and select an effective model for teaching literacy; within months professional development sessions were organized and offered to selected grade-level teachers. At the end of the year, the Literacy Committee collected classroom data to determine the impact of the professional development on teachers' practices, attitudes, and student performance. The positive responses they heard from teachers encouraged them to redouble their efforts the next year. The District Leadership Team also communicated these results to all the principals with a clear message that the focus on literacy would continue.

In the meantime, Bleke broadened his community outreach, meeting with parents and community members to talk about the district's critical focus on literacy. He called on the business community and the local university to get involved. By consistently framing the literacy focus in a "no shame, no blame" fashion, he helped create community-wide understanding of the problem, a hallmark of the envisioning phase.

**Laying the Foundations for Reciprocal, Relational Accountability.** The change leaders who accepted and developed their own accountability earlier now work to help educators and others throughout the community reach agreement and clarity about what the district will be held accountable for. This agreement helps produce increased purpose and focus for what the community is working toward. Simultaneously, educators in schools and districts gain a beginning sense of what they, as individuals, will be held accountable for in order for the district to deliver on its goals. As they do so, the seeds of horizontal accountability begin to take root. This clarity is reached through open dialogue among and across roles, where educators and community members explore what they individually and collectively must do if they are to reach all students.

These new forms of accountability began to grow in Corning when their Steering Committee decided to establish a broadly representative community advisory committee of teachers, parents, community, and union leaders. Its charge was to review the progress of the project and to advise the Steering Committee on strategies for a forthcoming public engagement campaign, the centerpiece of the second phase of their initiative. This intensive public engagement project was designed to expand the urgency to improve learning and teaching, provide greater clarity about the new skills needed by all students in a knowledge economy, and create a heightened sense of visible, shared responsibility for student results.

The Steering Committee organized community-wide small-group discussions, called focus groups, led by trained facilitators.[5] Many parents, teachers, and community members volunteered to facilitate the conversations, and were taught how to introduce the guidelines for discussion, sequence the questions for consistency across groups, and script summaries of the main discussion points. Eventually, more than 140 people served as facilitators for the focus groups that engaged about 1,800 people in the community, including all the district's educators. The questions offered for discussion were:

1. What are some of the most important changes that have taken place in our society in the last quarter century that we need to understand as we think about teaching and learning today?

2. Given these changes, what are the few most important things we want all Corning graduates to know and be able to do to be prepared for the world of today and tomorrow?[6]

3. How could we assess student performance so we know they've mastered the skills you identified? What would be evidence of mastery?

4. How will our schools and classrooms need to change to enable all students to master these skills?

5. How can the community help? How can the community be more involved in the process?

One of the most important outcomes of this process was a sharply defined—and very public—set of goals and priorities to which the district agreed to be accountable. Discussion of question 5 also helped generate a shared sense of accountability for results and an understanding of the respective roles and responsibilities of educators, parents, and community members in helping all students succeed. In addition, new expectations of accountability for improved instruction arose from discussions the teacher focus groups held on the Seven Disciplines, including assessments of individual school and district efforts on each discipline.

In contrast, in this phase, Grand Rapids was focused on literacy, and included school principals. Bleke worked with the District Leadership Team to help them understand their critical role in the improvement process. The Leadership Team, in turn, helped the principals understand their role. Members of the Leadership Team designed the bimonthly principal meetings to build principals' understanding of what they needed to do and to develop their capacity to carry it out. In doing so, they helped the principals (especially K–6) see why an instructional model needed to be districtwide and how students' success depended on successive years of consistent and effective literacy teaching. Principals began to understand that they needed to hold all their teachers accountable for implementing the new literacy model.

Meanwhile, the Leadership Team and the Literacy Committee began to feel overwhelmed by the magnitude and complexity of their challenge and the size of the tasks they faced in such a large district. After careful reassessment, they could see that they were at risk of doing too much and with insufficient coordination, and they responded by adjusting their tasks and time lines so that everything was more tightly aligned with and focused on literacy. In doing so, they became clearer about what was expected of them and what they could expect from others—a more robust system of accountability.

**Developing More Trusting, Respectful Relationships.**  In the envisioning phase, trust and respect must deepen, as the success of the improvement work depends on the quality of the conversations among individuals and groups. Vital conversations about the nature of the problem, different visions of the solutions, and assignment of responsibility for the improvement effort require a commitment and ability to actively listen, especially when there is disagreement. Working through differences in frank and respectful ways ultimately enables the collective problem solving and decision making required for successful change.[7] Where there is growing trust, the quality of discourse increases, again helping stimulate greater engagement and real collaboration.

---

*Where there is growing trust, the quality of discourse increases, again helping stimulate greater engagement and real collaboration.*

---

The quality of relationships in Corning was improving because the focus groups provided a safe space for people to talk about important issues. The structured format of the conversation explicitly provided for every voice to be heard, and thereby fostered respect. Many community members remarked on the productive nature of their conversations, acknowledging the need to promote more respectful dialogue—rather than acrimonious debate—in all discussions of local civic affairs and especially in matters related to education. Parents and community members were also able to talk frankly about the ways in which Corning's educators had in the past appeared disinterested in what parents had to say. The schools had sometimes appeared to them as forbidding fortresses rather than welcoming community centers. The opportunity to talk openly about these issues began to build new trust between the community and its educators. Teachers said that the small-group discussions in their buildings provided them with important opportunities to get to know one another in new ways. In their evaluations, many said the day that had been set aside for teacher focus groups was the best professional development experience they had ever had in the district. These dialogues were instrumental in generating greater purpose and focus, engagement, and collaboration among all shareholders.

Although the focus groups helped the district take a giant step toward better relationships at many levels in Corning, administrators recognized that communication at Administrative Council meetings was strained. They asked one of their consultants to conduct a series of confidential interviews with each of the subgroups that made up the council, including elementary principals, middle and high school principals, and the central office administrators. What emerged from these interviews was a clear pattern of low trust between building leaders and central office administrators, as well as a need for guidelines or group norms for their discussions. To the great credit of the administrators, they requested the data from the interviews be shared (without attributing names) at their year-end retreat so that they could discuss how to build trust, create a greater sense of mutual accountability, and have more fruitful, inclusive discussions at their meetings. Each group committed to paper what they thought they should be held accountable for and what they needed from the other groups to accomplish their work, and then the groups compared notes. The entire council also forged agreement around a set of group norms they believed would make future discussions more productive. These steps vastly improved the quality of discussion and the extent of participation for everyone on the council, particularly the new administrators.

Relationships among those in the Grand Rapids Leadership Team also grew during the envisioning phase and required some difficult self-scrutiny and stocktaking. The team acknowledged that they were not truly utilizing each other's expertise or fully exploring multiple perspectives. Instead, each member tended to take a position and defend it, deferring resolution of the team's differences to the superintendent. This honest self-reflection also led the team to understand more deeply how they needed to lead the improvement work through their own example. As a consequence, they made an explicit agreement to work collectively to discuss fully and resolve their key improvement effort dilemmas. Setting these new goals did not immediately translate into changed team dynamics, yet the team now had a clearer idea of what they were striving for, which was necessary for them to dedicate themselves fully to the change.

Discussions about their patterns of relationship arose again when the team began focusing some of their bimonthly principal meetings around problems of practice. Again, early collective problem solving was minimal, and the leaders of those meetings sometimes fell back into old patterns of "telling" principals what to do. They recognized that if they were to foster greater levels of collaboration and engagement, they must struggle to change deep-seated behaviors and beliefs. Although such recognition was a sign of growth and would have been impossible in phase one, these leaders knew that even greater trust was necessary if leaders were to make themselves vulnerable by talking openly about what they didn't know and how much they needed help. They committed themselves once again to deepening that trust.

To take stock of where you see your school or district on this journey of envisioning change, see Exercise 8.2.

## Exercise 8.2: Change Phase Diagnostic: Envisioning

Use the indicators below each continuum to help in your assessment of where you believe your school or district falls in respect to the change levers in the envisioning phase. The indicators are illustrative, not complete.

### Envisioning Phase

DATA FOR COMMUNITY-WIDE UNDERSTANDING AND URGENCY

| 1 | 2 | 3 | 4 |
|---|---|---|---|
| Not present | Emerging | Developing | Well underway |

**Indicators of Data in Envisioning Phase:**

- Qualitative and quantitative data sets concerning the functioning of the school system (for example, indicators of student achievement and student engagement) are widely and transparently shared with the greater community.

- A large number of shareholders understand the gap between where the district needs to be and the current reality.

- An open and honest assessment of how professionals within the district work together and how the district functions as a system is the focus of district dialogue and action.

- Data are gathered (for example, by conducting learning walks) around current teaching practices.

LAYING THE FOUNDATION FOR RECIPROCAL, RELATIONAL **ACCOUNTABILITY**

| 1 | 2 | 3 | 4 |
|---|---|---|---|
| Not present | Emerging | Developing | Well underway |

**Indicators of Accountability in Envisioning Phase:**
A few clear districtwide goals and strategies, focusing on improving teaching and learning, are established.

- The community develops a deep understanding of the current gap between what graduates presently know and are able to do and what they need to know and be able to do to thrive in twenty-first century.

- Community shareholders have been brought together to help develop goals and foci for the change work.

- Community shareholders develop a sense of what they are accountable for in relation to helping all students develop the necessary new skills.
- Greater clarity is reached concerning what district leadership is accountable for to the community shareholders.
- Teachers and administrators have an emerging understanding of the need for everyone in the system to improve professional practice.

DEVELOPING MORE TRUSTING, RESPECTFUL **RELATIONSHIPS**

| 1 | 2 | 3 | 4 |
|---|---|---|---|
| Not present | Emerging | Developing | Well underway |

**Indicators of Relationships in Envisioning Phase:**

- Patterns of forthright communication and positive collaboration between (and among) the district and its constituent groups have been developed.
- School-level collaboration among teachers has increased.
- The quality of discourse in working meetings throughout the district has increased, creating the opportunity for all educators to engage in collaborative and productive ways.
- Educators understand the need to work more collaboratively on instructional practice and have begun grade-level and cross-school discussions.
- School-level meetings are more directly focused on the issues of teaching and learning and the meetings tend to model powerful instructional practice.

## Enacting Whole-System Change

Change leaders are well positioned to enter the enacting phase once they've built a solid foundation on a clearer definition of the problem, greater urgency for change, increased clarity about the desired outcomes, and a beginning sense of what this work entails. In this phase, steady improvement begins. This improvement rests on implementing plans and strategies developed in previous phases, constant monitoring, and ready revisions to the plans and strategies as needed.

Laying the foundation for lasting success requires focus and progress toward implementing the organizational practices that are related (directly and indirectly) to the improvement of teaching and learning in every classroom. The Seven Disciplines for Strengthening Instruction move educators from simply understanding the problem they are trying to solve (Preparing) and envisioning what success might look like (Envisioning), to helping schools and districts undertake new practices that will result in improved instructional practice and results for students (Enacting). The disciplines will continue to add to the rightward movement on the three continua, yielding even sharper focus and purpose, greater engagement of all adults, and the creation of new forms of collaboration among professionals.

**Data for Continuous Improvement of Teaching and Learning.**   The work of reinventing schools and districts—or any adaptive venture for that matter—is seldom straightforward. Even well-designed and implemented strategies may not always generate the intended results, and change leaders need to relentlessly examine data to assess the effectiveness of strategies underway. Any differences between the intended and actual results of these strategies require shifts or redirection to better increase the learning of all students. Change leaders also use data to help identify and consolidate any general learnings about the change process itself. Leaders must recognize the cyclical aspects of change and the systemic nature of organizations, and must have the flexibility to adapt where necessary to meet their goals.

Corning took a number of steps to make better use of its data. In the 2003–04 academic year, teams from every school received extensive training from an outside consultant on how to understand and use their building's test score data to inform the continuous improvement of instruction. A team of central office administrators also used state test data to determine where curricula might need to change to align with state standards. Throughout 2004, administrators scheduled meetings with building teams and K–12 committees in these two academic areas to share their analyses so that the alignment work could be better informed.

Districtwide learning walks to gather data on the quality of instruction at every level also began in 2004. To further develop a common standard for good teaching, monthly faculty meetings in every building were devoted to text-based discussions of strategies for improving teaching and learning.[8] At the end of 2004, every educator in the district also participated in small-group, building-level discussions about what they thought was going well and what they needed to be more successful in doing as teachers. Data from this "midcourse" review was then used to revise both building and district-level professional development strategies and priorities.

The classroom data that the Literacy Team in Grand Rapids had collected in the envisioning phase confirmed their thinking that developing teacher capacity to teach literacy skills was an effective strategy. In particular, the data showed that the new methods had met with widespread enthusiasm and optimism among teachers, who saw how their teaching could reach more students. The core Leadership Team began to devise new K–6 literacy assessment tools and school-level protocols for looking at student performance data. The leadership team wanted to collect student performance data so that teachers could have timely information about how the new methods were and were not working with each of their students. By the fall of 2004, all elementary schools were required to use these tools and strongly encouraged to form improvement teams to use the data from these new tools productively. The Leadership Team supported the schools by providing them with coaches who had been trained to interpret how these data should inform teaching. The District Leadership Team also accepted new responsibility for overseeing the quality and districtwide effects of the K–6 literacy strategy. To do so, they needed data that would help them monitor teachers' success with students, principals' capacity to support teachers, and the improvement teams' examination of schoolwide data and the overall success of their strategies. They identified particular kinds of information throughout the system that would accurately indicate these performances, and began to collect and interpret these data regularly.

**Shared Accountability for Continuous Improvement of Teaching and Learning.** Accountability deepens and becomes a more meaningful guide to individual and collective action as individual educators take on new classroom practices and collaborate in new ways. Administrators and teachers reach greater understanding of what they need to be held accountable for and why. Horizontal accountability emerges more clearly and is recognized among professionals who hold a collective sense of purpose and integrity, with public expectations for themselves and each other. The existing professional culture is strengthened and the entire school or district develops greater capacity to work collaboratively.

By August 2004, Corning had moved a long way toward its goal of an aligned, coherent system with shared accountability for improvement of instruction. The launch of the Quantum Leap Project signified a consistent and continued emphasis on improving teaching and learning for all students, despite significant changes among school board members and in the leadership of the district. The

Administrative Council took time during their retreat that summer to codify practices that had evolved somewhat unevenly over the previous year into a set of Public Agreements to which they committed to hold themselves and one another accountable.[9] These agreements included the following:

- All adult meetings (both building level and administrator) will continue to be about instruction.
- We will create a plan to move from awareness of best teaching practices through text-based study to successful implementation in every building, as measured by increased student performance.
- The Administrative Council will meet twice a month (instead of just once a month) to continue its learning together, and this work will be shared widely with all staff.
- Elementary and secondary principals will communicate what they work on in their separate meetings.
- All administrators will continue their regular learning walks, and these will be expanded to include cross-level involvement in learning walks (that is, elementary and secondary administrators visiting different grade levels together).

During the 2004 calendar year, additional forms of horizontal accountability began to emerge in Corning. Language arts teachers hammered out a new curriculum for the teaching of writing, specifically addressing how they would be accountable for its implementation. They also agreed to create portfolios of student written work and to discuss common writing performance standards within and across grade levels. Elementary and secondary math teachers conducted an item analysis of test data, which led them to review their curriculum and determine collective expectations for more articulated mathematics instruction and higher levels of achievement.

Once the core leadership team at Grand Rapids accepted responsibility for crafting interventions in schools that were not making sufficient progress, the team came increasingly to understand the need to speak plainly and directly, especially with those principals who were not on board with the literacy strategy. Although they had long seen the role of principal as pivotal and had worked intensively to develop principals into effective change agents within their own buildings, the team had not held principals accountable for the improvement work. They began developing a strategy intended to both support principals and effectively hold them accountable.

These examples underscore the need for accountability to flow appropriately, both horizontally and vertically. Horizontal accountability does not negate the need for supervision or for structures and processes that reinforce the publicly held values and aims of an organization. Optimally, all individuals rise to the challenge of *all students, new skills,* and hold themselves accountable to the standards of performance that goal demands. This kind of accountability must be fostered; leadership must intentionally and explicitly move all adults toward these kinds of behaviors. Nevertheless, as was the case in Grand Rapids, sometimes supervision takes precedence over facilitation, but leaders must recognize this as an interim measure. As a long-term approach to accountability, this practice will hold an organization to a state of compliance. Throughout each phase, leaders must therefore exercise their sense of balance, judgment, and clarity about their expectations and the results they seek. They must carefully consider what accountability measures are necessary to achieve those ends.

**Relationships Improve Teaching and Learning.**   In the enacting phase, the trust that has emerged grows and deepens, allowing educators to work together in new ways—ways that would have been considered impossible in the past. These trust-based relationships are essential if schools and districts are to fundamentally disrupt the extreme isolation of educators and help build a profession of teaching based on standards of practice. These new relationships are also necessary to ensure that leaders can work with people in various roles to promote the changes necessary to benefit all students.

---

*These trust-based relationships are essential if schools and districts are to fundamentally disrupt the extreme isolation of educators and help build a profession of teaching based on standards of practice.*

---

Indicators of profound changes in the quality of working relationships were apparent throughout the Corning District. Judy Stapes, who became the Corning superintendent in 2003, met regularly with the association leadership to collaboratively and proactively identify and solve problems. Contract negotiations were concluded in record time through conversations around a table. The Quantum Leap Project Executive Committee, reconstituted after the public engagement phase of the project, began to include the association president at the table with central office and building administrators to represent the voices and concerns of teachers. They met weekly to assess the progress of the initiative and refine and develop new strategies where needed, becoming a highly effective leadership practice community that worked and learned together.

In previous years, building administrators rarely spoke up in meetings and never discussed their leadership challenges, yet they now participated regularly and discussed leadership challenges with one another. Districtwide curriculum meetings, once little more than opportunities for mutual blaming, were now cochaired by teachers and administrators and productively addressed the tasks at hand. Increasingly, teachers opened up their practice for discussion, grew less fearful of learning walks, and began videotaping their lessons. Deeper levels of trust at every level of the Corning School District provided a foundation that enabled adults to become increasingly collaborative in ways characteristic of communities of practice. Quantum Leap was no longer viewed as just another district project, but represented powerful new ways of working together in continued efforts to improve teaching and learning.

Deeper trust among the adults in Grand Rapids was also visible. The leadership team continued to honor its agreement to use its meetings for collective problem solving of key improvement effort dilemmas. They grew increasingly successful in bringing problems of practice to the group, and individuals took turns presenting the personal challenges they faced in their work, spurring genuine dialogue among group participants. Progress could also be seen in principals' meetings. Perhaps most telling is that many principals set up communities of practice within their buildings so that teachers could work with each other to improve their practice by using student data and learning how to implement new literacy strategies.

When the central office leaders who were overseeing the elementary academic program conducted learning walks in multiple schools, they reported common experiences: teachers who warmly invited them into classrooms and who demonstrated real interest in what the central office administrators observed. Some teachers, in fact, demanded to hear honest feedback on their teaching and on the school's implementation of the literacy model. By many accounts, this openness was new to the professional culture of Grand Rapids, and reflected the positive results of their work in the preparing and envisioning phases.

To take stock of where you see your school or district enacting at the moment, see Exercise 8.3.

---

## Exercise 8.3: Change Phase Diagnostic: Enacting

Use the indicators below each continuum to help in your assessment of where you believe your school or district falls in respect to the change levers in the enacting phase. The indicators are illustrative, not complete.

### Enacting Phase

DATA FOR CONTINUOUS IMPROVEMENT OF TEACHING AND LEARNING

**Indicators of Data in Enacting Phase:**

- Systems of data collection and analysis are constructed to monitor the implementation and impact of improvement strategies.

- Data are being used at the district level to identify pockets of success from which to identify best practice.

- Data concerning the quality of instruction are continuously gathered and analyzed by administrators and teachers.

- In each school, data are used diagnostically at frequent intervals by teams of teachers to refine school assessments and goals, monitor student progress, and continually improve instruction.

- Assessments of school quality and effectiveness rely on multiple and varied sources of data concerning student achievement and engagement (test scores, promotion rates, dropout rates, and the like).

SHARED **ACCOUNTABILITY** FOR CONTINUOUS IMPROVEMENT OF LEARNING AND TEACHING

**Indicators of Accountability in Enacting Phase:**

- District leadership has developed and has implemented a structure for providing frequent, rigorous, and focused supervision of school principals' instructional leadership.

- School leadership has developed and implemented a structure for providing frequent, rigorous, and focused supervision of classroom instruction.

- The structure and content of teacher supervision at the school level are aligned with the focus of district improvement efforts.

- Schools have begun to create vivid and clear standards of professional practice based on research-tested and practice-based understandings of how students learn. In other words, teachers and administrators share collective definitions of what constitutes effective instructional practice.

- Expectations and responsibility for student outcomes are clarified for and aligned through grade and school division (elementary, middle, high) levels.

- All educators have a greater sense of what they are being held accountable for, and these more collectively held expectations form the basis of more horizontal accountability.

- All professionals at the district and school levels understand the relation between their work and role and the improvement of instruction.

TRUSTING **RELATIONSHIPS** FOR WORKING IN NEW WAYS

|   | 1 | 2 | 3 | 4 |
|---|---|---|---|---|
|   | Not present | Emerging | Developing | Well underway |

**Indicators of Relationships in Enacting Phase:**

- Schools have been reorganized to provide the conditions necessary to facilitate collaborative teamwork among adults and to foster personalized learning communities for students.

- Professional relationships become increasingly effective as trust throughout the system increases and deepens.

- Professionals begin to open up their practice among colleagues, working to improve their respective competencies while simultaneously developing consistent and increasingly effective standards of practice.

- Parents and community members are welcomed into schools and are more actively involved in the collective enterprise of improving student learning (for example, community members are involved as mentors or parents, providing students a time and place for studying at home).

Now that you have identified where you see your school or district in all of the three phases, you can use your assessments to generate a fuller picture of where you might need to add to your initiative or circle back to address some earlier phase work. Exercise 8.4 provides questions and steps to help you consider the implications of your assessment.

## Exercise 8.4: Review and Revise Your Strategies

### Step One

Take a moment to reflect on your completed phase diagnostics (Exercises 8.1, 8.2, and 8.3) by answering the following questions.

1. What is going well? What should the school or district celebrate?
2. Which change levers might require greater attention? What might we have missed entirely?

### Step Two

Go back to the *As Is–To Be* picture that you created in Chapter Six. Look at the systemic strategies (currently underway or planned) in light of your new understanding of data, accountability, and relationships and the phases of change, and your assessment of where your school or district is on these. Answer the following questions:

1. Do any strategies (underway or planned) need to be revised? If so, which ones? Why?
2. What would be a more effective strategy? Take a moment to explain your thinking about why this strategy would be more effective.
3. What are next steps toward developing more effective strategies?
4. What evidence will indicate that it is time to move to the next phase of this work?

### Step Three

Use the following template to organize your ideas for new or revised strategies.

| Lever | Preparing Phase | | Envisioning Phase | | Enacting Phase | |
|---|---|---|---|---|---|---|
| | Strategies | Actions | Strategies | Actions | Strategies | Actions |
| Data | | | | | | |
| Accountability | | | | | | |
| Relationships | | | | | | |

## PUTTING THE PIECES TOGETHER:
## THE ECOLOGY OF EDUCATIONAL TRANSFORMATION

Over the course of several years, both the Corning-Painted Post School District and the Grand Rapids Public School District developed progressively greater purpose and focus, engagement, and collaboration in all their meetings. Corning's districtwide discussions in the first year helped educators and parents understand the new context for teaching and learning—the changing nature of the family and the new skills needed for learning, work, and citizenship. In Grand Rapids, the discussions were more focused on the literacy skills needed by all children in the twenty-first century, which enabled adults within the school buildings, parents, and community members to understand that the district was not meeting the current needs of the majority of its students.

The culture of both districts changed profoundly in this process. Trusting relationships became the norm, as did the expectation that people would talk through their differences directly. Both districts developed a culture of higher expectations—for all students and adults. Both districts also effectively developed the competencies of administrators and teachers to work on instructional improvement, including critiquing their own and their colleagues' teaching, assessing, and aligning curricula.

Still, at the end of the two and a half years, leaders in both settings knew that theirs was a work in progress. Naturally, each district had reached different thresholds in the work and began grappling with new dimensions of the improvement process. In Corning, much more remained to be done to develop the teaching and supervision competencies that could increase rigor in every lesson. Grand Rapids' leaders had just begun the work of sharpening their picture of what supervisors needed to be able to know and do, and how the central office needed to support them. Creating performance standards for student work at every level was another longer-term goal of the Corning district that was necessary to further strengthen efforts to define and assess rigor. Grand Rapids was not yet ready to take on this work. In both districts, central office administrators recognized the need to deepen collaboration across departments and to spend more time in schools.

Another of Corning's challenges was to design a new schedule that would improve the conditions of adult learning for teachers and allow for more time in buildings to discuss instruction and ways to make the curriculum more active and more relevant for students. Corning needed to resume work—which had been suspended because of the defeat of a facilities renovation plan in May of 2003—on how best to improve the conditions of teaching and learning at the secondary level to strengthen teacher-student relationships. Rethinking the structure of the two high schools would likely require another public engagement campaign, and parents throughout the district needed help in learning how best to support their children's learning. Grand Rapids was facing unprecedented financial constraints and needed to learn how to keep the improvement priorities alive and well in a climate of shrinking financial support.

Both the Corning and Grand Rapids stories illustrate the kinds of issues a district or school leadership team might need to consider in a systemic improvement process. The stories are not intended as prescriptions for how to undertake change, telling leaders exactly what to do. Rather, they represent two different pictures of what it looks like to phase reinvention according to the unique problems, resources, goals, and tactics of each district. One size cannot fit all. Leaders must be well aware that their work is ongoing in nature and that school transformation is necessarily adaptive. Changing strategies need not indicate a weakness in planning, but a culture of inquiry, evidence, and reflection that acknowledges the ecological nature of change and the application of tools that promote progress and continuous improvement.

These stories also illustrate how the phases themselves are cyclical and must be considered and reconsidered as new insights, opportunities, or challenges present themselves. Corning, for example, learned that their secondary initiative represented a level of change sufficient to require strong preparation and clear vision before enactment. As much as anything, this recognition represents how well they had grasped the concepts of engagement, purpose and focus, and collaboration—and phased their work to sustain these concepts and ensure successful implementation.

## MEASURING SUCCESS AND THE CHALLENGE OF HIGH-STAKES TEST SCORES

So far, we have said nothing about test scores in either Corning or Grand Rapids and have made scant reference to improving test scores. We have several reasons. First, with respect to Corning and Grand Rapids, it is simply too early to expect to see meaningful improvements in test scores. As we write this book, the enacting phase of improving instruction and the curriculum has been going on, in both places, for only a little more than a year. But we have deliberately chosen to deemphasize test scores for other reasons as well. Although we know how important they are, especially with the heightened accountability requirements of the No Child Left Behind legislation, we have seen too many districts focus on the improvement of test scores as the goal, rather than seeing them as just one indicator of a successful systemic initiative to improve teaching and learning. Districts that take a "test prep" approach may see test scores improve for a few years, but without a focus on substantive improvements in teaching and learning, their modest gains soon plateau.

Item analyses of test results show that, in most districts, students perform the weakest on elements of tests that assess reasoning, analysis, problem solving, and application—so-called higher-order skills that cannot be improved significantly simply by giving students more drills and practice tests. In the long run, it is only through a systematic focus on improvement of instruction that student achievement gains will be sustained over time. There are no shortcuts to ensuring that all students master new skills. Test scores will inevitably go up as a result of a relentless focus on improvement of instruction and the creation of a rigorous "thinking" pedagogy and curriculum in every class. Certainly that has been the case for some of the highest performing districts in the country, including District 2, as we saw in Chapter Six.

We have further evidence from West Clermont. When we began working with this district in 1999, only 46 percent of its elementary students—not including special education students—were reading at grade level. By 2004, 81 percent of all elementary students in the district—including special education students—met the reading standard on a tougher test. The district also now has a coherent strategy to push these gains to the secondary level. And West Clermont is today one of the best examples in the country of a district that led a successful suburban high school transformation.

We believe the techniques used in West Clermont will be successful for many others. We further believe that these ways of planning and envisioning also apply to the work *individuals* undertake when they seek to overturn their personal immunities to change. As we explore further in Chapter Nine, it is equally important to track the incremental changes that occur in this work because having a clearer picture of how you overturn your immunities and what these changes look like as they are in progress will improve your capability and maximize your own efforts to change.

## Endnotes

1. Readers may want to refer to Charles Abelmann and Richard Elmore's discussion of internal and external accountability in Charles Abelmann and Richard Elmore with Joanna Even, Susan Kenyon, and Joanne Marshall, *When Accountability Knocks: Will Anyone Answer?* (Philadelphia: University of Pennsylvania, Consortium for Policy Research in Education, 1999).

2. In their study of Chicago schools, Anthony Bryk and Barbara Schneider uncovered three lenses critical to understanding how trust manifests itself in an educational organization: (1) the individual assumptions and expectations held about how people in particular roles should behave—principals, teachers, and parents (Do they behave the way we expect them to?); (2) four distinct elements that must be present for trust to exist: respect (Does he or she listen to me?), integrity (Does this person stand behind stated values and do what he or she claims?), competency (Is this person able to do what I expect him or her to do?), and personal regard (Does this person care about me?); and (3) the uneven power structure inherent in education and how that reality collides with a mutual dependency for results. In other words, principals are dependent on teachers to achieve results with students for which they are both accountable; teachers are dependent on principals to provide certain supports but lack the power to require these supports; both are dependent on parents to send students who are rested and ready to learn. Bryk claims this third component is particularly influential in creating vulnerability for all parties and one that must be intentionally addressed in developing trusting relationships. See Anthony S. Bryk and Barbara Schneider, *Trust in Schools: A Core Resource for Improvement* (New York: Russell Sage Foundation, 2002).

3. In *Building a New Structure for School Leadership*, Richard Elmore explains that improving schools at their core—in classrooms—is an enterprise that cannot be controlled. Instead, because of the complicated nature of improvement, leadership throughout the organization can at best "guide and support" the process. See Richard Elmore, *Building a New Structure for School Leadership* (Washington, D.C.: Albert Shanker Institute, 2000).

4. John Kotter, *The Heart of Change: Real Life Stories of How People Change Their Organizations* (Boston: Harvard Business School Press, 2002).

5. For a longer discussion and case study on the use of community-wide focus groups in setting education goals and priorities, see Chapter Two of Tony Wagner's *Making the Grade: Reinventing America's Schools* (New York: RoutledgeFalmer, 2002). See also Daniel Yankelovich, *The Magic of Dialogue* (New York: Touchstone, 1999).

6. Participants first brainstormed an inclusive list. When all the suggestions were in, participants were each given three sticky dots and asked to place them on the learning

goals they considered most important. The dots then gave everyone a visual cue of consensus.

7. Bryk and Schneider, *Trust in Schools*.

8. The text used was Robert Marzano, Debra Pickering, and Jane Pollock, *Classroom Instruction That Works* (Alexandria, Va.: Association for Supervision and Curriculum Development, 2001).

9. For a discussion of the formation and use of public agreements, see Chapter Nine of Kegan and Lahey's book, *How the Way We Talk Can Change the Way We Work* (San Francisco: Jossey-Bass, 2001).

# Overturning Your Immunities to Change

It is not easy to call into question and potentially alter the assumptions we have taken as truths. Often we have held particular Big Assumptions for years and years; their roots are lodged deep in our pasts and in our identities. The busy pace of our lives, the pressures of immediate deadlines, and the force of our own immune system can easily get in the way of our good intentions and plans. Habits of mind can be as intractable as habits of behavior. But it is possible to alter them, as Arthur demonstrated. As you may recall, Arthur's Big Assumption was, "I assume that if others recognize that I am not exactly clear about every step of the way, or see that I am at all uncertain, they will lose confidence in me as a leader, see me as an ineffective leader, and I will be a failure."

Holding this assumption meant that he avoided taking any risks that might lead others to discover that he was uncertain about how to take the next steps toward progress and realize the district's improvement goals. Though he had some ideas about what might work, none of these plans felt solid or secure enough to promise results. Because the right answers were not materializing for Arthur, district progress had stalled.

Yet eventually, Arthur found a way to get unstuck. We'll see exactly how he was able to do so later; first, here's what he accomplished. He announced and implemented learning walks in several classrooms. Principals and other district leaders began to systematically observe instruction and discuss what they saw. They all took notes and compared their impressions with each other, according to the standards they had developed for what good instruction would look like. Their conversations were at first hesitant but then grew more and more animated, often leading to new questions and sometimes to new insights.

Arthur's excitement grew. Although his plan for the learning walks and resulting conversations initially seemed rather hazy to him, his experiences helped him clarify his plan. Each month he thought back on what he and the others were learning about how to support improved instruction. He kept systematic notes about what he was hoping and expecting to happen with this plan, what kinds of evidence he was gathering to suggest the plan was working, what kinds of worries and questions still existed, and what all these data could tell him about what to do next. "I still don't know all the steps we'll need to take," Arthur explained, "but I'm learning that's okay. I can and need to take action even when I'm not 100 percent sure that things will work the way I want them to. Risks are part of this job, and I don't believe that there is any superintendent in this day and age who always knows what to do next. So, instead of working toward certainty, I'm working on getting better at deciding which risks to take and how."

So how did Arthur accomplish these changes? What did his change process look like? How did he alter his Big Assumption in order to allow these new achievements? In this chapter, with Arthur's work as an example, we describe a series of steps necessary for individual change.

## STEPS TOWARD INDIVIDUAL CHANGE

In delineating the steps of individual change, we lay out a picture of an unfolding process. However, unlike the phases of an organizational change process, which explain *what looks different* as a result of change leadership (as described in Chapter Eight), the steps toward individual change describe *what to do* to enact the changes you desire. Throughout this chapter, we offer a series of exercises designed to help individuals overturn their immunities to change.[1] These steps can be taken in the order listed. We have found that individuals often want to repeat steps, refining their responses as they learn more about their immunities. In practice, people generally revise their original maps several times, clarifying their commitments and assumptions, and adding new and related assumptions. With each iteration, their maps grow more powerful as descriptions of their internal systems.

---

### Steps Toward Individual Change

- Design the metrics to identify costs and progress.
- Observe the Big Assumption in action.
- Stay alert to challenge to the Big Assumption.
- Write the biography of the Big Assumption.
- Design a test of your Big Assumption.
- Run the test.
- Develop new designs and new tests

---

We strongly suggest that before beginning this work you schedule several regular meetings with your immunities work partner, one to two weeks apart, in order to coordinate your movement through the exercises. Report back to each other on what you are learning, ask each other questions, and provide feedback to each other. We believe that by deliberately creating a schedule and structure, and by enlisting a partner to hold you accountable, you can accelerate the work ahead in overturning your immunities.

---

*By deliberately creating a schedule and structure, and by enlisting a partner to hold you accountable, you can accelerate the work ahead in overturning your immunities.*

---

### Design the Metrics to Identify Costs and Progress

Designing the metrics allows you to clarify the goals of your immunities work and imagine what successfully overturning immunities would look like. We believe a vision of success will increase your motivation to engage in this work; we define victory in two ways:

1. Dramatic reduction of the costs created for you and your school or district by your immune system

2. Significant strides forward (a quantum leap) in realizing your first-column commitment

The purpose of having you identify more specifically what progress would look like is *not* to begin immediately trying to accomplish it. The immune system concept is not as straightforward a matter as people often think. Rather, the purpose of this step is to create a context to make changes that will eventually become more visible. It allows you to elaborate on your individual *To Be* picture already stated conceptually as your first-column commitment.

We begin with an assessment of the current costs to you if your immune system continues unchallenged. Arthur, for example, was immediately aware of how his own hesitation was affecting his district. Progress was stalled. "If we continue to wait," he acknowledged, "we'll continue to do about as well as we've been doing. Test scores will still be pretty good. I would probably still be seen as a good superintendent. Most kids will learn. Many won't, though. As a whole, we won't get better. The teachers won't get the supervision and the professional development that they need to improve. Principals won't have any ideas about how to do their own jobs more effectively and how to be instructional leaders, which most have never been before. We didn't expect it of them, didn't train them for it. And the biggest cost is that every day that we wait, there are kids who aren't learning as much as they could be, kids who aren't realizing their potential. All kids in this district could be learning more, doing better. I really believe that in my heart of hearts. And so then I also have to admit that by not taking action, I'm holding them back, holding us all back. That's hard for me to accept, but I know that unless I do better, instruction won't get better."

By this point, Arthur had identified his costs as follows:

- Progress on the district improvement plan stalls.
- Results (student learning and test scores) stay the same—we don't get better.
- Teaching and teachers don't improve significantly.
- Principals and leadership don't improve significantly.
- I hold kids back from realizing their potential.

Now it's your turn. How would you assess the costs of continuing to produce the behaviors and nonbehaviors you've listed in column 2? It is unlikely that you will be able to quantify these costs, but it may be possible to describe a number of performance categories—to your own effectiveness and your organization's change process. The more specific you are about how the costs show up, the better. Try to come up with at least as many identified costs as Arthur did.

By successfully completing this first step, you (and anyone else with whom you might be sharing your personal immunity work) should be reminded just why it is so important to do something to disrupt our immune systems. If you are working through this guidebook in a leadership practice community, the collective pooling of your individual costs should impress on you that (1) the school or district is paying *a very large price* for these personal immune systems and (2) the prospect of disrupting these systems raises the possibility of *very large gains* for the school or system. We now turn your focus to these potential gains.

When asked to think about what "success" would look like, Arthur had a harder time answering. He could imagine powerful teaching and learning. He could imagine principals effectively supervising teachers in their schools. At first, however, it was hard for him to imagine what he would be doing differently. Finally, Arthur decided, "At first, I think I just have to start taking action. I have to acknowledge that it is going to be very difficult to start doing learning walks in classrooms. Teachers will be defensive. The union will certainly have something to say. But my first step is to act anyway, to push forward, to take the risks and accept the flak they give me. What makes it a first step is that I imagine that I'll feel all kinds of doubts, and I probably won't do anything so drastic that the pressure and complaining will get too great. I'll probably be very aware of how others— the principals, my board members, central office folks—are perceiving me. It'll be hard not to dwell on that.

"And then, what would the finish line look like? Well, I guess that would be that I could take action, even if I'm not always sure what needs to be done exactly, and I would not get all twisted up and worried about it. I would just know that something has to be done, and we'll take our best shot. If that's not quite right, then we'll make the necessary adjustments. But I guess, ideally, I'll feel better about it—pretty good about it, even—because we'll be watching carefully to see what happens, and what is getting better, and learning how to do this change work, and taking the risks that just go along with this sort of thing. That really would be the finish line."

Arthur's vision of success is shown in Exhibit 9.1.

| Exhibit 9.1 | | |
|---|---|---|
| **Arthur's Vision of Success** | | |
| Column 1 Commitment → | First Noticeable Step Forward → | The Finish Line → |
| I am committed to moving my district from "good" to "great" by creating a common vision of rigorous instruction. | I take action, pushing us forward. I take the risks and accept the flak that others give me, but I don't do anything so drastic that the pressure and complaining is too great. I still feel doubts and remain very aware of how others perceive me. I realize that I can't dwell on that but have difficulty not worrying about it. | I take action, even when I'm not sure what needs to be done exactly. I know when something has to be done, that we need to take our best shot, and then we constantly monitor our progress and make adjustments. These habits mean I don't worry about taking risks as much. |

Now, in thinking about your own immunities, what would constitute a quantum leap forward in your realizing more of your own first-column commitment? What would constitute just an appreciable first step forward? Answer these questions in Exercise 9.1. Doing so should begin to enable you to create a continuum of progress that can eventually be fleshed out further as a metric of "column 1" progress.

### Exercise 9.1: Your Vision of Success

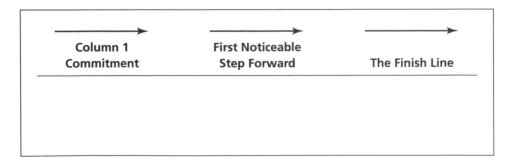

| Column 1 Commitment → | First Noticeable Step Forward → | The Finish Line → |
|---|---|---|
| | | |

Partner's Reflections:

_____

_____

_____

_____

_____

## Observe the Big Assumption in Action

What happens, or fails to happen, as a result of holding your Big Assumption as true? By observing the Big Assumption in action, you can keep track of those situations where you can see (or have recently seen) your Big Assumption at work— for example, influencing how you look at things, feel about things, take action (or don't take action), make choices, spend your energies. For some of you, these situations will be so abundant that it will make sense for you just to keep track of several salient instances. For others, there may only be a few such situations that occur. Some of you may wish to confine your observing to the work sphere; others may want to make note of wherever the Big Assumption is seen to be influential. Some of you may wish to confine your observing to your present circumstances. Others may want to think back over the last few months.

Arthur recorded his thoughts about where he could see his Big Assumption in action during a two-week period. After listing several instances, he highlighted the following particular interaction as key: "My Big Assumption is, *I assume that if others recognize that I am not exactly clear about every step of the way, or see that I am at all uncertain, they will lose confidence in me as a leader, see me as an ineffective leader, and I will be a failure.*" As he said, "the biggest thing I noticed is how hard I work to prevent anyone from recognizing that I don't know something. For example, I was talking to a woman in charge of special education here who was just recently promoted to her current position. She was asking me lots of questions about her role, what she can expect, what I want from those people who have positions similar to hers. I gave her pretty clear answers whenever I could. But I was also aware that some of my answers were pretty vague and that I was speaking quickly. And my voice was getting more and more hurried and clipped. I was sort of signaling to her that I had someplace I had to be, and that I was late, and that her questions were slowing me down. (I did have someplace to be, but I wasn't late yet.) She was trying to write it all down and ask questions, but I could tell that I didn't give her everything she wanted.

"I couldn't tell her that I didn't know all the answers! I mean, what would she have thought? I couldn't even suggest that we talk more at another time. I just started feeling nervous, like I was such a fraud, and I didn't want her to see that. But later, when I started to write down what happened, I realized that I never asked her what *she* thought. We promoted her because obviously we think she's pretty good, and yet I didn't use her expertise at all. I didn't ask her anything! I was only concentrating on what was happening to me and how I needed to look as a leader. I just saw that she was asking me to give her answers, to tell her what to do, and the crazy thing is, she really could have helped *me* figure out what she should be doing. I just didn't see that at the time. It really makes me see how much all this immunities stuff is getting in my way."

Your Big Assumption may bring you to different conclusions. For the next two weeks, do not attempt to change your behavior or your Big Assumption. Just attend to its influence in your life and use Exercise 9.2 to keep track.

 ## Exercise 9.2: Your Big Assumption in Action

What do you notice does or does not happen as a result of holding your Big Assumption as true? For each observation, write down two things: (1) details concerning what happened and (2) how it is an instance of your Big Assumption at work.

| Observation | What Happened? | How Does This Show Your Big Assumption at Work? |
|---|---|---|
|  |  |  |
|  |  |  |
|  |  |  |
|  |  |  |
|  |  |  |
|  |  |  |

Partner's Reflections:

_____

_____

_____

_____

_____

_____

## Stay Alert to Challenges to the Big Assumption

Once you've found examples of your Big Assumption in action and shared them with your partner, next you need to be on the lookout for any experiences that might lead you to question the truthfulness or widespread applicability of your Big Assumption. Because of the "certainty" quality of our Big Assumptions (our difficulty in considering how things could be anything *other* than this), our Big Assumptions actually inform what we see and how we see the world. They lead us to attend systematically to certain data and to systematically avoid or ignore other data.

> *[Our Big Assumptions] lead us to attend systematically to certain data and to systematically avoid or ignore other data.*

In completing this step, Arthur began to take particular notice of one of the principals in his district. "This woman," Arthur explained, "is really one of our better principals. And she has the respect of pretty much every other principal in our district. She's been in the system for about 30 years and knows a great deal. I send newer principals to her all the time for mentoring and support. And she's good at that. She's good at helping the new ones.

"What I've been really noticing lately is how she often talks about what she's still learning, what she thinks she needs to get better at, what the new ones are teaching her. And she says it in a way, in a tone, that suggests that it's perfectly natural that she doesn't know everything. She is completely confident about the importance of learning in her job, always getting better. I respect that so much and I think the other principals do too. So, it occurs to me that not knowing isn't necessarily a bad thing, and saying that you don't know, and getting ideas from others—all of that, if done right—can actually help you to *gain* other people's respect. It can help them be okay with what they don't know and are still learning. At least that's how it seems to work for *her*. That runs completely counter to my Big Assumption! I think you have to do it right—with the kind of confidence and conviction that she has. And she really is good at her job—nobody would question that—and so nobody sees her not knowing something as an indication that she's weak.

"I don't know how to do what she does. I don't know how to be okay with not knowing. I can't imagine being that calm and fine about it and having others be fine with me too. But watching her suggests to me that I could learn this."

### Exercise 9.3: Challenges to the Big Assumption

For the next two weeks, take the opportunity to search for data and experiences—whether in your professional life or personal life—that would counter or cast doubt on the absolute quality of your Big Assumption. You might want to take notes about specific situations, interactions, and feelings. Do not intentionally change anything you do (or think) relative to your Big Assumption. Just take account of any spontaneously occurring experiences that might cast doubt on its absolute quality.

_____
_____
_____
_____
_____

Partner's Reflections:

_____
_____
_____
_____
_____

## Write the Biography of Your Big Assumption

The next step is to explore the history of your Big Assumption: When was it born? How long has it been around? What were some of its critical turning points?

Arthur began to write about the competitive relationship he had with his brother when they were growing up. Arthur had often suspected that he wouldn't be able to stay ahead of his precocious younger brother, who seemed to succeed at everything so easily. By contrast, Arthur remembered feeling dull and untalented and was convinced that it was only a matter of time before others found this out and saw him in that way too. As the boys got older and their lives took very different directions, these feelings slowly faded. But every once in a while his brother's accomplishments could still generate in Arthur familiar pangs of rivalry and anxiety. He began to wonder whether something of this powerful dynamic was creeping into his present-day situations of uncertainty

---

### Exercise 9.4: The Biography of the Big Assumption

As you reflect on the origins and development of your Big Assumption, take notes about specific situations, feelings, important events, and "moments" in the life of your Big Assumption. Again, this step is not about you intentionally changing anything you do relative to your Big Assumption, but about noticing and paying attention.

_____

_____

_____

_____

_____


Partner's Reflections:

_____

_____

_____

_____

_____

---

## Design a Test of Your Big Assumption

In this step, we want you to design a safe, modest test of your Big Assumption in *preparation* for actually running the first "formal" test of your Big Assumption. In designing this first simple experiment, your "test" will lead you (in the next step) to do something different from what you ordinarily would do when routinely holding your Big Assumption as true.

---

*A good test is safe, modest, actionable, and allows you to collect data related to your Big Assumption.*

---

A good test has three criteria:

- It is both safe and modest. You might ask yourself, "What can I risk doing, or resist doing, on a small scale that might seem inadvisable if I held my Big Assumption as true, in order to learn what the results would actually be?"
- A good test will allow you to *collect data* related to your Big Assumption (including data that would qualify your assumption or call it into doubt).
- Finally, a good test will be actionable in the near term. The test is relatively easy to carry out. Ideally, it doesn't require you to go out of your way; rather, it is an opportunity to do something different in your normal day. Also, you should be able to carry it out within a week or two (before you next meet with your partner, if you have enlisted one).

An example of a first test might be to do something small and novel in a work meeting, where you can get feedback from a trusted colleague—someone also present at the meeting—on "what happened." Your partner can be especially helpful as a sounding board as you design this experiment. You may also want feedback from your partner on whether your test meets the three criteria for a good test.

Arthur's test was for district leaders to begin the process of learning walks. In his district, learning walks are used as a way for all instructional specialists, coordinators, supervisors, and principals to gain the same understanding of criteria for good instruction in action and for progress toward the vision. Arthur planned to begin with a small team of leaders in one school, but move eventually to all schools randomly, as a way of "taking the temperature" of how instruction is going—and changing.

Arthur admitted that this test might not initially seem very safe or modest, but he also knew that he couldn't keep stalling. In fact, stalling any longer was starting to feel like the very thing that would cause others to question his effectiveness. "Basically," Arthur concluded, "I'm testing my assumptions if I act. And I'm testing them if I don't. So I might as well act! But I know that I have to do some careful planning so that we are more likely to succeed." Arthur therefore decided to:

- Begin with a small team of instructional leaders.
- Make clear to the teachers who would be observed that the purpose of the learning walk was for the professional development of the supervisors, that it was not a formal evaluation of instruction.
- Share the learning walk protocol with all the teachers, asking them to identify a few criteria that they believed would be evident in their teaching and that the instructional leaders should look for.

Having completed this preparation for the test, Arthur confirmed that it felt modest, safe, and actionable. Now it's time for you to design your own test (see Exercise 9.5).

---

### Exercise 9.5: Test Your Assumption

Describe your own modest, safe, actionable test.

_____

_____

What data do you plan to collect?

_____

_____

How modest and safe is it? How actionable?

_____

_____

Discuss your test with your partner. Describe any modifications made to the design of your test.

_____

_____

_____

_____

Partner's Reflections:

_____

_____

_____

_____

## Run the Test

In this step, we ask you to actually run this first test and take some notes about what happens. Share the results with your partner and consider the implications for your Big Assumption as well as the best design for your *next* test. The overall purpose of the test is to see what happens when you alter your usual conduct and then reflect on the results in light of your Big Assumption.

> *The overall purpose of the test is to see what happens when you alter your usual conduct and then reflect on the results in light of your Big Assumption.*

Arthur's small team of instructional leaders completed their first learning walk, which he described as "a wonderful experience." Most teachers welcomed the team into their classrooms and, if they were nervous, they were also quick to agree that "We are professionals. This is what we need to be doing." Arthur marveled, "So what actually happened was the complete opposite of what I expected, what I feared. We thought there would be mutiny, but there wasn't!" He and his team immediately began to plan visits to other schools in the district.

As Arthur reflected on what this experience taught him about his Big Assumption, he came to several insights. "I see that I had a pretty stubborn assumption that was related to my Big Assumption, even though I didn't identify it until now. I assumed that if conflict can occur, it will. I focus on that potential and my fears get all blown up until I'm sure things won't go well. I think that if we had started these learning walks without doing all the work we did—laying the groundwork—we could have had some nasty conflict. But now I can see that there are ways to prepare that can really minimize the chance that people will revolt. We can take things one step at time. There are ways to prevent things from getting nasty.

"I was also surprised to realize that other people on this instructional team are more knowledgeable about and committed to the district mission and vision than I had thought. It's not just my mission, my vision. It really is theirs too. So, they aren't just looking for whether or not I know what to do; they're pretty intent on us all thinking about and working on what to do. I see now that I had assumed I had all the responsibility for whether this worked or failed. I see that others are right there with me. And they want to be. It's their district too. So now I have added a new assumption to my map: *If I am not exactly clear about every step of the way, I don't have to be alone in that. I can look to others to help us come up with a plan that might work. And we'll all take responsibility for it.*

"I think it will still be hard for me to keep pushing these changes forward when I fear that I'm not always sure we're going in exactly the right way. I'll still worry about what it would be like to fail, or to have others see that I'm unsure. But now it's really clear to me that I was trying to hold back a process that was already in motion. I had already generated some momentum by bringing others into the planning. It was actually taking energy to hold them back. I could be using that same energy to move forward. And holding back might get me the same result I feared in the first place—people would begin to see me as incompetent. Once you start creating urgency and expectations, you had better find ways for people to act! And you'd better act yourself! So, now I think I have an assumption that runs counter to my Big Assumption: *I now assume that if others are ready to act, and I hold them back, they will lose confidence in me as a leader.* How could I not have seen that before?"

## Exercise 9.6: Running the Test

Your assignment now is to describe what happened during your test and make a list of any data that you collected. With that description and list in mind, what do the results of this test tell you about your Big Assumption?

_____

_____

_____

_____

Partner's Reflections:

_____

_____

_____

_____

### Develop New Designs and New Tests

If your first test bore fruit, you now have some good initial feedback about your Big Assumption. We suggest that you think about this new information as hypotheses about different ways you could be operating in your leadership work. In subsequent tests, you have the opportunity to explore these hypotheses further, experiment with new behaviors, and generate additional hypotheses. Ultimately, new hypotheses that yield successful results can become new assumptions that guide your leadership of your school or district.

Often, the first test generates many new ideas for additional tests. Arthur, for example, noticed that as much as he had learned from his first test, it did not give him the opportunity to actually share his uncertainties with others to see how people reacted. He began to consider ideas for how he might share his uncertainty about next steps with his colleagues in one of their leadership meetings, explicitly proposing that the team take on the planning collectively.

What do you want to explore further about your Big Assumption as a result of running your first test? What feedback does your partner give you regarding this question? What would be a good test design for this further exploration? Is your test safe enough? Is it likely to yield the information you need? Is it actionable? Does your partner agree? Use the form provided in Exercise 9.7 to guide your explorations.

## Exercise 9.7: Your Big Assumption, Revisited

Describe your next modest, safe, actionable test.

_____

_____

List the data you plan to collect.

_____

_____

Clarify how modest and safe your test is. How actionable is it?

_____

_____

Discuss your test with your partner. Describe any modifications made to the design of your test.

_____

_____

Partner's Reflections:

_____

_____

Describe what happened during your test. List any data that you collected.

_____

_____

What do the results of this test tell you about your Big Assumption?

_____

_____

## CONSIDERING STEPS FOR THE MOST POWERFUL LEARNING

As you complete each of the steps we have described in the previous sections, you also might want to consider whether and how your responses are leading to the most robust learning possible. To that end, we make three recommendations—maintain your focus on your Big Assumption, think of the steps as iterative, and solicit input throughout—each of which should deepen and enhance your experiences of these steps.

---

*Maintain your focus on your Big Assumption, think of the steps as iterative, and solicit input throughout.*

---

*Maintain your focus on your Big Assumption.* As you plan for and complete each step, try to maintain your focus on how what you are doing, thinking, and learning affects your Big Assumption. As powerful as it is to experience yourself behaving in new ways or getting results you never thought possible, these changes are likely to become permanent, fully realized new ways of leading only when you directly challenge, test, and amend the fundamental ideas and beliefs (the Big Assumptions) that generated your old ways of being.

*Think of all the steps as iterative* (not just last ones). Individuals often find that after completing a step, they now have several new ideas for how they could have done it in a way that would lead to greater personal learning. Perhaps writing the Biography of the Big Assumption leads to new ideas about what a "Quantum Leap" toward success in overturning the Big Assumption would look like. Perhaps a test leads you to see that your first-column commitment was not worded accurately. Think of the steps as pieces of a complex puzzle—the sequence you use in the beginning may alter completely during the solving process. As we work further through the puzzles of our own immune systems, we are better able to look back at what we have done in terms of how well it will lead us to our personal solution.

*Solicit input from others* about the impact you are having before, during, and after engaging in this work. Individuals often perceive their own effectiveness quite differently than do others. It is very hard to know if we are working on the right issues, changing in valuable ways, and learning all we could be without honest feedback from others. We are not recommending that you publicize each and every step you take, nor are we suggesting that any and all feedback is helpful. But we do want to emphasize that there might be particularly opportune moments or issues when feedback that is solicited and specific can help us see ourselves in important new ways.

## PHASES IN OVERTURNING YOUR IMMUNITIES

Arthur engaged in some hard and ultimately very rewarding work to overturn his immunities. We have described this work chronologically, illustrating how he undertook it step by step. Our hope is that these steps will provide you with a clearer sense of how to begin and proceed yourself. But we also think it is useful to describe the changes in Arthur, and in others we have worked with, in terms of the phases of change, describing what these changes look like in a way that is general enough to apply no matter what the individual's particular immunities issues are.

This sequence shown in Exhibit 9.2 depicts the basic rhythm of overturning our immunities to change, in which we go from being *unconsciously immune,* to *consciously immune,* to *consciously released,* and finally to *unconsciously released.* We all start the process not knowing what we don't know: we are unconscious of our own immunity to change (we are *unconsciously immune*). We alter our unconsciousness and become conscious of our immunity when we develop a powerful "diagnostic" immunity map. In this map we get a snapshot picture of what our immunity to change looks like, what basic Big Assumptions give rise to our

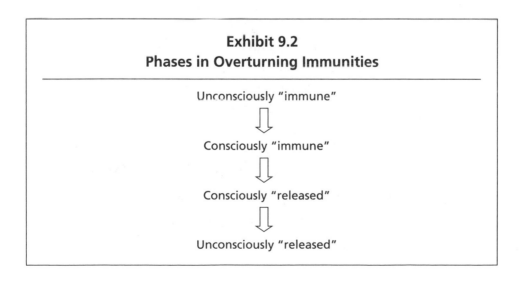

**Exhibit 9.2**
**Phases in Overturning Immunities**

Unconsciously "immune"

⇩

Consciously "immune"

⇩

Consciously "released"

⇩

Unconsciously "released"

immunities. Although seeing this immunity does not alter the immunity itself, it alters our relationship to our immunity and we move from being unconsciously immune to being consciously immune. We are now able to make an informed decision about whether we want to engage in the work required to be less subject to our assumptions, to be less captive of them and released from their power over us. For example, after Arthur became consciously aware of his own immunities, identified his assumption about how others would view him if he didn't always know what steps to take, and realized the continuing costs of leaving his immunity unchallenged, he made the choice to work at overturning his immune system. Perhaps you have, too.

The move toward being consciously released from the power of the immune system comes from recognition that the Big Assumption may not be true, or at least not so pervasively true. For Arthur, this was the moment when he identified a leader who was able to admit to not knowing without losing credibility or others' confidence. Often people learn new behaviors and new ways of thinking about what they do and how they react. When you can act on your newly discovered knowledge to interrupt the Big Assumption (and the old behavior and self-talk patterns associated with it) from operating in those situations where it is not valid, you are demonstrating the new capacity to be consciously released. A changed relationship to the Big Assumption inevitably disturbs the system that keeps producing the obstructive behaviors and ultimately enables you to deliver more of what you've committed to. Being consciously released means that you can begin to break free of the familiar pattern, but you have to work at it, think about it.

This takes mindful practice. The journey is not bump-free or necessarily a straight one. It is normal to fall back into old patterns associated with the Big Assumption. Still, knowing that you're falling back and knowing how you can get yourself unstuck are all signs of development. By running his test, reflecting on it, and creating new assumptions, Arthur had become consciously released.

---

*When you no longer need to stop, think, and plan*
*in order to interrupt your Big Assumption,*
*you have developed the capacity to be*
*unconsciously released from it.*

---

But we can see that he has not yet become fully released; he has yet to move into the final phase of the work. When you no longer need to stop, think, and plan in order to interrupt your Big Assumption, you have developed the capacity to be unconsciously released from it. At this point, you automatically act and think in ways that run counter to your previously held Big Assumption in those situations where it is not valid. New beliefs and understandings, informed and developed mindfully throughout the process, have taken the place of the Big Assumption. It usually takes (and will likely take Arthur) a good deal of practice, self-monitoring, and reflection before individuals reach this final phase of the work. To conclude this chapter, we share with you another story, in compressed form, of how one district leader was able to reach this final phase.

## BECOMING FULLY RELEASED FROM IMMUNITIES TO CHANGE

Katherine had recently taken a job as the "change coach" for a large midwestern district. Eager to prove that she deserved the job and could be successful at it, her first inclination was to work extremely hard and keep a very close eye on all of the various projects she was running. She soon realized that others were quite happy for her to take on all of these responsibilities and she was pleased to feel like she was making a real contribution. But as time passed, Katherine realized that as long as she was doing so much work and watching over it all so carefully, others did not have to change, learn, or grow. Those who reported to her did what she asked them to do, but their work was often of lower quality than what Katherine expected. She found herself frustrated by their reluctance to work as hard as she did.

Therefore, when she created her immunities map, she based it on a first-column commitment to:

*Help others take on and successfully fulfill greater responsibility for our work.*

Admitting that she had been focusing largely on how others were working against this goal, Katherine realized that she was also getting in the way of it herself. She then identified the following behaviors in her second-column commitment:

- *I take on responsibilities too quickly by volunteering for them or taking over when they're not getting done well.*
- *I don't ask others to volunteer for work (or wait for them to accept responsibility once we've collectively identified a need).*
- *I don't delegate as much as I should.*

But when she thought about changing these behaviors, Katherine was aware of several fears that arose within her:

- *I'm afraid that if others are doing more of the work, I'll have less control over it.*
- *I'm afraid that if I'm not in control, then others either will not do the work or they won't do it well enough.*
- *I'm afraid that if any of these projects fail, I'll be held responsible.*
- *I'm afraid that if others are doing more of the work, then my contributions won't be seen or valued as much.*

These fears were pretty powerful ones, and they led her to realize she was holding a third-column commitment that enabled her to continue doing too much of the work.

> *I am committed to always being in control and having things go my way, according to my plans.*

Underlying her immune system were a couple of Big Assumptions about what would happen if she couldn't enact her third-column commitment.

- *I assume that if I let go of my control, things won't be done the way I want them done.*
- *I assume that if I let others do the work, it won't be done or won't be done correctly and I'll lose my credibility with others.*

Katherine admitted that her tendencies to take control and do the work had costs: she limited others' opportunities for learning and growth and she limited her own opportunities to gain input from others' ideas. She also was not able to do all of the work she was taking on in an efficient, high-quality way and was not able to focus enough on high-priority projects. But, particularly as she began observing her Big Assumption in action, she found that in most instances, it seemed to be quite accurate. Several meetings and projects in which she was not directly involved were not executed to her standards.

Katherine began to wonder what kinds of things she could do that might lead to a different result. She began to run tests and to reflect on the results. She decided to meet with those she directly supervised to discuss their own expectations for the work, to compare these expectations with those Katherine held for them, and to come to common agreement. These meetings represented new behaviors for her, an attempt to not have her "fingers in everything" but to give people "the tools and resources they need to make their own decisions and then to support them in what they do." Once others had a clearer sense of her expectations and a voice in determining the standards for their work, Katherine found that the quality of their work began to improve. As she continued running and learning from her tests, she was able to delegate more and worry less about others' performance.

Relating these new behaviors and results back to her Big Assumption, she realized that her Big Assumption no longer held true as long as she held effective preliminary conversations with her team to create shared expectations. But she felt it was important to add that she had already developed a relationship with those on her team and that her Big Assumption might still hold true for those with whom she did not yet have a relationship.

Katherine was also aware that these new behaviors and insights were not yet completely natural for her; she was still only consciously released. "I feel I still need to build on where I am. It's not a done deal. I have to intentionally remind myself to do these things. I would like it to be my natural behavior. If it didn't keep working, I would probably revert to my former behavior. It feels like a rubber band that would just snap. I still have anxiety when I go to meetings because I worry about the quality of them."

As she continued to practice new behaviors and the assumptions she brought to her work, Katherine reported feeling more relaxed at work and therefore better able to put others at ease. When others came to her with questions or wanting help, she was often giving that work back to them. She saw these projects now "as an opportunity for them to grow. I'll be there if they need me." There were times when the work wasn't always getting done well, and she could see how these disappointments implicated her own leadership. "I'm figuring out what they can and can't do. I'm also seeing what I need to help them learn in order to take the work on that they currently can't do."

Slowly, Katherine also began to appreciate that when other people completed the work differently than what she had expected, they weren't necessarily doing it wrong. She explained, "Before I would have seen 'different' only as 'not good enough.' Now, I can see 'different' as just different. I can add a new assumption to my framework: *Work that is done differently from what I expected is not necessarily not good enough. It is often just that—different.*"

And she listed other revised assumptions she now held:

- *When I am more controlling, I become ineffective in everything.*
- *You can't create a community if you have your hands on everything.*

As she grew more released from her immunities, Katherine found that she was getting better and better at thinking through what others needed to know in order to take on and complete projects successfully. She felt that the quality of relationships in her organization was improving and became very deliberate and thoughtful about how she communicated with others about their and her expectations and how to maintain trust. An organizational climate that had been characterized primarily by compliance was slowly changing into one of true engagement. By working through her assumptions and immunities, Katherine changed herself and her organization.

### Endnote

1. These steps are drawn from and elaborate on Robert Kegan and Lisa Lahey, *How the Way We Talk Can Change the Way We Work* (San Francisco: Jossey-Bass, 2001).

# Reflections

In Chapters Eight and Nine, we looked at key milestones in two different but complementary journeys. One is an organizational journey toward improving all students' learning that requires new approaches to working more strategically. The other is a personal journey that helps you as a leader recognize your contributions to the aims of your school or district and overcome any beliefs and behaviors that get in the way of essential progress in this first journey. Both chapters provided exercises that you can use along the way to gain greater awareness of how your assumptions guide your behavior. Taking the time to contemplate the questions we've raised and completing the exercises can help you make greater progress toward your personal goals. In doing so, you should find yourself moving through four phases of growth, from being ensnared by your immunities to being fully released from them.

When leaders undertake both the organizational and personal journeys concurrently, the chances of success for all students are greatly enhanced. Each involves risks, as well as potential rewards. Each requires leaders to think and act in substantially new ways. Perhaps, then, the first and most important challenge for all of us in education is to rethink our understanding of what it means to be an educational leader in the twenty-first century.

In Chapter Ten, the final chapter of the book, we weave the outward and inward focus together and provide still further guidance for change leaders preparing for the future.

# Conclusion: Bringing the Outward and Inward Focus Together

Throughout *Change Leadership*, our main premise has been that leaders must understand and bring together the challenges of both organizational and individual change to successfully lead improvement processes in schools and districts. We have structured the core chapters in a way that suggests these two fronts are two learning tracks, with an outer and inner focus, parallel to each other. In this chapter, we clarify how the inner and outer changes are two sides of the single coin of school improvement. We discuss the implications of this integrated curriculum for a new kind of improvement leadership in our schools and districts.

You should by now have a personalized, fully elaborated four-column immunity map that shows a private, personal learning challenge (an inner focus) tightly bound up with some public, shared expectation or understanding of what is called for from you to succeed with the work (an outer focus). For example, you may genuinely want to be a better delegator and create a more collaborative form of leadership in your school or central office. Everything you've read about school improvement suggests that the kinds of changes you and other superintendents or principals want to bring about cannot be achieved through the heroic efforts of a single leader alone, no matter how inspired, tireless, or charismatic, and you strongly believe this yourself. Yet your four-column immunity map has also surfaced another kind of belief, one that is more personal and that you do *not* find in the things you read about school reform. This belief is headlined in your Big Assumption. Let's say you uncovered a belief that you may not experience your work as fulfilling enough if your job becomes more about enabling others rather than yourself being in the center of the action, the hero of the work. However genuinely committed you are to being a better delegator, this belief—if it remains unsurfaced and unengaged—is going to undermine your ability to improve. We trust that you now see how your own four-column immunity map expresses *one* vital intersection of the outward and inward foci.

*Every one of the* outward *changes we have been suggesting needs to occur, for successful whole system improvement has a similarly challenging inward dimension for any individual or team that is having a hard time bringing that change about.*

In fact, we believe that every one of the outward changes we have been suggesting needs to occur, for successful whole system improvement has a similarly challenging inward dimension for any individual or team that is having a hard time bringing that change about. Chapters Two, Four, Six, and Eight have each worked on sharpening an aspect of our outward attention—clarifying a focus on instruction, generating increasingly effective collective energy for change, thinking more systemically, acting more strategically. Although each of these ideas has an inner demand (discussed in Chapters Three, Five, Seven, and Nine), some of these outward agendas tend to generate personal learning challenges more frequently than others. We look at a small number of these now to illustrate the critical interconnection between individual and organizational change.

- We must hold high expectations for all our kids.
- Building and central office level administrators need to get more involved in instruction.
- If we have many improvement priorities we actually have none; so we must choose a priority and stay relentlessly focused on it.

- We must foster a widespread feeling of urgency for change.

- We need a new kind of leader, one whose expertise is more invested in helping a group create the shared knowledge necessary for sustained improvement than in being the certain source of the answers and solutions.

- We need a new kind of administrative team, one that can take on two jobs at once—running the school or district we have, and leading an improvement process to create the school or district we must become.

We have found that these ideas strike the many hundreds of school leaders with whom we have worked as eminently sensible. These school leaders are all smart and conscientious people. So if these ideas make so much sense to bright, caring people, why aren't they put into practice? We've presented a wealth of answers to that question. One overarching response would be to say that the ideas involve a host of adaptive challenges. If we actually knew how to put the ideas into practice we would have, long ago.

Recalling Heifetz's distinction,[1] technical challenges are those for which the knowledge to solve the problem already exists (as is evident in tried-and-true procedures, effective tools, and established means of training). The challenge may be complicated, and meeting it may be very consequential, so technical challenges are not trivial. (Removing someone's inflamed appendix and landing a jet airplane are technical challenges.) Adaptive challenges are those for which the necessary knowledge or capacity to solve the problem must be created during the work of solving it. The individuals or organizations undertaking these efforts must themselves change—they must adapt. They must not just use the available knowledge (as in meeting technical challenges) but create new knowledge. When we describe the job of remaking our schools so that no child is left behind as similar to trying to rebuild an airplane while flying it, we are talking about an adaptive challenge. There need be no embarrassment in acknowledging that we don't yet know exactly how to do this.

But we do need to be at work learning how. A big part of learning how, in our view, is by coming to see that although any list of organizational "should-do's" may shine brightly in its clarity and reasonableness, we are only looking at half of the picture, at the illuminated side of "the moon of school improvement." We need to also shine a light on the usually unseen side—the inner dimensions, demands, and assumptions. What is it like to travel through that same sensible list, via paths that cross into the dark side of the moon?

## HOLD HIGH EXPECTATIONS FOR ALL OUR STUDENTS

Two of us recently worked with the leadership team—the superintendent, an assistant superintendent of curriculum and instruction, several school principals, assistant principals, a few lead teachers—of a hard-working district in Southern California (SoCal District). Its student body was over 80 percent Latino; the professional staff was over 80 percent white. The majority of students came from families needing financial assistance. We asked this group to try constructing a four-column immunity map, only we asked them to do it together as a leadership team and to construct a single, collective picture, which is depicted in Exhibit 10.1. (A form for doing this with your group is included in Appendix A.)

As shown in Exhibit 10.1, the group had no trouble identifying a shared first-column commitment that felt important to all of them. Although it was a less comfortable experience filling out the second column (designed to answer the question, "What do we do or not do that works against this?"), they arrived fairly quickly at their answer, indicating, "We do not hold high expectations for ELL or SpEd students." As is usually the case, they found the third column (the hidden, competing commitment) to be the most difficult and ultimately their biggest learning opportunity. At first, they identified concerns about the new kinds of work they would have to take on if they were really to hold higher expectations for the ELL

---

### Exhibit 10.1
### SoCal District's Four-Column Immunity Map, in Process

| 1 | 2 | 3 | 4 |
|---|---|---|---|
| Collective Commitment | Doing/Not Doing | Collective Hidden/Competing Commitment | Collective Big Assumption |
| We are committed to accelerating the rate of academic achievement of ELL and SpEd students.* | We do not hold high expectations for ELL or SpEd students. | We may also be committed to not having to revise what we teach and how we teach our ELL and SpEd students. | |

*ELL = English Language Learners; SpEd = Special Education

---

and SpEd students—the need to create new kinds of curricula and supports for the students. Although the third-column commitment they settled on technically created a picture of an "immunity to change," the exercise did not seem to produce much energy for the group or usher in some productive, new vantage point. It was late in the day and we decided to adjourn until the following morning.

The next morning, an agitated assistant superintendent came to find us at breakfast. "I've been thinking about that exercise since we ended yesterday. I thought about it last night, and I dreamt about it. We are not telling each other the truth about what should really be in that third column!" We asked him what he thought was going on.

"The hardest thing for us to really talk about, in this mostly white group," said the assistant superintendent, who was himself Latino, "is race. We all get along, and we are all people of goodwill, and we are all committed to helping these kids—but that may be exactly why we can't say what really belongs in that third column."

We asked him what he thought should go in the third column.

"If we were honest, it should say something like, 'We are also deeply committed to preserving a *povrecito* culture.' But I'm not sure I can say that to this group." He explained that a "povrecito culture" ("povrecitos," or "poor little ones," is a term of endearment) was full of protective concern and sympathy. "It's a stance that says, 'These kids are already facing so many obstacles, bearing so many burdens, how can we possibly increase their suffering by holding them to rigorous academic expectations?'"

We kept talking, and eventually he concluded that he owed it to the group to suggest a revision of their third column. "If I can't raise this, who can?" He decided that, however difficult it would be for him, "it would be impossible for one of the white administrators to raise it. They would fear they'd end up looking racist, or offending us, or damaging the spirit of goodwill on our team."

When he brought this to his team that morning, "it was like putting a match to dry tinder," he said. It was as controversial as he'd expected it might be, and although not every member of the group was immediately willing to accept the new picture, they all agreed they had taken an important next step in their joint leadership. The four-column immunity map they came up with is shown in Exhibit 10.2.

The idea that reduced expectations could come not only from a place of discrimination or disregard but from love and concern brought a previously unilluminated side of the group's operations into plain view. The team now sees

**Exhibit 10.2**
**SoCal District's Four-Column Immunity Map, Revised**

| 1 | 2 | 3 | 4 |
|---|---|---|---|
| **Commitment** | **Doing/Not Doing** | **Collective Hidden/Competing Commitment** | **Collective Big Assumption** |
| *We are committed to accelerating the rate of academic achievement of ELL and SpEd students.* | *We do not hold high expectations for ELL or SpEd students.* | *We may also be committed to not having to revise what we teach and how we teach our ELL and SpEd students.*<br><br>*We are committed to preserving a "povrecito" culture.* | *We assume if we really did push our students they would not succeed; they would be crushed; we would feel defeated.* |

more deeply and accurately how they work against their own genuine commitment to their ELL and SpEd students. They now can address the core question of whether pushing these students will always lead to failure and suffering, as they had unknowingly assumed. And they create the possibility for revising this assumption, for coming to see that they *can* succeed with their ELL and SpEd students—and that their ELL and SpEd students can succeed. (Chapter Nine describes the process through which the team could go about overturning their immunity to change.)

## INVOLVE BUILDING AND CENTRAL OFFICE ADMINISTRATORS IN INSTRUCTION

Over the last several years, school improvement advocates from many quarters have called for a dramatic reconstruction of the role of school principal—from capable building administrator to chief instructional officer. The old role is that of a plant manager who is buried in the office with concerns about bells, busses, and building maintenance, succeeding or failing on a set of criteria having little to do with the unique core enterprise of the school—teaching for learning. The new role is that of principal educator, the school's leader in directing the attention of all the school's participants to its central function and enhancing their capacity to engage it. This is the image of a principal who is out of the office and observing in classrooms, convening ongoing conversations about what constitutes good teaching and how we can have more of it.

However compelling this new picture may be, and despite ever mounting evidence of the critical value for student achievement of principals playing this new role,[2] it is enormously difficult for principals to make the shift from building manager to chief instructional officer. A recent study from *Education Week* Research Center, polling nearly 10,000 principals, found that only 27 percent spend part of each day guiding the development or evaluation of curriculum and instruction, whereas 86 percent say they spend part of every day managing the school facilities and maintaining security within their buildings. Only 53 percent can report spending at least some time every day facilitating student learning; and 55 percent of 56,000 teachers polled strongly disagree or somewhat disagree that their principals talk with them frequently about their instructional practices.[3]

## Conditions, Culture, or Adaptive Challenge?

When Gerry House came on as the superintendent of the Memphis schools, she was appalled at the number of broken windows in many of the school buildings. She could have said to the principals, "You are not doing as good a job as plant managers as I'd like. The state of these windows sends a terrible message to everyone inside and outside your school. Get on this." Having the principals clean up the "broken windows problem" could have been seen as a strong stand for improving the culture of the Memphis public school system. It might have sent the message that "We care about your kids and we care about the places where we educate them. A lot is broken around here, and we are going to start fixing it, right away."

But if Dr. House also wanted to support the new cultural value of principals shifting their priorities from plant managers to instructional leaders, it would have been a costly way to send this good message. So instead, she hired an outside contractor to coordinate window repair throughout the district. She got the first message across ("We care about your kids . . .") and she did it in a way that also said to the principals, "We care about you, too. Your time is better spent as leaders of our central enterprise. I'm not here to add one more management function; I'm here to get you out of one business so you can take up the other."

Of course, there are many places to look for the sources of difficulty in making this shift—conditions and culture play major roles—but we believe a main reason for the difficulty is that the challenge is not only a technical one, but an adaptive one. Even when the conditions have been altered and the culture is saying that our number one priority is learning, it turns out that many, many principals have a hard time making the shift, a sure sign that there is a major part of the moon in shadow. We can almost hear Einstein whispering at times like these, "Get a better grasp of the problem before moving to the solution."[4]

David, a candid principal in one of the districts with which we have had a multiyear relationship, gave us a rich example of his version of why this shift is difficult and what can lie on the other side of the moon. His superintendent has demonstrated that he means it when he says he wants to support every principal to become an instructional leader in his or her school. And David will be the first to admit that—as much as he himself is committed to making this shift—it isn't going very well.

As Exhibit 10.3 shows, David's first-column commitment is perfectly aligned with his superintendent's goal. When David took the "fearless inventory" required to complete column 2, he said: "Two things especially stand out. I have long believed in an open-door policy for my faculty, but the result is that I am continuously drawn in to providing advice and counsel on a whole host of personal issues, personnel disputes, life counseling. You can't believe all the kinds of things people want to come in and talk to me about! And the other thing is that I did a weeklong tracking of where my time goes, and I realized that monitoring the lunch periods every day, which I have always done, ends up taking a huge amount of time when you add it all up."

Considering what he would least like or would be most concerned about were he to do the opposite of what is in column 2 catapulted David from the illuminated to the unilluminated side of his terrain. David realized that even though his open-door policy and lunchroom monitoring distract him from his primary goal, he really *likes* what he gets from the roles he plays as a warm, friendly, open, and available presence for both the faculty and the students. As he contemplated really making these things "peripheral" (in the language of his column 1 commitment), his demeanor became visibly subdued. It was clear that much of the joy he derives from his work is associated with what it means to him that faculty trust him enough to bring their problems to him, that they experience him as someone who is giving them something they clearly value, that the students feel emotionally attached to him and he to them.

## Exhibit 10.3
## David's Four-Column Immunity Map

| 1 | 2 | 3 | 4 |
|---|---|---|---|
| Commitment | Doing/Not Doing | Hidden/Competing Commitment | |
| To make "Instructional Leadership" the predominant center of my work as principal and limit the time and energy that I spend on peripherals. | Open-door policy with faculty leads to many conversations not directly related to instruction; daily monitoring of cafeteria is huge expenditure of my time. | I am committed to being the Good Shepard, Father Confessor, amateur therapist, Friendly Mayor of the school, loved by and accessible to faculty and students alike. I am committed to not having conflictual relationships with faculty. | |

"And I'll tell you something more," David said, with a groan and a wry smile, warming to the opportunity to have an even better look at the dark side of the moon, "I can see it's not just that I would hate for the students or the teachers to start feeling I was inaccessible. I start to think what I would be doing more of with the teachers if I wasn't being their benevolent Father Confessor. I'd be riding their rear ends about changes in their instruction, and I know there'd be a lot of strife and struggle in all of that. Things are on a wonderfully even keel around here these days, and I can see a big part of me wouldn't be thrilled about giving that up."

At the very least, David now sees that for him the work of truly becoming an instructional leader carries a broad set of learning challenges, including some internal ones. He is now aware that his success will depend, in no small measure, on his willingness and ability to grapple with his various assumptions about what he would have to give up and what he'd need to start doing. With his current beliefs and assumptions, David can't yet imagine how satisfying and meaningful he might find it to be an effective instructional leader. But over time, he may find that the strife and agitation created in the short run actually lead him—and others—to deeper satisfaction in the longer run.

By doing this inner work, David will have a much better chance of delivering on the outer work of being an effective instructional leader.

## CHOOSE A PRIORITY AND STAY RELENTLESSLY FOCUSED ON IT

It's true that if we have many improvement priorities, we actually have none. We must choose a priority and stay relentlessly focused on it. So why don't we? We regularly see districts in which everyone is "dancing as fast as we can," heroically expending energies on an impressive variety of initiatives, any one of which, on its own terms, may make all the sense in the world. No one can fault the effort, or the sincerity, of all this hard work. But in most cases no significant progress is made. This is a costly situation on multiple fronts: the leadership team fails to get traction toward its present goals, and it becomes increasingly difficult to enlist people's energies in future efforts. "Look how hard we tried last time, and we still didn't get anywhere," goes the logic. "So what is the use?"

Trying harder may be an effective strategy for technical challenges. But for adaptive challenges we need a way to step off the dance floor and move to the balcony, away from the crowd and its frenetic pace, to have a look at the bigger system that is preventing us from doing the "relentless focusing" we know we need to do.

We don't yet know *all* the possible hidden commitments that can make starting an abundance of initiatives seem like a brilliant strategy. Leaders must discover their own answer to the question, "What would be most troubling to you about achieving a laserlike focus?" especially if they have been frustrated in their honest efforts to focus. Their answers will reveal the personal and specific learning agenda they will need to adopt if they are to succeed in focusing. Choosing a priority and staying relentlessly focused requires that we first see the personal contributions that prevent us from such focus. Having done so, we can then explore and test our specific assumptions in order to free ourselves and our organizations from the grip of overinitiating.

Superintendents have sheepishly told us (with an expression that suggests they've never before thought it, let alone said it to others), "To be honest, I really don't know which of these initiatives is going to work. It's like the idea of a 'differentiated portfolio,' where you spread out your risk. Or like fishing with many lines. I'm afraid to remove a line from the place where a big fish might swim. I'm afraid of putting all our capital into one stock." The irony is that this very strategy to avoid failure might, in the end, assure it.

Exhibit 10.4 shows three superintendents' contributions to a four-column immunity map illustrating their quite different hidden reasons for *not* prioritizing.

Why is it so important that these superintendents illuminate their hidden side? Let's take a minute to consider the implications of their not doing so. In a nutshell, each will continue to believe in the importance of focus and act inconsistently with that belief. Principals, in turn, will pick this up. They will hear how important focus is and get the message that focus isn't really a priority; everything has to get done. So although they may know and believe that their success in the eyes of the superintendent is to focus, focus, focus, they also believe that focus needs to happen in addition to all the other things already on their plates!

A principal's immunity map might then look something like that shown in Exhibit 10.5.

---

*The forms of our personal learning challenges
are not infinitely different. There is more
than one crater on the dark side of the moon,
but not an endless number.*

---

We see how the principal can repeat the same pattern as the superintendent and we can then imagine how teachers in that building will also not focus and prioritize. Without explicit messages from the principal about what they can let go of, or what they can loosen up on, teachers will understandably feel pressure to do it all too. Self-protection, in its varied forms, will cascade throughout the system. Focus will be absent. People will hedge their bets and do as much as they believe they need to do to avoid the dire outcomes their hidden worries and guiding assumptions predict. Yet if we all could see these worries and unearth our assumptions about the risks of focus, we would be in a position to radically alter our behaviors. For the first

# Exhibit 10.4
## Four-Column Map Reflecting Three Superintendents

| 1 | 2 | 3 | 4 |
|---|---|---|---|
| Commitment | Doing/Not Doing | Hidden/Competing Commitment | Big Assumption |
| I am committed to leading an improvement process that is relentlessly focused on a single priority. | I/We take on too many things at once, have a host of "balls in the air," keep adding without subtracting. | **Superintendent A:** I am committed to not making a mistake, to not betting on the wrong horse. | **Superintendent A:** I assume I will make the wrong choice. I assume an initial choice is not modifiable. I assume if I am shown to be mistaken I will lose all credibility. |
| | | **Superintendent B:** I am committed to not being bored, to feeling stimulated and energized by having a lot going on at once. | **Superintendent B:** I assume that if I relentlessly focus on just one or two initiatives I will feel unsatisfied, restless, and turn into the kind of person I disdain. |
| | | **Superintendent C:** I am committed to being responsive to the enthusiasms, needs, or expectations of internal and external constituencies. | **Superintendent C:** I assume if I do not respond positively to internal enthusiasm and external pressure I will lose my bases of support. |

time, we might be able to see, for example, the inevitable costs for students of our not focusing.

The *forms* of our personal learning challenges are not infinitely different. There is more than one crater on the dark side of the moon, but not an endless number. Being aware of the basic moon landscapes can help us see what we might be hiding

## Exhibit 10.5
## Principal's Four-Column Immunity Map

| 1 | 2 | 3 | 4 |
|---|---|---|---|
| **Commitment** | **Doing/Not Doing** | **Hidden/Competing Commitment** | **Big Assumption** |
| *I am committed to focusing on a single priority.* | *I take on too many things at once, have a host of "balls in the air," keep adding without subtracting.* | *I am committed to not making mistakes by letting the wrong things go.*<br>*I am committed to not putting myself out on a limb by not delivering the status quo.* | *I assume that if I let the wrong things go, it will be my fault, my job, and my livelihood here. I won't have the superintendent's backing.* |

from ourselves. We can use that knowledge as a resource when, try as we might to imagine what we are protecting, we don't see anything noteworthy.

Over the last five years, we have seen hundreds of four-column immunity maps, bravely created by school leaders and teams of leaders working at educational improvement. The learning challenges that arise often share common features and forms and can therefore be grouped. As illustrated in Table 10.1, each of these challenges can involve new definitions or new tolerance for risk.

For example, Leader A assumes that "if I do not respond positively to internal enthusiasms and external pressure I will lose my bases of support." This personal learning challenge exemplifies the challenge of redefining and renegotiating relationships with others.

Leader B illustrates immunities in the top right quadrant. He is in the grip of a Big Assumption implicating his own self-definition, what he must expect of himself in order to feel fulfilled: "I assume that if I relentlessly focus on just one or two initiatives, I will feel unsatisfied, restless, and turn into the kind of person I disdain." To move past his immunity, he needs to change his self-expectations.

Leader C's immune systems were anchored in risk. She was committed to focusing on a single priority, and her Big Assumption led her to act inconsistently with this commitment because she could not risk making the wrong choice. As she

**Table 10.1   Adaptive Challenges of Change Leadership**

| | Personal Learning Required for the Adaptive Challenges of Change Leadership | |
|---|---|---|
| | New Work with Others | New Work with Self |
| **New Definitions** | *Renegotiating Relationships*<br>(Leader A, for example)<br><br>• Disappointing expectations (for example, by not having all the answers)<br>• Giving the work back to the people<br>• Collaborating/mutual accountability/ being receptive to upward feedback<br>• Shifting loyalties to new reference group<br>• Pushing back or dissenting in new ways or with new people | *Changed Self-Expectations*<br>(Leader B, for example)<br><br>• Possible to be a good and effective leader without having the answers, being able to solve it all oneself, knowing at the outset how to get from "here to there"<br>• New definitions of old roles (for example, from superintendent as public relations manager to getting people to look at hard realities; from principal as building manager to chief instructional improvement officer; from assistant superintendent of instruction to systemwide change leader)<br>• New sources of satisfaction in the work; new definitions of what it is to be personally "successful"<br>• That in addition to being masterful at X in my work, I am also an "emergent learner" at Y |
| **New Risk Tolerance** | *Allowable Uncertainties for One's Group*<br>(Leader C, for example)<br><br>• Willingness to lead a process that puts others at risk of failing (students or staff)<br>• Willingness to lead a process that puts others at risk of feeling overwhelmed<br>• Willingness to set out toward a destination without a clear map of how we get from here to there | *New Self-Allowances*<br>(Leader C, for example)<br><br>• Risk learning what I "don't want to know" or find out (for example, that I can't do it; that I or others don't really believe all kids can learn to high levels)<br>• Risk not being in control of the process, or risk losing control<br>• Risk others' disapproval, loss of regard, respect, loyalty, affection<br>• Risk becoming more aligned with, or identified with, subgroups I had passionately regarded as "other"/not me<br>• Risk making a mistake, missing something valuable |

put it, "I assume I will make the wrong choice. I assume an initial choice is not modifiable. I assume if I am shown to be mistaken I will lose all credibility." Her challenges fall in the bottom half of the figure: she needs to work on risk tolerance with others and with herself.

When you review Table 10.1, consider whether you see the hidden commitment you have identified in one (or more) of these quadrants. If nothing seems to fit, does trying on the various learning challenges described prompt any "ah ha" for you?

## FOSTER A WIDESPREAD FEELING OF URGENCY FOR CHANGE

John Kotter, in *Leading Change*, says "allowing too much complacency" is the "number one error" change leaders make: "By far the biggest mistake people make when trying to change organizations is to plunge ahead without establishing a high enough sense of urgency."[5] But in explaining why, Kotter never gets to the leader's own inner work. As an organizational theorist, Kotter's focus tends to be on the complications of the organizational dynamics. He talks about leaders "overestimat[ing] how much they can force big changes," or "underestimat[ing] how hard it is to drive people out of their comfort zones."[6] We believe Kotter is absolutely right about this part of the picture, but it is not the whole picture.

Consider again the predicament of Corning's Superintendent Don Trombley (discussed in Chapter Eight) or another CLG learning partner, Superintendent Mike Ward of West Clermont. For several years both men led districts considered by their communities to be highly successful. Their communities felt this way, in part, because many good things were going on in their districts, and, in part, because these superintendents were doing a very good job selling their constituencies the proposition that the districts were succeeding!

Anyone who has been a superintendent knows that a large part of the job includes managing public perceptions. There is nothing evil or corrupt about this. As Boston Superintendent Tom Payzant has told us, "The kind of leader you want, someone who is closely tied to the improvement of instruction, is exactly what we need. But if a school or district head is not also a good politician, it doesn't matter how much they know about instruction. They might not last ninety days."[7] Yet the public relations dimension of leadership can make it exceedingly difficult to generate sufficient urgency.

Sometimes a superintendent brand-new to a district can more easily stand up and talk about the urgent need for things to improve because doing so casts no shadow on the quality of his or her own prior work. It is also easier to sound the alarm in a troubled urban district. (It is also, unfortunately, commonplace for a new superintendent to be brought into an urban district as a hero to clean up a mess perceived to be the product of his or her predecessor, who, two years earlier, was likely ridden in on the same white horse.) Although the prior superintendent may not have talked about it, district and community members are not surprised to hear that their urban district needs significant improvements. But most superintendents are not new superintendents. Most, like Ward and Trombley, understandably feel enormous reluctance to publicize their own district's problems and launch an initiative calling for systemic improvement.

"After standing up, year after year, telling the good people of my community what a great job we are doing," began Mike Ward, "how do I now say, 'We are not doing a good enough job by your children. We must and we can do better'?" Most leaders do not make this clear declaration. At best, they may borrow the frame suggested by Jim Collins' book, *Good to Great*;[8] as Arthur did, saying, "We have been a very good district, but now we must go from good to great." Such a frame appropriately does not find fault; however, it can also fail to generate sufficient urgency. "If we are doing well," people say to themselves or out loud, "and it is going to take an extraordinary amount of work or expense to do a little better, is it really worth it?" "Are we letting the Perfect be the enemy of the Good?" "If it ain't broke, why fix it?"

But Ward and Trombley each made a clear declaration. They found a different kind of frame that also had the merit of making the present situation no one's fault. They talked repeatedly about the way the world has changed. Trombley made dramatically visible how many kids were not reading at grade level and what this meant for their futures in a changing economy. Ward practically made a mantra out of "'Good enough' is no longer good enough for our kids." "We are ordinary people," he would say about everyone working to reinvent the district, "who are going to do extraordinary things."

What Ward and Trombley did took courage and required a willingness to disappoint expectations, to renegotiate relationships (see Table 10.1). In other words, what they did often requires overturning one's own immunities to change. It is not just the leader who wants to say, "everything is fine"; followers want to hear this from the leader as well. Superintendents feel this expectation from the community, from parents, and from their boards. Many superintendents believe they must continue to tell the public that things are fine or getting steadily better in order to maintain the political and financial support both they and their district need for survival. And although we have seen public support for superintendents and their districts actually *increase* when superintendents are more open and honest about the challenges that educators face, there does exist a powerful, persistent cross-cultural preference for the leader or teacher as reliable authority.

Some theorists attribute this preference to the psychology of early childhood relationships. Others seem to want to take us back further to our cross-species inheritances. (Heifetz, for example, evokes the image of the silverback gorilla whose signals the others continuously track.[9]) Whatever the source of the gravity, it is a difficult orbit to escape. It takes enormous courage to defy social expectations.

Social psychologist Stanley Milgram, best known for the infamous "simulated shock" experiment, once designed a study to test the difficulty of defying social expectations under even the thinnest of conditions. He directed his doctoral students to stand on crowded New York City subways and simply ask sitting passengers for their seats. The students found the task enormously stressful despite the fact they were talking (or just considering talking) to complete strangers they would never see again. They wanted to claim they were ill (and thus not really in violation of the norm or expectation). People did usually surrender their seats, no questions asked. Many students reported, after claiming the seats, they actually did begin to feel ill, as if reflexively they needed to create an internal condition that would preserve the norm![10] If it is very hard for us to disappoint others, even when they are complete strangers, imagine how much more difficult it will be for us to disappoint those with whom we have worked for many years. To overturn a third-column commitment not to disappoint others' expectations, we need to expose and then modify Big Assumptions about the dire consequences of doing so (as we saw in Chapter Nine).

## ENCOURAGE A NEW KIND OF LEADER

We need leaders whose expertise is more invested in helping a group create the shared knowledge necessary for sustained improvement than in being the certain source of the answers and solutions. We find the difficulty in "leading from behind" is that not only is it hard to disappoint others' expectations of the good leader as the authority but also that it is much harder than we realize to convince ourselves of a new definition of leadership. We can quickly agree that our schools and districts are not going to improve because of the heroic service of a charismatic leader working alone—that we must build teams (and build them not simply so there will be an army to follow our orders and pursue the plans we have masterfully created ourselves). Rather, we need a kind of team that can work together at "rebuilding the airplane while flying it," a team that can share the work of deciding, assessing, and revising on a path to improvement that is almost never a straight line. As with a first-column commitment, we say we believe this because we actually do; it makes sense to us. But we may not realize how powerful and how deep-seated are our countering beliefs (third-column commitments).

This is no different from the challenges teachers often face in successfully enacting a learner-centered pedagogy. In recent doctoral dissertations on teacher education, Jennifer Berger[11] and Jim Hammerman[12] each found that teachers (preservice teachers in a teacher preparation program, and veteran teachers in an intensive summer institute, respectively) espoused genuine, well-considered intentions to teach in the more learner-centered ways they learned in their programs. Yet they don't. In some cases, they do not even know that they don't. Within the teacher education field there is a growing body of research that documents how the powerful, and usually unrecognized, beliefs teachers hold (about the teacher-as-authority) counter the beliefs they may enthusiastically embrace in their programs. The teachers they become are much more a function of the former than the latter.[13]

As leaders, we are no different. A few years ago we conducted an "immunity to change" workshop with a group of urban high school principals, each of whom received Annenberg grants for school improvement. Along with approximately fifty principals and assistant principals, there were a dozen or so representatives of the foundation. One of the participants generously volunteered to "go public" with her developing "immunity map," speaking elegantly and passionately about her aspirations for her high school in her first-column commitment: "I am deeply committed to leading an improvement process that will make our school a place of learning and self-respect for all of our kids." She said it with such conviction that the group broke out into applause.

When it came time to hear examples from the second column ("doing and not doing"), she was less boisterous but no less dedicated to honestly speaking her truth: "I am not pushing for results. I am not eliminating dysfunctional processes that slow down the change process. I am not really actively 'campaigning' for the changes."

When we got to the third column, which reveals why all the obstructive behavior makes sense, she rose up from her chair. With a voice that resonated with the same deep conviction, and now with a half-smile, she proclaimed, "I am also committed to dragging my heels and keeping things from moving forward a single inch!" This was met with gasps and laughter, as people thought about their foundation benefactors in the room. "I am damn well committed to not being the one who takes my people out into deep water and then lets them drown because we don't know how to get to the other side!"

Although the group was hearing a declaration of stuckness from one of its most inspiring colleagues, they broke out into spontaneous applause and laughter in appreciation for the sheer authenticity of her words. Later one of her colleagues mentioned that he thought it was a particularly brave thing for her to admit, given all who were in the room. "Yeah," another said, "I thought one of those Annenberg people was going to come over and take back your check!" "Well, the thing I was most struck by," said a third, "was that the Annenberg people were among those clapping the loudest."

The Annenberg people knew that leading change was not simple. They in fact were feeling increasingly frustrated by the lack of results they were seeing overall. But they recognized that the principal was bravely getting down to her role in the matter, maybe for the first time. They did not doubt for a moment that she meant every word of her first-column commitment, but they must have intuited that human beings comprise multiple truths, and they appreciated that she was now expressing not just one, but two of hers.

Her bigger story, which came out in her fourth column, was that she had been coleading this improvement process with a mentor who had come out of retirement to be a "bench coach" with her. A trusted advisor, who had lately decided he needed to return to retirement, his departure left the principal feeling very uncertain that she had what it takes to bring off the changes they were working on. She wrote, "I assume I cannot do this alone. I assume I cannot lead without being clearer how we get from here to there."

These Big Assumptions led to other assumptions. "I assume *someone* must know exactly how this is going to go." "I assume no self-respecting leader will set off toward a worthy destination without knowing how to get there." "I assume if I cannot do it alone, the only course of action is inaction."

Her "change immunity" reminds us of Arthur's, whose journey we have chronicled throughout this book. His earlier reluctance, like hers, to take real steps forward may teach us that no matter how easily we acknowledge the limits of a traditional command-and-control conception of "the good leader," most of us, should we take on the hard work of school leadership, will discover its vestiges still have a hold on us. This conception may be better suited to leaders facing technical challenges rather than adaptive ones, for which it is never possible, even for the very best leader, to know everything needed before setting out. Like Columbus' exploration, the voyage inevitably requires us to revise our own mental models (from a flat world to a global one) in the process. This is the learning work of remaking our own self-expectations and self-conceptions (see Table 10.1).

We know such learning happens. Mike Ward, the Ohio superintendent, is just one example. Ward understood that meeting adaptive challenges in reinventing West Clermont's district required both outer and inner work and that he needed to model being a learner on both fronts himself. In August, two of the authors attended the district's annual start-of-the-new-year, multiday leadership retreat. At its conclusion, when people had a chance to say how they'd experienced the meeting, several people made comments like these: "I've been to many of these annual meetings, and many with Mike. To be honest, they have always had a similar quality for me: you come in, already feeling a little overwhelmed thinking about everything that has to be done to be ready for the start of school, and then the superintendent comes in and adds to your stress by giving you this year's set of additional marching orders. You walk out feeling even more overwhelmed. The meeting this year was a unique experience and I am walking out with a kind of energy I have never had before!"

What made such a difference? Along with the fact that the "marching orders" this year were collaboratively created during the retreat, instead of being "handed down," a turning point in the meeting came early on, when Ward decided to share his own four-column immunity map. He began by telling the team that he was committed to further developing a more collaborative, distributed form of leadership. This came as no surprise, and they expected him next to tick off the initiatives they knew about that demonstrated that commitment. Instead, he took them through his second column, naming the variety of ways he was actually holding back or undermining his own commitment. This got their attention. He then told them he realized he still had very strong commitments to retaining various kinds of unilateral control that actually contradicted his first commitment and that he probably held a Big Assumption like, "I assume if I really do lead in this new way *you all will screw things up!*"

On paper, this might look like a bizarre way for him to be communicating with his team. At the least it could seem rude, and at worst it could seem to severely damage bonds of trust between the leader and his group. But in reality, it had a very different effect. First, all members of the group, some time before, had gone though the exercise of creating a four-column immunity map themselves, both individually and collectively, so they understood the kind of "bigger picture" it creates. Second, they deeply appreciated that Mike was making clear how their new work together was a learning challenge for him, too. And, finally, they experienced his first-column commitment as much more "real" when it was paired with his understandable worry that they might "screw things up." They laughed when he said it—and they began to take more seriously the way he was counting on them.

---

*When we get rid of our idea of a leader as the source of all answers and solutions—the sure-and-certain, command-and-control, top-down authority—we don't replace it with a picture of a lost, inept bumbler, serene in his cluelessness.*

---

When we get rid of our idea of a leader as the source of all answers and solutions—the sure-and-certain, command-and-control, top-down authority—we don't replace it with a picture of a lost, inept bumbler, serene in his cluelessness. Instead, we picture a highly capable "leader-*learner*," someone with the courage and capability to learn, and help those around him learn, as they collectively create a path toward a previously unattained destination. Becoming this kind of leader is a long process for any of us, a kind of work that inevitably calls on us to be learning more about ourselves at the same time we are learning more about our organizations.

## DEVELOP A NEW KIND OF ADMINISTRATIVE TEAM

One of our strongest invitations throughout *Change Leadership* is for school or district leaders to develop a new kind of leadership practice when they are taking up the work of complex, long-term, whole system improvement. We believe that the team needs to learn to take on two jobs at once—running the school or district they have, and leading an improvement process to create the school or district they must become. Our concept of leadership practice communities (LPCs) is meant to signal that educational improvement or transformation cannot be seen as merely one more big initiative taken up by the administrative team as it currently operates.

In our work with district leadership teams, we have noticed that a critical moment in the early evolution toward an LPC occurs when the team decides that:

1. It needs one meeting time for doing its accustomed administrative work and another for leading the improvement process (often prompting the idea that perhaps we do not have all the right people for the second kind of regular meeting as we are currently constituted).

2. It needs to change its name (suddenly, it no longer seems quite right for a team to keep calling itself something like the "Administrative Council," even though this name has never felt problematic before).

These seem like spontaneous realizations of what it means that "we are taking up a second, different kind of leadership work" (not more important, but different). To do this work well, teams must give themselves the opportunity to develop over time a new form of practice appropriate to this different kind of work.

However leadership groups do it, this new form of practice must steadfastly maintain a dual focus to internal learning and external leadership (that is, it is not just a professional development space; it needs to *get things done*). This new practice must also enable the group to reconstitute itself from a collection of conscientious, semiautonomous operatives (each of whom is tending to his or her particular leadership responsibility in the system) into a genuinely collaborative team that is collectively assuming responsibility for a whole system improvement effort.

### Leadership Practice Communities: A Personal Learning Challenge

Better understanding of what a leadership practice community looks like is quite different from actually being able to bring one about. The LPC is one of our favorite ideas; in a sense, this whole book is meant to be a resource for it. The LPC is therefore one of those "should do's" about external organizational change that burns even more brightly—is perhaps more "illuminated"—than any other. And we are beginning to learn that bringing an LPC about may require us to turn inward as well, to meet individual and collective personal learning challenges. So again, there is a less illuminated side of the picture. We do need to bring into view a fuller picture of the moon in order for an LPC to be more than a first-column commitment (a good intention), but a reality.

The ideas that "we need to be more of a team," "we are all responsible for the improvement of each part of the system," and "we are at work on this together" frequently live alongside other, hidden, competing commitments that will undermine the LPC if they are not exposed. Despite all the goodwill, friendly banter, and even effective cooperation a leadership group may exhibit, very often its members are isolated from each other in many important ways. Even when a typical district leadership team begins to meet with the explicit intention to form an LPC, its members are not typically leaders *in the life of this meeting.*

We do not mean they behave unprofessionally or irresponsibly. They are more often followers, typically of the superintendent, or they are going to be leaders of their particular "franchises" ("X High School," "Y Middle School," "the SpEd program"), carefully weighing the proceedings relative to the needs, opportunities, or vulnerabilities of "their" turf. The meeting then is more like an assembly of subgroup leaders: the superintendent may need to coordinate these subgroup leaders; a member may need to advocate before the group or the superintendent on behalf of the needs of his or her subgroup. The district-as-it-is-now can be run this way. The district-we-want-to-become cannot be realized this way.

To be a leader in the life of the leadership meeting (rather than only a good steward of one's separate leadership realm), each member has to develop a second identity and loyalty. We refer to this as the ability to "wear two hats." (One high school principal said he felt relieved to hear us phrase the need this way, because it had seemed to him, when he was first trying to do it, that it felt more like having to "grow two heads.") Imagine that you are a principal of one of the high schools. There may well be times in the meeting when you are listening and reacting predominantly as the leader of that subgroup. But you also have to have the ability, as needed, to put on your other hat, not as the X High School leader, but as a coleader of the district improvement team. In that role you might, for example,

- Consider positions that will not be popular with your constituents back in the high school.

- Take positions concerning something going on in a colleague's school that normally you would consider none of your business.

- Be willing to respond to colleagues whose queries about something happening (or not happening) in your high school you might normally feel was not really their business.

- Make demands on colleagues to take actions or modify behaviors that have no direct relationship to your high school.

- Take an active interest in, or critique the work of, a colleague in an elementary or middle school.

## Definitions for Change

Developing a second identity and loyalty can stir up exactly the kinds of learning challenges suggested in the upper quadrants of Table 10.1—the need to alter your own self-definition and the definition of your relationships with others. One means of shifting from how we typically relate (as a group of separately enfranchised advocates who are followers of one or two leaders on the district team) to more of a team of coleaders is through making Team Agreements[14] and taking the time to discuss with each other what each agreement actually means. In these discussions, people have the opportunity to clarify their particular "dark side" learning challenge as it relates to being in the group as coleaders.

For example, we worked with a district leadership group in the Northeast that wanted to function more as a team. They thought this would improve their internal work and that it would improve their stature with their external clientele (they knew they had a reputation for not being a very cohesive group). Asked to identify a single agreement among themselves that could go the furthest toward improving matters, they came up with something they called the Fight-in-Private, One-Voice-in-Public Agreement. They valued their ability to take diverse positions and their superintendent's appreciation for the benefits of "spirited debate." They didn't want to lose that. However, they did see that their tendency to carry these fights outside the door, to make these differences known, even after the group had come to a decision, was not conducive to strengthening their own team.

Often groups can come to an agreement like this one fairly quickly. When they do, we invite group members to test their understanding of what the agreement actually means. This test is key because often when people make an agreement quickly, it will later turn out they each were comfortable with their own version of the agreement. We ask people to think of situations that are likely to arise, and how they might handle them, in keeping with the agreement as they understand it. This gives us a chance to ask, "If Ellen actually did X, would she be keeping the agreement as you understand it?"

A school principal on this team, Bernie, had a situation he wanted to test: "If my own leadership group at the high school and I have come up with our position on an issue I know is going to come up at a district meeting, and I come here and argue our view, and this group decides the other way, ordinarily I'd go back to my people and say, 'I gave it every shot, but you won't believe what those bozos decided this week.' [Hooting and hollering.] Okay, I realize this would not be in perfect keeping with our new agreement and I wouldn't say that. But let's be real. How can I really be 'One Voice in Public' with my own crew when they already know my position? I won't call you bozos, but I'm probably going to tell them I gave it every shot. I'm probably going to tell them what I said. Would I still be keeping our agreement?"

This led to spontaneous combustion, with six people talking at once and then a very lively conversation. Some people thought Bernie made complete sense and that he would not be violating the agreement. Some people thought it would violate the agreement, and that once a district team decision had been made he had to stand with the district team. His own team would know, of course, that he had taken a different position, but they also had to experience Bernie as a member of both groups. They would ultimately respect the district team more for witnessing that Bernie kept a kind of integrity with this team, too. "They need to see your other hat, Bernie!"

Other people said Bernie's issue made them think that they all should anticipate such situations. Maybe it was not a good idea in the first place to come to such a fixed position with their own teams before heading into the district team. That made them into advocates for their franchise and didn't really allow them to play a full role on the district team.

Other people wanted to go off on a related but more general issue: Is it okay to tell others outside the group just what your own position was concerning a contentious issue around which the team had rendered a public decision? "Isn't that just freedom of speech?" The group was divided about this, too. Some thought they ought to have this right and others said, "How can we possibly be keeping an agreement about 'One Voice in Public' if we are making known our dissenting view all the time? Isn't that basically what we are doing now?" We asked the following question of those who thought they should be able to make their views known to others outside the team: "Since you all seem to agree it would definitely be a violation to tell someone outside the group what someone else's position was [to which they all agreed], why would you think it would be any different to share a different part of the team's private conversation—namely, what you said?"

The group eventually saw what all these conversations are really about: they suggest the beginnings of a new organism taking shape, of a living entity with its own integrity. They suggest the possibility of collaboratively preserved boundaries that begin to make the leadership team a true space of its own, with conversation that all members own (rather than a place for "free speech" and advocating for one's subgroup). They suggest how weak or porous the current boundaries between this group and the rest of the system have been; how much more rooted in and loyal to their subgroups, to their separate franchises, many of the leaders have been. They suggest a group beginning to do the work that may be required to reconstitute itself as the kind of team needed to be an effective, cohesive agent of systemwide change.

In effect, they are beginning to do this work by manifesting their competing commitments. They may genuinely want to be a more collaborative team, but in getting into the details of how they would have to conduct themselves differently, outside the group as well as inside it, they are coming to terms with the power of their commitments to preserving a certain autonomy within the system and preserving a loyalty and identification with their subunits. If the team is to cohere as a group of coleaders who collectively plan for and tend to the adaptive work of reinventing the school or district, they will need to surface their individual immunities and work to overcome them.

## SHINING A BROADER LIGHT ON CHANGE

In *Change Leadership*, we have urged a number of significant visible changes in the ways schools and their leaders should operate. In this chapter, we have taken an unusual tour through the most prominent of these changes, focusing on the systematic nature of the less visible, personal learning challenges that may be a part of enacting any of them. Our goal has been to sketch this usually "dark side of the moon" much more broadly than the one example you created for yourself in the earlier chapters. We took this tour to bring to life the proposition with which we began: every one of the outward changes that we suggest needs to occur for successful whole system improvement has some kind of similarly challenging inward dimension; any individual or team that is having difficulty bringing that change about must address the inward dimension.

Enlightening this side of the picture suggests a number of implications for leaders. In keeping with our recommendation that leaders form an improvement team that functions as an LPC, in Appendix A we provide a groupwide exercise for diagnosing immunity to change.[15] This process can be most useful in helping a team see its "dark side of the moon" if they get stuck making progress on any critical "outer" change. This, as you'll see, is a close relative to the individual immunity tool we've asked you to engage throughout the book. Conducting this group activity can create a space for a new kind of group conversation. Issues the group has not before been able to discuss (either because it was not aware of them, or did not know how to bring them up constructively) should now be more discussable (such as the example earlier in this chapter about the inappropriately protective environment of the "povrecito culture"). The emphasis on clarifying a contradiction not between different factions within the group, but contradictory beliefs held by the group as a whole, allows the group to look deeply at itself without individual defensiveness.

The process allows the group to rather swiftly bring out hidden commitments and assumptions that have often never been voiced because it would feel too risky for any one person to be associated with them—such as the idea (which commonly arises in the third column) that we may also be committed "to *not* changing," or "to preserving the status quo," or the idea (which commonly arises in some form in the fourth column) that "we assume all children *cannot* learn at high levels," or that "it is actually impossible to leave no child behind." If we hold these beliefs (along with our more hopeful ones) but must pretend we do not, they continue to exercise their influence, and we have no chance, individually or collectively, to explore them. If we cannot talk about them in a safe and private space because they are "unacceptable," then all our learning, problem solving, and school improving will deal with only a piece of what needs to be engaged.[16]

A group should not be afraid or ashamed to discover it is bedeviled by a contradiction. Every adaptive challenge is beset with contradictions that require us to adapt. A contradiction is not a fatal flaw. Potentially, it is a rich resource for the group's learning and greater effectiveness. It gives the group an additional change strategy, besides merely trying to "fix" the limitations it identifies in its second column.

The groupwide immunities exercise invites leaders to dig deeper into the causes of the limitations before trying to "solve" them, especially to consider why these "limitations" may actually make complete sense. If every system is brilliantly designed to produce exactly the results that it does, then perhaps before we try to improve our system, we need to better grasp its current "brilliant design." If this "brilliance" escapes us, so likely will any lasting solution.

---

*If every system is brilliantly designed to produce exactly the results that it does, then perhaps before we try to improve our system, we need to better grasp its current "brilliant design." If this "brilliance" escapes us, so likely will any lasting solution.*

---

Finally, the group needs the opportunity to consider "where do we go from here?" with the new ideas and insights the exercise has generated. In some cases, this can lead to the group equivalent of "testing the Big Assumption," as described in Chapter Nine. What kinds of "experiments" can the group (or its delegates) conduct that will generate information on the Big Assumption?

In many cases, a more productive next step is continued and deeper conversation: a group might drill more deeply into the implications of its Big Assumptions. If its Big Assumption is, "We assume if we do try to do it we will fail," has the group discussed what "success" and "failure" mean in the context of a large, long-term initiative like the one it has just begun? Does the group need to clarify (and perhaps be relieved of) worries about who will make this determination? Or when? Or on what grounds? And with what consequences? Do group members assume they are supposed to already know how to do everything that will be required of them to succeed ("We assume if we do discover the problem is us it shows we are frauds"), that they are not allowed to learn "on the job" when taking on an adaptive challenge?

When the exercise is done in a multigroup format, often the next steps become self-evident once all the groups have reported. A warning to leaders: the experience  of getting so much useful and revealing information all at once can be intense. The subgroups of one district team came back and reported contradictions that showed why the leaders of each subgroup were not advancing the change initiative. In every case, there were third- and fourth-column entries reflecting a desire not to get the superintendent in trouble with his board, or not to risk disappointing or angering the superintendent by focusing on a small number of priorities. (Despite the fact that the superintendent was specifically asking them to focus on a few priorities, they weren't sure he really meant it.) The results were a revelation for the superintendent, who then made clear the need for conversations that would help the group members take new risks.

## IMPLICATIONS FOR THE CHANGE LEADER: TOWARD ADAPTIVE WORK

The work of organizational change inevitably runs smack into the work of personal change no matter what direction one turns. Yes, it is vital for schools and districts to be relentlessly focused on instructional improvement; for leadership teams to think systemically and act strategically; for leaders to generate the energies for change through increased collaboration, co-ownership, and urgent priorities. *And to succeed in these worthwhile activities, we may need to reexamine previously hidden beliefs, assumptions, or mental models that could stand in the way of our doing so.* This fundamental idea carries with it a variety of implications for the change leader. In this section, we briefly consider five: leaders need to embrace the fuller picture, set an example, encourage others to take up their own personal learning work, welcome contradictions, and create organizations that increase personal capacities. We describe them as a set of stances for change leaders to consider.

### Embrace the Fuller Picture

Embracing the fuller picture may be the least visible and the most important stance. It doesn't involve necessarily *doing* anything. It is about an inner disposition. It means acknowledging the existence and importance of the "fuller picture"—or at least taking seriously the possibility that success may depend on cultivating both a stronger outward and inner focus. We know this is not an easy thing to do. We know it makes new demands on leaders cognitively and emotionally.

From the cognitive side, the change leader's arena may be more complex than customarily described. If this has been one of your reactions, please know that you are not alone. How should you regard this suggestion that the work ahead may be harder than previously understood? Perhaps a brief story will suggest one kind of answer.

---

*"The driving ideas here," the Gates Foundation evaluator wrote, "are complex. But school reform has always been difficult, and we have tried many easy 'fixes' before. The ideas are complex, but then so are the schools and the adults working in them."*

---

Four years after the Gates Foundation awarded a grant to launch the Change Leadership Group at Harvard, it hired a third-party evaluation team, a group that had no prior need or potential advantage in rendering a verdict in one direction or another. These assessors interviewed people in the districts where we consulted, talked to people who attended our trainings, read or listened to the ideas you've been exposed to in this book, and tried to understand the use people made of the tools we have provided you throughout these chapters. Although the evaluators had a great many favorable things to say, the central conclusion they drew was that the framework we presented, and the work we did with district leaders, was "complex." What interested us especially was the stance they took toward this complexity. In their report to the Gates Foundation, they wrote: "The driving ideas are complex . . . but school reform has always been difficult, and we have tried many easy 'fixes' before. The ideas are complex, but then so are the schools and the adults working in them."[17]

This last sentence brings us back to thoughts of Einstein, who said: "No problem can be solved from the same consciousness that created it."[18] We may need a more complex way of thinking about educational transformation because the schools and adults working in them may be more complex than we have given them credit for.

And we know that adopting a stance that stays mindful of the "dual focus" is emotionally demanding. When Superintendent Mike Ward said, "We set out to work on our schools, and discovered that, in order to really succeed at it, we had to work on ourselves, as well," the expression in his voice had as much to communicate as the words themselves. Having begun to see the results of his work, there was undeniable exhilaration; but the wry tone also reflected the fatigue and the anxiety that have been an equally undeniable part of the journey. Growing is hard work, made all the harder if we continue to believe it is the primary province of the young—that "grown-ups," especially those in leadership positions, are supposed to have done all the growing they will ever need to do to successfully carry out their work.

## Set an Example

If we, as leaders, deny ourselves the opportunity to "grow on the job," how likely is it that those around us, those who work for us, are going to feel genuinely entitled to the same right themselves? The second stance recognizes that actions speak louder than words. If we want our colleagues to identify and engage those personal learning challenges that stand directly in the way of accomplishing goals to which they are genuinely committed, we are asking them to make themselves vulnerable. We are asking them first to name ways in which they are currently less effective in their work!

> *If we, as leaders, deny ourselves the opportunity to "grow on the job," how likely is it that those around us, those who work for us, are going to feel genuinely entitled to this same right themselves?*

What has been so remarkable and inspiring to us is the courage we have seen teachers and administrators display in their willingness to take on this work. Even when the "boss" makes his or her own learning challenges more visible, those who work for the boss are still taking a risk ("We can't fire *you* for *your* limitations"). But we have certainly seen that the leader's willingness to model the stance of "learning while leading" goes a long way toward fostering a community of personal reflection.

But what kind of "community of personal reflection" is the leader trying to foster? What is the optimal kind of example for the leader to share? Modeling the dual focus does not mean demonstrating that, along with the organizational changes one is trying to bring about, one is also willing to participate in and promote self-reflective activities of any sort, which may or may not have tight connections to those very organizational changes. A genuinely dual focus is not interested in personal reflection or personal disclosure for its own sake. However bravely undertaken, however personally illuminating the journey, personal learning among school professionals that is not tightly joined to the organizational changes designed to transform the quality of teaching and learning is not a dual focus; it is only a parallel focus. Improved teaching so that all students can develop the new skills required for them to succeed must be visibly connected to our individual learning agendas. The optimal example for the leader to share should clearly demonstrate a personal learning goal that, if not accomplished, will put at risk the collectively owned improvement priority, or the ability to carry out a publicly understood strategy for accomplishing that priority.

### Encourage Others to Take Up Their Own Personal Learning Work

We have yet to meet a single teacher or administrator participating in an ambitious whole school or whole district transformation effort for whom *no part* of their work presents an adaptive challenge. Nor do we expect to meet such a person. Adaptive challenges require provisions for our own growth. Trying to meet adaptive challenges through technical means is the most common error Heifetz sees.[19] Not bringing everyone into the dual focus (providing a kind of professional development for many, for example, that tries to input new skills without considering the way people may need to change in order to own and implement the new skills) is essentially an invitation for people to commit this error.

Each leader will find his or her most comfortable way to encourage others to take up their personal learning. This stance does not suggest that leaders should encourage their colleagues to make a "personal learning program" out of every challenging aspect of their work. This is unrealistic, unnecessary, and impossible.

We encourage an apparently more modest but actually quite transformational stance: Are you helping the people with whom you work identify even *one* good learning problem that neither you nor anyone else expects them to solve overnight?

And what is a good learning problem? It has the following traits:

- It is directly related to the work one needs to get better at, in order to succeed with the public, organizational improvement goal. In other words, it connects in a direct way to the challenge of improving teaching and learning.
- It is a problem one is personally very interested in working on.
- Its exploration (via the four-column immunity map or by any other means) should reveal both previously hidden contradictions in one's commitments and any Big Assumptions in need of testing.

The leaders of the district in the Northeast we discussed earlier (see p. 30) provide us an example of a "good learning problem," applicable to nearly every member, as each sought to work more collaboratively. Even when we divided them up into their role-alike subgroups (all the elementary principals; the middle school principals and vice principals; the high school principals and vice principals; the central office people) and had them work through a four-column map around their common commitment to work together more collaboratively, they each discovered myriad ways in which they did not, *even within their own role-alike groups!* (1) The problem—working collaboratively— is clearly related directly to their success in leading a whole-district improvement process. (2) It is a problem they were each interested in working on (in fact, they found it maddeningly interesting, especially when they discovered it was not just about factions *between* the subgroups, but just as difficult for them to bring off with their own peers). (3) Its exploration easily led them to contradictory commitments (for example, to protecting one's turf; to leading the top elementary school) and constraining assumptions (for example, the belief that no matter how much superintendents talk about the need for collaboration, they will be judged only on their individual accomplishments).

## Welcome Contradictions

At the very least, the ideas in this chapter might encourage leaders to take a more expansive and generous stance toward colleagues and subordinates who may not be delivering at the fastest pace or in the most desirable fashion. Might we less readily conclude the individual was not on board with the change in the first place or lacked the skills to perform at the level we expect? Is it possible there are "hidden commitments" and obstructive Big Assumptions at work here? Even if we bring this bigger picture only to our own thinking about another's work and never share it explicitly with the other, might we find a greater set of choices about how next to be helpful? Or work with a less "made-up mind" about the other's capabilities?

Imagine how much more benefit might be derived if there were a more widespread "friendliness" toward our contradictions (and the possibly limiting mental models or Big Assumptions that fuel them). Contradictions can be a rich resource for generating good problems to grow on—a curriculum, so to speak, for individual and collective change. As we describe in the group immunities tool in Appendix A, leaders can take the position that collective contradictions are inevitable (and not a shameful sign of their own inadequacy or the fatal dysfunction of their group) and ultimately valuable because they help a group bring to the surface possible distortions in its shared thinking. When leaders make clear that such contradictions are not "grounds for firing," but new opportunities for learning, it makes it much easier for everyone to bring this "fuller picture" into conversations and considerations about one's own work, and that of one's subordinates or supervisees. The question, "What 'hidden commitment' might you or I hold that makes these ineffective behaviors 'brilliant'?" becomes now, not punitive, but an invitation for valuable and prized learning.

## Create Organizations That Increase Personal Capacities

We believe leaders and leadership practice communities have a better chance of success when they develop what we have called here a dual focus—a simultaneous attention to cultivating both a greater organizational savvy and a more effective habit of personal reflection. One reason for this success is that a dual focus tends to increase personal capacities, a critical condition for meeting adaptive challenges. As people have a chance to expose and rethink limiting mental models, beliefs, and assumptions, their behavioral repertoire expands. They see a wider range of choices and possibilities. They don't simply redefine their working relationships or their self-expectations; they do so in a fashion that makes them more effective.

Of course, our schools and districts do not exist for helping the adults who work within them grow; they exist for helping our children and youth grow. But we may need to accomplish the first to accomplish the second—the adaptive challenge of helping all our young learn new skills at new levels. Writing over seventy years ago, educational sociologist Willard Waller said a similar thing: "It is necessary to consider the personalities of *all* who are involved in the social settings of the school, for it is not possible . . . to liberate students from present inhibitions without also liberating teachers."[20] To that we add that other adults in the schools must be liberated as well.

We have tried to be honest, both in our workshops and in this book, about the ways in which this leadership work is difficult. Significantly altering the quality of our schools is very hard work. But it is equally true that very deep satisfactions are also possible in a kind of leadership that supports the ongoing growth and development of all the people who are spending important parts of their lives in our schools—children and adults alike.

Research shows that the greatest cause of burnout comes not from simply having too much to do, but from being too long in a place of work without experiencing one's own ongoing development.[21] Conversely, the increase in energy and morale generated from experiencing one's work as personally expansive is geometric. And no one benefits more from this enhanced morale than our children. As Roland Barth has written, "Probably nothing within a school has more impact on children, in terms of skills development, self-confidence, or classroom behavior, than the personal and professional growth of teachers."[22] (Naturally, we add administrators as well.) When the adults in the school, says Barth, "individually and collectively examine, question, reflect on their ideals, and develop new practices that lead towards those ideals, the school and its inhabitants are alive. When [the adults in the school] stop growing, so do their students."[23]

## CONCLUDING . . . OR COMMENCING?

We want to suggest that you have patience with yourself and your colleagues as you work to develop this new way of seeing. This dual focus—attention outward and attention inward—takes time. The temptation to drop one focus or the other (perhaps, most often, the inward focus) is powerful. If it feels too hard or unfamiliar, it can gradually fall into disuse.

We may have to be on our guard not to become like the man who is looking for his lost watch under a lamppost. "Do you think you dropped it here?" a companion asks. "No," says the man. "I actually think I dropped it across the street, a ways from here." "Then why are you looking for it here?" asks the companion. "Because here," replies the man, "the light is so much better."

If one focus is so much more familiar to us, so much more illuminated, we may pour all our energies in that direction. We can be hard at work, with the greatest sincerity and devotion. We can support those around us to work tirelessly as well. We know we are all doing "all we can," so we are especially dismayed and discouraged when all this hard work seems not to be making the difference we are hoping for. The changes do not penetrate the classroom door. The achievement gap does not lessen. Children are still left behind.

Our work in learning to develop the dual focus may itself best be seen as taking up the ultimate "immunity to change." You genuinely want to sharpen both an outward and an inward focus (column 1). The more you work with *Change Leadership*, the more you will learn the ways you tend to undermine this genuine commitment (column 2). If you then take the time to work out your own hidden commitments (column 3) and Big Assumptions (column 4), you may help yourself, over time, develop your own version of the dual focus to which you (and we) aspire.

Our hope is that you can use this book to shine more light on those previously unilluminated places where you may also need to be looking to find what is missing. If your progress is slowed or stuck, consider that your light needs to shine more broadly, not more intensely; use the lessons we've provided to illuminate both sides of the street. We hope you will use this book as a "renewable resource" that you can return to over time, rather than something that is read through once and "finished."

The work of change leadership suggests a new kind of administrator and a new kind of administrative team. Although the language and enterprise of "leadership" has lately been vested with dignity and promise, the label and role of the "administrator" unfairly retains a gray, uninspiring pallor. The following words, attributed in the original to the Chinese poet Du Fu, from the Tang Dynasty more than a thousand years ago, cast a different light on "administration," and give us the chance to end by wishing you the strength to continue swimming against the tide:

> It is not that I lack the desire to live beside rivers and among hills,
> Hearing the wind scatter leaves, watching the rain breed fish;
> But the thought of disproportion in public affairs
> Offends my sense of rhythm, and disposes me

To expend the passion that normally takes form in song and painting,
On matters of administrative interest.
Knowing that all things have their intrinsic nature
I imitate the whale
That perpetually aspires to change the currents of the sea.
Torn by contradictory thoughts, I drink deep.

Drink deep—within the work, and within yourselves. Please know how much we admire what you do, and how important we believe it to be to the quality of our children's futures. We have no illusions that the work of transforming education has its source at Harvard University or Washington, D.C. It has its source in your classrooms, in your schools, in your district offices, and in the work you are doing each day.

## Endnotes

1. R. Heifetz, *Leadership Without Easy Answers* (Cambridge, Mass.: Harvard University Press, 1994).
2. J. Archer, "Tackling an Impossible Job," in Leading for Learning (series), *Education Week* (September 15, 2004). http://www.edweek.org (accessed October 27, 2004).
3. *Education Week* Research Center, "Instructional Leadership," in Leading for Learning (series), *Education Week* (September 15, 2004). http://www.edweek.org (accessed October 27, 2004).
4. As quoted in *The Evolution of Physics* (New York: Free Press, 1967), 92.
5. J. Kotter, *Leading Change* (Cambridge, Mass.: Harvard Business School Press, 1996).
6. Ibid., 5.
7. Personal communication, Change Leadership Group Advisory Board Meeting, Cambridge, Mass., June 14, 2004.
8. J. Collins, *Good to Great: Why Some Companies Make the Leap . . . and Others Don't* (New York: HarperBusiness, 2001).
9. Heifetz, *Leadership*.
10. Michael Luo, "Excuse Me? May I Have Your Seat?: Revising a Social Experiment and the Fear That Goes With It," *New York Times* (September 14, 2004): 1.
11. J. G. Berger, "Exploring the Connection Between Teacher Education Practice and Adult Development Theory." Unpublished doctoral dissertation, Harvard Graduate School of Education, 2002.
12. J. K. Hammerman, "Experiencing Professional Development: A Constructive-Developmental Exploration of Teachers' Experiences in a Mathematics Professional Development Program." Unpublished doctoral dissertation, Harvard Graduate School of Education, 2002.

13. E. Brantlinger, "Influence of Preservice Teachers' Beliefs About Pupil Achievement on Attitudes Toward Inclusion," *Teacher Education and Special Education* 19, no. 1 (1996): 17–33; C. T. Fosnot, "Learning to Teach, Teaching to Learn: Designing a Continuum to Strengthen and Sustain Teaching," *Teaching Education* 5, no. 2 (1993): 69–78; D. Holt-Reynolds, "Good Readers, Good Teachers? Subject Matter Expertise as a Challenge in Learning to Teach," *Harvard Educational Review* 69, no. 1 (1999): 29–50; D. M. Kagan, "Professional Growth Among Preservice and Beginning Teachers," *Review of Educational Research* 62, no. 2 (1992): 129–169. M. F. Pajares, "Teachers; Beliefs and Educational Research: Cleaning Up a Messy Construct," *Review of Educational Research* 62, no. 3 (1992): 307–332; M. A. Price, *Beliefs of Secondary Preservice Teachers: A Case for Foundations?* (Montreal, Canada: American Educational Research Association, 1999).
14. See Chapters Six and Nine in Robert Kegan and Lisa Lahey, *How the Way We Talk Can Change the Way We Work* (San Francisco: Jossey-Bass, 2001).
15. The concept of group-level "immunities to change" first appears in Robert Kegan and Lisa Lahey, "The Real Reason People Won't Change," *Harvard Business Review* (November 2001): 85–92; and Constance M. Bowe, Lisa Lahey, Robert Kegan, and Elizabeth Armstrong, "Recognizing Organizational Contradictions That Impede Institutional Change," *Medical Education* 37 (2003): 723–733.
16. This is akin to treating a patient's chest cold as energetically and conscientiously as we can while ignoring the patient's cancer, because cancer (as it once used to be) is a disease that cannot be discussed. (When the patient dies we are then perplexed because we were working so hard and so well on the chest cold.)
17. The evaluators continued, saying, "In all probability, our best chance for success will be found in coaching organizations like the Change Leadership Group." J. Fouts and Associates, *Learning to Change: School Coaching for Systemic Reform—An Evaluation of Programs Prepared for the Bill & Melinda Gates Foundation* (Mill Creek, Wash.: Fouts & Associates, LLC, 2004).
18. Jerry Mayer and John P. Holms (Eds.), *Bite-size Einstein: Quotations on Just About Everything from the Greatest Mind of the Twentieth Century* (New York: St. Martin's Press, 1996), 38.
19. Heifetz, *Leadership*.
20. W. W. Waller, *The Sociology of Teaching* (New York: Wiley, 1932), 445.
21. See H. J. Freudenberger, *Burnout: The High Cost of Achievement* (Garden City, N.Y.: Anchor Press, 1980); R. Kegan, *In over Our Heads: The Mental Demands of Modern Life* (Cambridge, Mass.: Harvard University Press, 1994), 171–172.
22. R. Barth, *Run School Run* (Cambridge, Mass.: Harvard University Press, 1980), 147.
23. Ibid.

---

## Team Exercise 1.1: Identifying the Problem

### Step One

In this exercise, we invite you to first reflect individually on the following questions:

1. From your vantage point in the classroom, school, or district office, what do you see as the greatest challenge you and your colleagues face related to improving your "system" in response to the new challenges we face in education? What is the number one problem you are trying to solve?

2. What are some of the organizational changes required to solve this problem? What practices, structures, or policies may need to change in classrooms, schools, and districts in order to solve this problem?

3. Are there organizational or individual beliefs and behaviors associated with this problem that may need to change, beginning with your own? From what to what?

4. Finally, what might be some of the implications for leadership at your particular level to solve this problem? What might you, as a leader or group of leaders, have to do differently?

### Step Two

If you are in a group, once you have had sufficient time to formulate an answer to each question, take turns sharing your answers to each question—making sure that everyone has an opportunity to contribute (but can pass if he or she chooses to) and that no one speaks twice until all who wish to have had a chance to speak once.

## Step Three

After everyone has had a turn responding to each question, we recommend that you first summarize on a flip chart the areas of agreement in your answers to each question. Then summarize the points where you may have had disagreement.

## Step Four

Put your notes and any summaries aside. We will ask you to refer to them later. For now, continue on to Chapter Two when you are ready.

---

## Team Exercise 2.2: Take Stock: Your Seven Disciplines for Strengthening Instruction

### Overview

This diagnostic tool can help you assess your efforts to implement the Seven Disciplines. We suggest you fill out this diagnostic individually first and then compare results with your colleagues, holding discussion among yourselves until everyone has a chance to weigh in. The discussion that follows will clarify your understanding of the disciplines themselves and almost certainly identify the most promising areas for further work in your school or district. We also encourage you not to skip over the identification of evidence. These indicators can be the most powerful discussion prompts and build a shared idea of what is, and what needs to be.

This diagnostic can be used with different groups—principals, teachers, and central office administrators—to see to what degree views differ and can be usefully explored. The diagnostic can also be given periodically as an informal assessment of progress in these areas.

Diagnostic:

Name _____

District _____

1. The district or school creates understanding and urgency around improving all students' learning for teachers and community, and it regularly reports on progress.

   • Data are disaggregated and transparent to everyone.

   • Qualitative (focus groups and interviews) as well as quantitative data are used to understand students' and recent graduates' experience of school.

   Not yet started   1   2   3   4   Well established

Evidence:

2. A widely shared vision of what is good teaching is focused on rigorous expectations, relevant curricula, and respectful relationships in the classroom.

Not yet started    1    2    3    4    Well established

Evidence:

3. All adult meetings are about instruction and are models of good teaching.

Not yet started    1    2    3    4    Well established

Evidence:

4. There are well-defined standards and performance assessments for student work at all grade levels. Teachers and students understand what quality work looks like, and there is consistency in standards of assessment.

Not yet started    1    2    3    4    Well established

Evidence:

5. Supervision is frequent, rigorous, and entirely focused on the improvement of instruction. It is done by people who know what good teaching looks like.

Not yet started    1    2    3    4    Well established

Evidence:

6. Professional development is primarily on-site, intensive, collaborative, and job-embedded and is designed and led by educators who model best teaching and learning practices.

Not yet started    1    2    3    4    Well established

Evidence:

7. Data are used diagnostically at frequent intervals by teams of teachers to assess each student's learning and to identify the most effective teaching practices. Teams have time built into their schedules for this shared work.

Not yet started    1    2    3    4    Well established

Evidence:

## Team Exercise 2.3: Grade the Videotaped Lesson

### Overview

To "observe" this teaching excerpt taken from a tenth-grade English class, go to our Web site, http://www.gse.harvard.edu/clg/, and view it with Internet video streaming. (Click on "News & Resources" on the main page and then the link for the "Change Leadership Book and Videos.") Our Web site also includes a video of a sixth-grade social science lesson that some readers may want to view instead of or in addition to the first video.

### Step One

Silently observe the video (up to the place where the teacher says to the students, "Now go to it"). Then, with no conversation in the group, answer the following question:

> *If you had to grade the lesson (from F to A, with plusses and minuses allowed), what would that grade be?*

Write your grade down on an index card. Do not put your name or your reasons for the grade on the card. Pass the card to whoever is facilitating this meeting.

### Step Two

Having made your decision, now think about what criteria you used for the grading. Consider what evidence led you to give the lesson the grade you did, whether high or low.

### Step Three

The facilitator should now array the results on the flip chart, as follows: list all possible grades vertically from A+ at the top of the page through F at the bottom. Place a check or hash mark after each letter grade horizontally to signify the grade indicated on each index card. This will make visually apparent how frequently each grade was chosen and the spread of grades.

While the facilitator is making this chart, group members are encouraged to discuss what criteria each person used for the grading.

### Step Four

Now the facilitator reminds everyone in the room that this is "no fault" work—that there are no right or wrong answers—and asks, first, for two or three volunteers to talk about what evidence led them to give the lesson a high grade—say B+ or above. Next, the facilitator asks the same number of volunteers who gave a significantly lower grade (C or below) to explain their reasoning.

We encourage the facilitator to let this conversation continue as long as it has energy, keeping in mind that the purpose is not, at this time, to solve or settle anything. The first purpose is to try to understand, as well as you can, the differing views that are in the room.

## Step Five

Finally, we invite you to step back a bit from the conversation to consider the bigger questions the exercise inevitably raises:

> *What does this distribution of grades, and our different views about what good teaching looks like, mean for our school or district?*

---

## Team Exercise 2.4: Define Rigor on a Learning Walk

### Overview

The New 3 R's are best understood as a framework for a conversation about instruction. With that in mind, we encourage your team to take the first steps in initiating such a dialogue. We begin with the idea of rigor, which we find to be the most ambiguous and difficult to define.

We want to stress, as we did in the text, that rigor by itself is an insufficient determinant of effective instruction. Its power is in combination with relevance and relationships. We suggest that you eventually determine what all three concepts might actually look like in the classroom at any grade level.

### Step One

Consider the following questions for reflection or discussion:

1. In a (pick a grade level) classroom where "rigorous" instruction is going on, what activities or behaviors would you expect to see? What would the teacher be doing? What would students be doing?

2. In (pick a subject content area and grade level), what might be some of the characteristics of "rigorous" student work?

3. List of some of the most important things that you might now look for related to rigor in classrooms.

Now "benchmark" your definition of rigor by considering to what extent the indicators on your list build the critical competencies needed in a knowledge economy (beyond mastery of the basic skills in reading, writing, and mathematics).

## Step Two

What might you need to revise or reconsider in light of the key competencies, the knowledge economy skills, such as those that Carnevale and Desrochers provided for the Educational Testing Service?

**Foundation Skills:** Knowing How to Learn

**Communication Skills:** Listening and Oral Communication

**Adaptability:** Creative Thinking and Problem Solving

**Group Effectiveness:** Interpersonal Skills, Negotiation, and Teamwork

**Influence:** Organizational Effectiveness and Leadership

**Personal Management:** Self-Esteem and Motivation/Goal Setting

**Attitude:** Positive Cognitive Style

**Applied Skills:** Occupational and Professional Competencies

## Step Three

When your "rubric for rigor" is completed to your team's satisfaction, take the indicators to the classroom, to see what they might really look like in practice and, most important, to foster a conversation that will begin to build a shared and concrete vision of rigor. We suggest you take an hour and a half, and visit ten or so classrooms in a school with your list. Observe each class for perhaps five minutes. If the purpose of the lesson is not clear, ask a student what he or she is doing and why.

How you record your observations is important, as these are the data that will ground your conversation later. Rather than check off the presence of an indicator on your rigor rubric, try to describe, verbatim, what you see that you believe illustrates a particular indicator. Try not to interpret, but instead describe what you actually see so that you and your colleagues can together determine if this activity, question, or performance is indeed an indicator of rigor. For example, rather than noting that a teacher's question was complex, record the question itself. Let the decision as to its complexity come later and be one that you determine together.

## Step Four

When you've finished your "learning walk," examine the data you've collected and reflect on what you saw by asking the following questions:

1. Were you able to identify some particular teacher or student behaviors that indicated rigor?

2. Did you see evidence of rigorous content? How did that differ across classrooms, teaching styles, disciplines?

3. Do team members agree that what you saw illustrates the rigor indicators on your rubric?

4. What areas of commonality can you build on?

5. Where do you disagree?

6. What questions do your disagreements raise?

7. What else do you need to learn?

Typically, these observations help educators become clearer about their individual definitions of key concepts such as "rigor." What is much more powerful, we find, is for a team of educators to observe the same lessons and share their responses to these questions. You can imagine how a conversation that addresses the previous questions not only challenges individuals to clarify, rethink, and refine their own definitions but can also allow the whole team to come to powerful, shared understandings.

## Team Exercise 4.1: Reaction Versus Purpose and Focus Diagnostic

You and your team can use this exercise to assess the way in which your district or school "does business" along this dimension.

### Step One

As a group, first decide whether you want to focus on the problem statement you generated in Chapter One and possibly rewrote in Chapter Two or on the district's work more broadly.

### Step Two

Individually, rate your district or school on the continua relative to your problem statement (or more broadly). We have provided some examples of what a system might look like at either end of this spectrum. Enter your ratings under the arrows and use the space below to jot down specific examples or evidence of your rating.

*Purpose and focus* refers to whether you have a goal that is clearly focused and understood. Note that it is not about how well you are doing in relation to your goal.

General questions to consider include:

1. Is there a clear district or school focus?

2. Is this focus widely known throughout the system?

3. Are we able to resist certain pulls and tugs because they are peripheral to our purpose?

Some indicators of what a system at either end of the spectrum might look like follow. Use these to rate your school or district on the continuum.

| Reaction | Purpose and Focus |
|---|---|
| • Insufficient attention to instructional improvement. | • Clear focus on instructional improvement. |
| • Absence of well-defined strategies for improving learning, teaching, and leadership. | • Well-defined strategies for improving teaching and learning. |
| • Highly responsive to external agendas. | • External pressures are assessed and filtered based on their relation to the focus on and strategies for instructional improvement. |
| • Many priorities—no sense of what is most important. | • All adults in system know and understand the key improvement strategy(ies), what they need to do, and how it is going to get them to the organization's goals. |
| • Multiple discrete strategies that are not aligned or connected. | • Strategies, time, money, and professional development are aligned in service of improving teaching and learning. |

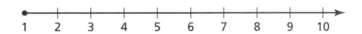

## Step Three

Take turns sharing individual ratings for this scale. Enter these ratings in the following graph. Explain why you gave the rating you did. Provide specific examples if you can.

| Purpose and focus | | | | | | | | | | |
|---|---|---|---|---|---|---|---|---|---|---|
| | 1 | 2 | 3 | 4 | 5 | 6 | 7 | 8 | 9 | 10 |
| Totals | | | | | | | | | | |
| | | | | | | | | | | |

## Step Four

Together, discuss the following questions:

1. What stands out when you look at your collective data?

2. How do you make sense of the rating disagreements in light of people's explanations for their ratings? Are there additional data you might want to collect to inform your understanding of where your district lands on this continuum?

3. What would it take to move even one notch higher (rightward) on the continuum?

---

## Team Exercise 4.2: Compliance Versus Engagement Diagnostic

You and your team can use this exercise to assess the way in which your district or school "does business" along this dimension.

### Step One

As a group, first decide whether you want to focus on the problem statement you generated in Chapter One and possibly rewrote in Chapter Two or on the district's work more broadly.

### Step Two

Individually, rate your district or school on the continua relative to your problem statement (or more broadly). We have provided some examples of what a system might look like at either end of this spectrum. Enter your ratings under the arrows and use the space below each to jot down specific examples or evidence of your rating.

As you assess the level of *engagement* in your school or district, here are some general questions to get you started:

1. How much ownership is there among all adults in the system and how do you know?

2. Is there ownership just at the top, or do people throughout the system feel genuinely committed to the instructional improvement goals?

3. How much does it seem people are working to meet someone else's goal versus meeting their own, or a goal they co-own?

4. Are people participating productively during meetings?

Here are some specific indicators of both ends of the continuum.

| Compliance | Engagement |
|---|---|
| • Teachers and principals are expected to "go along" with mandates; no procedures exist for generating conversation and collaborative decision making. | • Productive dialogue and debate regarding organizational strategies and goals are nurtured. |
| • Communication tends to be one-way. | • Communication is multidirectional. |
| • Culture tends to be rule and procedure driven. | • Culture is characterized by strong sense of personal and shared responsibility for the strategies and goals of the district. |
| • Teachers and principals do not take risks and do not investigate successes and failures. | • Professional discourse is focused on learning from professional challenges. |

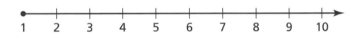

## Step Three

Take turns sharing individual ratings for this scale. Enter these ratings in the following graph. Explain why you gave the rating you did. Provide specific examples if you can.

| Engagement | 1 | 2 | 3 | 4 | 5 | 6 | 7 | 8 | 9 | 10 |
|---|---|---|---|---|---|---|---|---|---|---|
| Totals | | | | | | | | | | |
| | | | | | | | | | | |

## Step Four

Together, discuss the following questions:

1. What stands out when you look at your collective data?

2. How do you make sense of the rating disagreements in light of people's explanations for their ratings? Are there additional data you might want to collect to inform your understanding of where your district lands on this continuum?

3. What would it take to move even one notch higher (rightward) on the continuum?

## Team Exercise 4.3: Isolation Versus Collaboration Diagnostic

You and your team can use this exercise to assess the way in which your district or school "does business" along this dimension.

### Step One

As a group, first decide whether you want to focus on the problem statement you generated in Chapter One and possibly rewrote in Chapter Two or on the district's work more broadly.

### Step Two

Individually, rate your district or school on the continua relative to your problem statement (or more broadly). We have provided some examples of what a system might look like at either end of this spectrum. Enter your ratings under the arrows and use the space below each to jot down specific examples or evidence of your rating. Here are some questions to consider:

1. Are meetings focused on learning, teaching, and leading?
2. Do organizational members possess and use the skills of dialogue and inquiry?
3. Do people share problems of practice at meetings?

Some indicators of what a system at either end of the spectrum might look like follow:

| *Isolation* | *Collaboration* |
|---|---|
| • Teachers and administrators work in *isolation*. | • The work of teachers and administrators is a public enterprise within the school. |
| • There is no opportunity or urgency for collective problem solving. | • Educators collectively solve problems that inhibit effective teaching and learning. |
| • Good leading and teaching exist as random acts of excellence in the system; there is little dissemination of best practice. | • Standards of practice for teaching and leading exist, and are shared and specific. |
| • There are few expectations for collaborative work among adults. | • There are clear and shared expectations around the nature and ends of *collaboration*. |

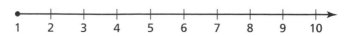

## Step Three

Take turns sharing individual ratings for this scale. Enter these ratings in the following graph. Explain why you gave the rating you did. Provide specific examples if you can.

| Collaboration | | | | | | | | | | |
|---|---|---|---|---|---|---|---|---|---|---|
| | **1** | **2** | **3** | **4** | **5** | **6** | **7** | **8** | **9** | **10** |
| **Totals** | | | | | | | | | | |
| | | | | | | | | | | |

## Step Four

Together, discuss the following questions:

1. What stands out when you look at your collective data?

2. How do you make sense of the rating disagreements in light of people's explanations for their ratings? Are there additional data you might want to collect to inform your understanding of where your district lands on this continuum?

3. What would it take to move even one notch higher (rightward) on the continuum?

## Team Exercise 6.1:  4 C's Diagnostic Tool—As Is

### Step One

Using a blank version of the 4 C's chart provided, put the problem you defined in Chapter Two in the center of the overlapping circles.

### Step Two

Now take some time to reflect on the contributors to your current system as they relate to the problem you've identified. The following questions can get you started.

**Competencies**

*How well do we:*

- Think strategically?
- Identify student learning needs?
- Gather and interpret data?
- Collaborate?

- Give and receive critiques?
- Productively disagree?
- Reflect and make midcourse corrections?

## Conditions

*How well do we create and maintain:*

- Time for problem solving, for learning, for talking about challenges?
- Relevant and user-friendly student data?
- Agreed upon performance standards?
- Clear priorities and focus for each person's work?
- District- and building-level support?

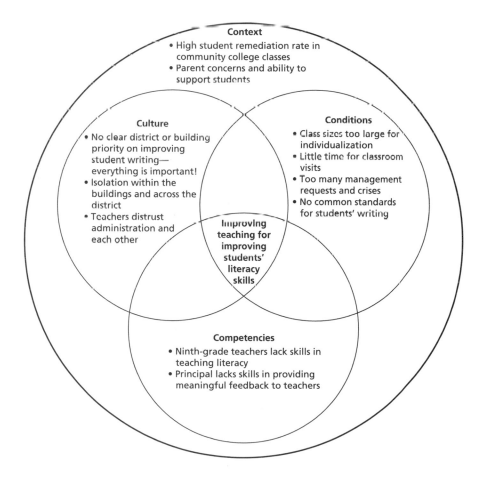

**Context**
- High student remediation rate in community college classes
- Parent concerns and ability to support students

**Culture**
- No clear district or building priority on improving student writing— everything is important!
- Isolation within the buildings and across the district
- Teachers distrust administration and each other

**Conditions**
- Class sizes too large for individualization
- Little time for classroom visits
- Too many management requests and crises
- No common standards for students' writing

**Improving teaching for improving students' literacy skills**

**Competencies**
- Ninth-grade teachers lack skills in teaching literacy
- Principal lacks skills in providing meaningful feedback to teachers

### Culture

*How would we characterize:*

- Our level of expectations for all students' learning? (Consistently high? Medium? Low? Or a mix of these depending on which students?)
- Our school's agenda? (Multiple and unrelated? Frequent changes? Steady, consistent focus? Related initiatives that build on each other?)
- The communications between district and school leadership to teachers? (Directive? Compliance oriented? Engaged in building cosponsorship and ownership?)
- Adult relationships with each other? (Lacking trust? Trusting?)
- Adult views of responsibility for all students' learning? (Blames others? Sees various contributors, including oneself?)

### Context

*How well do we:*

- Understand and work with students' families?
- See clearly the core competencies students will need for work, citizenship, and continuous learning?

## Step Three

Now add brief, bulleted descriptions of the strengths or assets your school or district has—as they relate to the problem you're trying to solve—to the appropriate circles or the overlaps between the circles. We encourage you to go back to the seven disciplines diagnostic (Chapter Two, Exercise 2.2) and the three continua diagnostics you completed in Chapter Four (Exercises 4.1, 4.2, and 4.3) and consider your responses as current contributors to your system.

## Step Four

Using a different color, insert bulleted descriptions into the appropriate circles, listing the weaknesses or challenges that will need to be overcome in order to solve your problem.

## Step Five

We encourage you to discuss with your group any new insights or questions that arise from your diagnostic work. Does your understanding of the problem change in any way? Do you see new or different ways of going at the problem? Does your diagnosis begin to suggest some work that needs to be done before other work can be undertaken? Do you feel ready to answer these questions? If not, what more would you need to know? Are there specific data you need to collect in order to develop a robust picture of the various 4 C's contributions? How might you collect these data? What is your next step?

## Team Exercise 8.1–8.3: Change Phase Diagnostic

This survey is designed to help identify where your school or district is within the phases of change.

### Step One

Please respond to each statement individually. Indicate where you believe your school or district falls in respect to the change levers in each of the phases. You can use the indicators below each continuum to help in your assessment. The indicators are illustrative, not complete.

#### Preparing Phase

DATA FOR LEADERSHIP UNDERSTANDING AND URGENCY

| 1 | 2 | 3 | 4 |
|---|---|---|---|
| Not present | Emerging | Developing | Well underway |

**Indicators of Data in Preparing Phase:**

- Leadership has created compelling data sets that have the potential to create urgency (they can mobilize the intellect and passion of people to alter the status quo and their individual behavior).

- Current qualitative and quantitative data have been gathered and then formatted in a way to generate urgency to change or address a specific problem or challenge.

- Leadership has developed an understanding of the gap between the current reality of the schools and the demands the twenty-first century puts on high school graduates.

- Leadership has developed a clear plan for how to educate the community about the specific challenge(s) using compelling data sets.

- Leadership oversees a general inventory of data systems to understand how useable and useful the current data are to the necessary consumers of it [for example, How accessible is data throughout the system? What form(s) is collected and disseminated? Do the people who need to use the data have the necessary skills to use it effectively?]

**ACCOUNTABILITY** FOR SOLVING A COMMON PROBLEM

**Indicators of Accountability in Preparing Phase:**

- The current state of schooling is openly examined in the context of a dramatically changing economy and society, reducing any sense of blame or victimization among educators throughout schools and districts.
- Educators throughout the system begin to understand that the challenge of educating students for the twenty-first century is everyone's responsibility, one where administrators and teachers share accountability for the problem and the solution.
- A leadership team is created or rechartered for the purpose of overseeing, guiding, and nurturing the overall reinvention process.
- Leadership understands the need for and agrees to next steps for engaging a critical mass of shareholders (inside the schools and among community members) in understanding the problem.
- Leadership gains a shared understanding of what graduating students need to know and be able to do, and this understanding begins to inform next steps.

BUILDING TRUSTING **RELATIONSHIPS** WITH COLLEAGUES AND COMMUNITY

**Indicators of Relationships in Preparing Phase:**

- Leadership team has a shared understanding of the cultural dimensions of a successful change process (that is, collaboration, commitment, and proactivity/redesign as cornerstones of an effective culture, and that norms of no shame, no blame, and no excuses enable these cornerstones to take hold).
- Leadership applies these values to how they work together as a team.
- Leadership works to surface and address dysfunctional relationships throughout the system so as to enable new forms of collaboration.

- Leadership creates new constructive relationships with and cosponsorship of the change efforts with necessary leaders among shareholders (for example, teachers associations, parent groups, community members, businesses).

## Envisioning Phase

DATA FOR COMMUNITY-WIDE UNDERSTANDING AND URGENCY

### Indicators of Data in Envisioning Phase:

- Qualitative and quantitative data sets concerning the functioning of the school system (for example, indicators of student achievement and student engagement) are widely and transparently shared with the greater community.
- A large number of shareholders understand the gap between where the district needs to be and the current reality.
- An open and honest assessment of how professionals within the district work together and how the district functions as a system is the focus of district dialogue and action.
- Data are gathered (for example, by conducting learning walks) around current teaching practices.

LAYING THE FOUNDATION FOR RECIPRICOL, RELATIONAL **ACCOUNTABILITY**

### Indicators of Accountability in Envisioning Phase:

A few clear districtwide goals and strategies, focusing on improving teaching and learning, are established.

- The community develops a deep understanding of the current gap between what graduates presently know and are able to do and what they need to know and be able to do to thrive in twenty-first century.
- Community shareholders have been brought together to help develop goals and foci for the change work.

- Community shareholders develop a sense of what they are accountable for in relation to helping all students develop the necessary new skills.
- Greater clarity is reached concerning what district leadership is accountable for to the community shareholders.
- Teachers and administrators have an emerging understanding of the need for everyone in the system to improve professional practice.

DEVELOPING MORE TRUSTING, RESPECTFUL **RELATIONSHIPS**

| 1 | 2 | 3 | 4 |
|---|---|---|---|
| Not present | Emerging | Developing | Well underway |

**Indicators of Relationships in Envisioning Phase:**

- Patterns of forthright communication and positive collaboration between (and among) the district and its constituent groups have been developed.
- School-level collaboration among teachers has increased.
- The quality of discourse in working meetings throughout the district has increased, creating the opportunity for all educators to engage in collaborative and productive ways.
- Educators understand the need to work more collaboratively on instructional practice and have begun grade-level and cross-school discussions.
- School-level meetings are more directly focused on the issues of teaching and learning and the meetings tend to model powerful instructional practice.

**Enacting Phase**
**DATA** FOR CONTINUOUS IMPROVEMENT OF TEACHING AND LEARNING

| 1 | 2 | 3 | 4 |
|---|---|---|---|
| Not present | Emerging | Developing | Well underway |

**Indicators of Data in Enacting Phase:**

- Systems of data collection and analysis are constructed to monitor the implementation and impact of improvement strategies.
- Data are being used at the district level to identify pockets of success from which to identify best practice.

- Data concerning the quality of instruction are continuously gathered and analyzed by administrators and teachers.
- In each school, data are used diagnostically at frequent intervals by teams of teachers to refine school assessments and goals, monitor student progress, and continually improve instruction.
- Assessments of school quality and effectiveness rely on multiple and varied sources of data concerning student achievement and engagement (test scores, promotion rates, dropout rates, and the like).

SHARED **ACCOUNTABILITY** FOR CONTINUOUS IMPROVEMENT OF LEARNING AND TEACHING

| 1 | 2 | 3 | 4 |
| Not present | Emerging | Developing | Well underway |

**Indicators of Accountability in Enacting Phase:**

- District leadership has developed and has implemented a structure for providing frequent, rigorous, and focused supervision of school principals' instructional leadership.
- School leadership has developed and implemented a structure for providing frequent, rigorous, and focused supervision of classroom instruction.
- The structure and content of teacher supervision at the school level are aligned with the focus of district improvement efforts.
- Schools have begun to create vivid and clear standards of professional practice based on research-tested and practice-based understandings of how students learn. In other words, teachers and administrators share collective definitions of what constitutes effective instructional practice.
- Expectations and responsibility for student outcomes are clarified for and aligned through grade and school division (elementary, middle, high) levels.
- All educators have a greater sense of what they are being held accountable for, and these more collectively held expectations form the basis of more horizontal accountability.
- All professionals at the district and school levels understand the relation between their work and role and the improvement of instruction.

TRUSTING **RELATIONSHIPS** FOR WORKING IN NEW WAYS

1  Not present
2  Emerging
3  Developing
4  Well underway

**Indicators of Relationships in Enacting Phase:**

- Schools have been reorganized to provide the conditions necessary to facilitate collaborative teamwork among adults and to foster personalized learning communities for students.

- Professional relationships become increasingly effective as trust throughout the system increases and deepens.

- Professionals begin to open up their practice among colleagues, working to improve their respective competencies while simultaneously developing consistent and increasingly effective standards of practice.

- Parents and community members are welcomed into schools and are more actively involved in the collective enterprise of improving student learning (for example, community members are involved as mentors, or parents are providing students a time and place for studying at home).

## Step Two

Share your individual assessments with your group, using the indicators to help explain your thinking. Be prepared to offer examples as evidence to help develop a shared understanding of what is meant by each phase and where your school or district really is in the change process.

## Step Three

Determine your areas of agreement and disagreement.

*What additional data might you gather to reach greater consensus?*

## Step Four

Once relative agreement is established among you, consider the following questions:

1. What is going well? What should we celebrate?
2. What change levers might require greater attention? What might we have missed entirely?

## Team Exercise 10: A Groupwide Approach to Diagnosing the Immunity to Change

### Overview

The purpose of this exercise is to provide a safe forum for a group to discover and act on the variety of threats, barriers, or impediments that get in the way of successful functioning and the shared beliefs or assumptions that hold them in place. After you read through the steps and discussion that follow—and before you decide to use this tool—we suggest that you consider your comfort level with the intense discussion the exercise can generate. You may decide that you would prefer to have someone from outside your group or team to facilitate this process. Whoever runs the process—be it someone from within or outside your school or district—should be personally familiar with the immunity concept and his or her own individual immunity.

If you are an individual reading this, you may be a member of an intact group or team that might value engaging in this exercise. If so, we suggest you introduce them to the idea of immunities to change, and then see if they are interested in first taking themselves through the individual immunities work (in the same way you have throughout this guidebook).

All participants should have had the experience of developing their own four-column immunity maps *at the individual level* so that they understand the "immunity to change" concept.

This exercise will take from one to three hours, depending on which format is being used:

**Format #1—Solo Group:** A single group (for example, a leadership team) generating results for its own internal reflection. This is generally accomplished in one hour.

**Format #2—Multigroup:** Several subgroups taking part together (for example, a district's high school principals and vice principals, middle school principals and vice principals, elementary principals, and district office), each doing its own work and then sharing their separate work with each other to examine trends across the organization (and contextual influences). Allow up to three hours.

**Materials:** Each participant will need a worksheet (provided), and you should have a common worksheet to keep track of the group's collective product. When a group works alone, the "common worksheet" is best drawn on newsprint on a wall, so that everyone can see it. If you are working with several groups at once, we find it best to use a transparency version of the common worksheet so that it can be projected for all groups to see when they share their work.

| 1<br>Collective Commitment | 2<br>Fearless Organizational Inventory (Doing/Not Doing vs. First Column) | 3<br>Collective Competing Commitment | 4<br>Collective Big Assumption |
|---|---|---|---|
|  |  |  |  |

## Step One

Together decide the focus of your exploration. This should be a collective goal that the group agrees is important and insufficiently accomplished (the group agrees it would like to be doing much better with this goal). Once the focus is determined, each person should enter it in column 1 of his or her worksheet, the "collective commitment."

## Step Two

Working silently and independently for the next ten minutes or so, each person considers the following question:

*What do we as a group (not "I as an individual," not "some members of our group") do and fail to do that works against our collective commitment in column 1?*

Enter these answers (still working individually) into column 2.

## Step Three

Still working individually, make a list of what you believe the group's biggest fears would be if it were to do the opposite of column 2. From this, craft the collective commitment you believe these fears represent. This should be very familiar to you from your individual work on the four-column immunity map.

## Step Four

Now it's time to reengage with your group and see what others have come up with. Your task here is to create a common picture of a possible groupwide contradiction or "immunity to change" by sharing your individual perspectives of columns 2 and 3. Let us remind you that powerful third-column entries:

- Are inevitably commitments to groupwide self-protection
- Show why the second-column behaviors make "perfect sense" just as they are
- Are almost never the sort of thing the group would be comfortable announcing to the press (unlike first-column commitments, which are)

## Step Five

Having created a picture of a contradiction you deem both powerful and plausible, you should turn to the fourth column and ask yourselves:

*What assumption must we be holding that makes the third-column commitment inevitable?*

## Step Six

Finally, as a group, consider "where do we go from here?" with the new ideas and insights this exercise has generated. *Have we uncovered a Big Assumption that needs to be tested to determine its validity? What experiments might we devise and run that will move us, as a group, through the phases of overturning an immunity to change (as identified in Chapter 9)?*

Examples of this process for another district are shown in the following tables.

Here is an example of one district leadership team's work:

| 1 Collective Commitment | 2 Fearless Organizational Inventory | 3 Collective Competing Commitment | 4 Collective Big Assumption |
|---|---|---|---|
| We are committed to creating a plan based on research and using data that addresses the needs of our English Language Learners (ELLs). | • We make plans but don't follow through on our commitments.<br>• We have district materials but people use them or not as they choose.<br>• There is no ongoing training for teachers.<br>• We don't consistently reinforce teacher skills and strategies/techniques.<br>• We don't have the expectation that we put in practice what we train staff to do.<br>• We don't continuously support programs with district resources.<br>• We don't have consistent district goals that money follows.<br>• We don't systematically monitor best practices.<br>• We don't make clear to all what programs and expectations all sites must support.<br>• We don't demonstrate our commitment to uninterrupted time for critical instruction.<br>• We (district) are not clear in direction to sites on what is negotiable or not.<br>• We don't analyze program success.<br>• We don't involve teachers and principals in change reform by connecting current practice and sharing data as evidence for a need to change.<br>• We want districtwide programs if we like them for our own school. | • We are committed to the status quo, to not trying to change.<br>• We are committed to not discovering (if all the programs, materials, training, and such, are in order) that the problem is just us—that we are ineffective, don't really have what it takes. | • We assume if we do try to do it we will fail.<br>• We assume if we do discover the problem is us it shows we are frauds, should not be in charge, may lose our jobs. |

# APPENDIX B: RECOMMENDED READING

## IMPROVING TEACHING AND LEARNING

Tina Blythe & Associates, *Teaching for Understanding Guide* (San Francisco: Jossey-Bass, 1997).

John Bransford, Ann L. Brown, and Rodney R. Cocking (Eds.), *How People Learn: Brain, Mind, Experience, and School: Expanded Edition* (Washington, D.C.: National Academies Press, 2000).

M. Suzanne Donovan and John D. Bransford (Eds.), *How Students Learn: History, Mathematics, and Science in the Classrooms* (Washington, D.C.: National Academies Press, 2005).

Robert Marzano, Debra J. Pickering, and Jane E. Pollock, *Classroom Instruction That Works: Research-based Strategies for Increased Student Achievement* (Washington, D.C.: Association for Supervision and Curriculum Development, 2001).

James Stigler and James Hiebert, *The Teaching Gap* (New York: Free Press, 1999).

## UNDERTAKING SCHOOL IMPROVEMENT

Richard F. Elmore with Deanna Burney, *Investing in Teacher Learning: Staff Development and Instructional Improvement in Community School District #2 New York City* (Washington, D.C.: National Commission on Teaching and America's Future, 1997).

Deborah Meier, *The Power of Their Ideas* (Boston: Beacon Press, 1995).

W. Togneri and S. E. Anderson, *Beyond Islands of Excellence* (Washington, D.C.: Learning First Alliance, 2003).

Richard Murnane and Frank Levy, *Teaching the New Basic Skills: Principles for Educating Children to Thrive in a Changing Economy* (New York: Free Press, 1996).

Tony Wagner, *Making the Grade: Reinventing America's Schools* (New York: RoutledgeFalmer, 2001).

## PROMOTING CHANGE

Robert Kegan and Lisa Laskow Lahey, *How the Way We Talk Can Change the Way We Work: The Seven Languages for Transformation* (San Francisco: Jossey-Bass/Wiley, 2001).

John Kotter and Dan S. Cohen, *The Heart of Change* (Cambridge, Mass.: Harvard Business School Press, 2002).

## DEVELOPING LEADERSHIP

Richard F. Elmore, *Building a New Structure for School Leadership* (New York: Albert Shanker Institute, 2000).

Ronald A. Heifetz and Donald L. Laurie, "The Work of Leadership," *Harvard Business Review* (January–February, 1997).

Ronald A. Heifetz, *Leadership Without Easy Answers* (Cambridge, Mass.: Belknap Press of Harvard University, 1994).

Andy Platt and Caroline Tripp, *The Skillful Leader: Confronting Mediocre Teaching* (Acton, Mass.: Research for Better Teaching, 2000).

## SUPPORTING TRUST AND PROFESSIONAL CULTURE

Anthony S. Bryke and Barbara Schneider, *Trust in Schools: A Core Resource for Improvement* (University of Chicago Press, 2002).

Douglas Stone, Bruce Patton, and Sheila Heen, *Difficult Conversations: How to Discuss What Matters Most* (New York: Penguin Putnam, 2000).

# INDEX

## A

Accountability: accountable collaboration, 31–32, 155; as change level, 134–137; culture and, 103; enacting systemic change, 155–157; envisioning systemic change, 147–149, 151; external, 165n1; horizontal, 135–136; internal, 165n1; modeling, 111; preparing for systemic change, 140–141; for students, 165n2; vertical, 135–136

Adaptive challenges: change leadership and, 221–227; conditions and culture, 199–200; and need for adaptability, 5; personal learning required, 206; preparing for systemic change, 138; systemic change and, 195; technical vs., 8–12

Administrators: developing new kinds of teams, 214–218; involving in instruction, 198–202. See also Principals; Superintendents

Agreements: enacting systemic change, 156; engagement and, 70; teams and, 217

Alvarado, Anthony, 30–31, 66, 110–111, 113–114

Ambiguity, tolerance for, 138

Annenberg grants, 210–211

"Arthur" case study: Big Assumptions, 167, 173, 175–181; identifying costs, 170–171; immunities to change, 90–92, 170, 185–187, 212; immunity map, 124–129; spotting obstacles through self-reflection, 55–56; vision of success, 171–172

*As Is-To Be* tool, 107–110, 119–120

Assessment standards: diagnostic data and, 31–32; rigor and, 40; shared vision, 29–30

Assumptions: change leadership and, 221; immunity map, 86, 91, 127–129; lenses of trust and, 165n2. *See also* Big Assumptions

Attitude: key competencies needed, 5; relationships and, 135

Authority: respect for, 7–8; unrecognized beliefs about, 210

Autonomy: as organizational belief and behavior, 13–14; principals and, 71

## B

Barth, Roland, 228

Basic skills, need for, 4–5

Behaviors: counterproductive, 57–58; organizational beliefs and, 11–14; relationships and, 135. *See also* Individual beliefs and behaviors

Berger, Jennifer, 210

Big Assumptions: about social expectations, 209; biography of, 177; challenges to, 175–176; change coach case study, 189; concentrating on change and, 220; designing tests, 182–183; immunity map and, 86, 91, 127–129; leading to other assumptions, 211–212; observing, 173–175; overturning, 167, 185–190; testing, 178–183; welcoming contradictions, 225–226

Bill & Melinda Gates Foundation, 80, 222
Bleke, Bert, 140–142, 147
Boston Public Schools, 14
Boy Scouts of America, 40
Bryk, Anthony S., 39, 69, 136, 165*n2*
Buckerey, Gloria, 111–114
*Building a New Structure for School Leadership* (Elmore), 165*n3*
Building administrators, 198–202
Bureaucracies, 25, 68

## C

Carnevale, Anthony P., 5, 10
Central office administrators, 198–202
Challenges: accepting the, 16–18; to Big Assumptions, 175–176; of change, 9; to collaboration, 103; effective instruction, 99–100; to effective supervision, 100–101; of high-stakes test scores, 163–165; to instructional improvement, 24–26; with time, 101. *See also* Adaptive challenges
Change: challenge of, 9; and change levers, 134–137; concentrating on, 218–221; and conditions of teaching and learning, 112; goal of, 98; inward and outward, 193–195; obstacles *vs.* momentum for, 64–74; recommended reading, 256; starting points for, 90–92; systems thinking and, 98–110. *See also* Immunities to change; Individual

change; Organizational change; Systemic change; Urgency for change
Change leadership: adaptive work and, 221–227; complacency and, 207; data and, 136; enacting systemic change, 153; envisioning systemic change, 145; personal learning required for, 206; recommended reading, 256
Change Leadership Group (CLG), 11, 25
Charter schools, 25
CLG (Change Leadership Group), 11, 25
Coaches: change coach case study, 187–190; enacting systemic change, 155; isolation and, 77–78; for teachers, 113
Coalition of Essential Schools, 43, 75
Collaboration: accountable, 31–32, 155; challenges to, 103; envisioning systemic change, 145, 150; isolation and, 71–74; lesson study process, 122*n8*; moving toward, 16–18; with parents, 103, 105; preparing for systemic change, 138; principals in, 114; professional development and, 31; relationships and, 142; teamwork and, 72
College-readiness of graduates, 2–5, 104
Collins, Jim, 208
Commitment: competing, 87–90, 124–126, 196–198; evaluating, 84–86;

horizontal accountability and, 135; to instructional improvement, 51–60; relationships and, 135–136; SoCal District example, 196; to teaching literacy, 66, 110–111; teamwork and, 210, 218. *See also* Hidden commitments
Communication: accountability and, 136; among leaders, 103; envisioning systemic change, 145–147; key competencies needed, 5; preparing for systemic change, 140–142; systems thinking and, 105
Communities: envisioning systemic change, 145–153; focus groups from, 165*n5*; preparing for systemic change, 136–145
Communities of practice: horizontal accountability and, 135; leadership practice communities, 76–80; lesson study process, 122*n8*; moving toward, 16–18; as strategy, 74–80. *See also* Leadership practice communities
Community School District 2: culture, 122*n8*; effective practices, 27; PS 198, 111–118; reorganization of, 110
Competency: communication and, 5; educational transformation, 162; mastering core, 39–41; systems thinking, 99–101; and transformation, 112–113; trust and, 136, 165*n2*

Competing commitments, 87–90, 124–126, 196–198

Complacency, 207

Compliance: communities of practice and, 80; generating momentum and, 74; as organizational tendency, 64, 68–71; vertical accountability and, 135

Conditions: adaptive challenges and, 199–200; for learning at home, 105; systems thinking, 101–102

Connecticut Center for School Change, 80

Consciously immune, 185–186

Consciously released, 185–186

Context, 104–106

Continuous improvement of instruction: ecology of change and, 136, 139–140, 154–157; generating momentum for, 74–78; obstacles vs. momentum, 64–74

Contradictions, welcoming, 225–226

Corning-Painted Post School District (New York): educational transformation, 162 163; enacting systemic change, 154–158; envisioning systemic change, 146–151; preparing for systemic change, 136, 139–142; urgency for change and, 208

Costs, identifying, 169–172

Counterproductive behaviors, 57–58

Craft knowledge, 24, 65, 76

Creative noncompliers, 14

Csikszentmihalyi, Mihaly, 7

Culture: adaptive challenges and, 199–200; Community School District 2, 122n8; defined, 102; educational transformation, 162; leaders and, 111; organizational, 17; povrecito, 197–198, 219; principals and, 103, 113–114; recommended reading, 262; systems thinking, 102–103, 105; transformation and, 113–119

Curriculum: autonomy with, 71; educational transformation, 162; enacting systemic change, 158; improved instruction and, 104; relevance of, 41–42

## D

Data: with accountable collaboration, 31–32; change leadership and, 136; as change lever, 134–137; collecting for Big Assumption test, 178; enacting systemic change, 154–155; envisioning systemic change, 145–147; instructional improvements using, 28, 133; preparing for systemic change, 139–140

Decision-making, 24, 142

Deming, W. Edwards, 75–76

Designing tests, 178–180, 182–183

Desrochers, Donna M., 5

Diagnostic tools/exercises: Challenges to the Big Assumption, 176; Change Phase Diagnostic: Enacting, 159–161, 245–250; Change Phase Diagnostic: Envisioning, 152–153, 245–202; Change Phase Diagnostic: Preparing, 143–145, 245–250; Compliance Versus Engagement Diagnostic, 70–71, 239–240; Define Rigor on a Learning Walk, 45–48, 235–237; Evaluate Your Commitment and Behaviors, 84–85; 4 C's Diagnostic Tool—As Is, 107–110, 242–244; Grade the Videotaped Lesson, 35–38, 234–235; Groupwide Approach to Diagnosing the Immunity to Change, 251–254; Identifying the Problem, 18–19, 231–232; Isolation Versus Collaboration Diagnostic, 73–74, 241–242; Look Inward: Your Four-Column Immunity Map, 86–92; Make the Commitment, 52–54; Moving Toward the Goal, via the 4 C's, 119–120; Protocol for Building Communities of Practice, 78–80; Reaction Versus Purpose and Focus Diagnostic, 67–68, 237–239; Recognize Counterproductive Behaviors, 57–58; Refining Problem Statement, 26; Review and Revise Your Strategies, 161; Running the Test, 182; Take Stock:

Diagnostic tools *(continued)*
  Seven Disciplines for
  Strengthening Instruction,
  33–34, 232–233; Test Your
  Assumption, 179–180;
  Your Big Assumption in
  Action, 174–175; Your Big
  Assumption, Revisited,
  183; Your Vision of
  Success, 172–173
Disciplines to improved
  instruction, 27–34. *See also*
  Seven Disciplines for
  Strengthening Instruction
Dropout rates, 139–140
Du Fu, 228
DuFour, Rick, 75

## E

Ecology of change framework:
  enacting, 133–134,
  136–137, 153–161;
  envisioning, 133–134,
  136–137, 145–153;
  midcourse correction,
  136; preparing, 133–134,
  136–145; Seven
  Disciplines and, 133
Edmonson, Amy, 69
Education system. *See* Public
  education system
*Education Week* Research
  Center, 199
Educational Testing Service, 5
Educators. *See* Teachers
Effective instruction:
  competencies, 99–100;
  conditions for, 101;
  culture and, 102–103;
  defining, 147; as discipline,
  30, 32; meetings about,
  29, 32; success as, 171;
  teaching literacy, 31.
  *See also* Instructional
  improvement

Effective supervision:
  competencies, 100–101;
  conditions for, 102;
  culture and, 103;
  as discipline, 30, 32;
  leadership practice
  communities and, 77
Einstein, Albert, 2, 200, 222
Elmore, Richard, 24, 165*n*3
Emotional intelligence, 5, 10
Enacting phase (systemic
  change), 133–134,
  136–137, 153–161
Engagement: agreement
  and, 70; compliance and,
  68–71
Envisioning phase (systemic
  change), 133–134,
  136–137, 145–153
Escalante, Hyamie, 72
Excellence, random acts of, 16
Exercises. *See* Diagnostic
  tools/exercises

## F

Failure, 221
Feedback, 178, 182, 184–185
*The Fifth Discipline*
  (Senge), 97
Fink, Elaine, 29, 66, 110–114
Focus: communities of
  practice and, 75;
  importance of, 112;
  on priorities, 198–207;
  reaction and, 65–68
Focus groups: community-
  wide, 165*n*5; envisioning
  systemic change, 148; instructional improvements
  using, 28; on respectful
  relationships, 42
Forrester, Jay, 97
Forster, Greg, 2
4 C's. *See* Competency; Conditions; Context; Culture

## G

Girl Scouts of America, 40
Goleman, Daniel, 5, 10
Good teaching. *See* Effective
  instruction
*Good to Great* (Collins), 208
Graduates, college-readiness
  of graduates, 2–5, 104
Grand Rapids School District
  (Michigan): coaching
  in, 77; educational
  transformation,
  162–163; enacting
  systemic change,
  155–158; envisioning
  systemic change,
  147, 149, 151; *As Is-To Be*
  tool, 120–121; preparing
  for systemic change, 136,
  140–143
Greene, Jay, 2
Group effectiveness, 5

## H

Hammerman, Jim, 210
Harvard Business School, 69
Harvard University, 223
Heifitz, Ron, 10–11,
  195, 209
Hidden commitments:
  change leadership and,
  221, 226; finding,
  87–90; personal
  immunities and,
  124–126; SoCal District
  example, 196–198
Hiebert, James, 75–76,
  122*n*8
Historical events, relevance
  of, 41
"Home alone," societal
  changes and, 7
Horizontal accountability,
  135–136, 155–156
House, Gerry, 199

**I**

Identifying progress, 169–173
Immunities to change:
    becoming fully released,
    187–190; concentrating
    on change and, 219–221;
    group-level, 230n15;
    individual, 83–92,
    124–129; overturning,
    185–187; SoCal District
    example, 197–198; steps
    for powerful learning,
    184–185; steps toward
    change, 168–184
Immunity maps: Annenberg
    grant recipients, 210–211;
    assumptions and, 86, 91,
    127–129; change coach
    case study, 187–190;
    exercise, 86–92; hidden
    commitments, 124–126;
    importance of, 193–194;
    of a principal, 201; SoCal
    District, 196; of
    superintendents,
    203–205, 212
Improved instruction. See
    Instructional
    improvement
Individual beliefs and
    behaviors: attending to
    countering, 83–85;
    considerations, 14–16;
    external risks, 14–15;
    hidden commitments
    and immunities, 124–126;
    investigating, 85–86;
    uncovering with
    immunity maps, 194
Individual change:
    immunities to, 83–92;
    leaders and, 193;
    organizational change
    and, 194–195; steps
    toward, 168–184

Influence, 5
Input. See Feedback
Instructional improvement:
    building and central office
    administrators and,
    198–202; challenges to,
    24–26; commitment to,
    51–60; conditions for, 102;
    creating systems based on,
    23–24; educational
    transformation, 162;
    envisioning systemic
    change, 145; 4 C's, 98–110;
    implications of term, 9;
    launching, 34; leaders and,
    165n3; new 3 R's of,
    38–49; recommended
    reading, 255–256; Seven
    Disciplines, 27–34, 133;
    shared vision for, 35–38;
    urgency for, 133; using
    focus groups, 28; using
    interviews, 28. See also
    Continuous improvement
    of instruction; Effective
    instruction
Integrity, 136, 165n2, 218
Interviews, 28
Isolation: coaches and, 77–78;
    communities of practice
    and, 80; culture and, 103;
    as organizational
    tendency, 64, 71–74;
    PS 198 motto, 113

**J**

Japan, 76, 122n8

**K**

Kearns, David, 3
Keating, John, 72
Kegan, Robert, 190n1
Kinsley, Dale, 16
Knowledge economy, 3–6
Kotter, John, 207

**L**

Labor force, 3, 5
Lahey, Lisa, 190n1
Larson, Reed, 7
Leaders: collaborative
    learning and, 16–18;
    communication among,
    103; communities of
    practice for, 76–80;
    concentrating on change,
    218–221; culture and, 111;
    educational transforma-
    tion, 162; enacting
    systemic change, 153–161;
    encouraging new kinds of,
    209–213; envisioning
    systemic change, 115–153;
    growing on the job, 223;
    immunities to change,
    83–92; improvement and,
    165n3, 193; learning and,
    175–176; "no shame, no
    blame, no excuses," 143;
    organizational beliefs and
    behaviors, 11, 13–14;
    preparing for systemic
    change, 138–145;
    principals as, 77,
    198–202; prioritizing
    goals, 100–101;
    recommended reading,
    262; self-reflection and,
    56. See also Change
    leadership
Leadership Academy
    (San Diego), 29
Leadership practice
    communities (LPC):
    concentrating on
    change, 217–221;
    evolving to, 17, 214–216;
    overview, 76–80.
    See also Communities
    of practice
Leading Change (Kotter), 207

Learning: accountability and, 136; change leadership and, 206; changing conditions of, 112; enacting systemic change, 154–159; encouraging, 224–225; leaders and, 175–176; moving toward collaborative, 16–18; PS 198 motto, 114; recommended reading, 255; societal changes and, 6–8; steps for, 184–185; success as, 171; systems thinking and, 105

Learning walks: Big Assumption tests and, 178–179; defining rigor on, 45–48; enacting systemic change, 154, 156

Lesson study process, 122*n8*

Levy, Frank, 3

Lieberman, Ann, 75

Literacy, teaching: action plan for, 111–113, 147; challenges in, 99–100; commitment to, 66, 110–111; ecology of change and, 140–142, 147, 155; professional development and, 31; systems thinking and, 104

LPC (leadership practice communities): concentrating on change, 218–221; evolving to, 17, 214–216; overview, 76–80

## M

MacArthur Foundation "genius prize," 14

Manhattan Institute for Policy Research, 2

Mason, Perry, 72

Meetings: about effective instruction, 29, 32; educational transformation, 162; enacting systemic change, 156, 158; engagement in, 69–70; improving, 113; LPCs and, 214–215; nature of, 13; preparing for systemic change, 139; principals', 114; professional development and, 64; systems thinking, 102–103

Meier, Deborah, 14

"Merit badge" approach, 40

Metrics, designing, 169–173

Midcourse correction, 136

Milgram, Stanley, 210

Momentum, 64–74, 138

Motivation, 4, 6–7, 42–43

Murnane, Richard, 3

## N

NAEP (National Assessment of Educational Progress), 1

Nagaoka, Jenny K., 39

Names, importance of, 214

*A Nation at Risk,* 1

National Assessment of Educational Progress (NAEP), 1

National School Reform Faculty, 75

New 3 R's framework, 38–49

New York City Public Schools, 14

Newmann, Fred M., 39

"No Child Left Behind," 1, 11, 164, 195

## O

Obstacles: immunities to change, 83–92; to learning walks, 48; political and structural barriers, 25;

self-reflection and, 55–58; *vs.* momentum for improvement, 64–74

Olmos, Edward James, 72

Organizational change: accepting the challenge, 16–18; change levers, 134–137; communities of practice and, 74–80; creating cultures, 17; ecology of transformation, 162–163; education "problem" and, 11–14; enacting systemic change, 133–134, 136–137, 153–161; envisioning systemic change, 133–134, 136–137, 145–153; generating momentum for, 74; increasing personal capacities through, 226–227; individual change and, 194–195; leaders and, 193; measuring success, 163–165; obstacles to, 64–74; phases of systemic, 133–134; preparing for systemic change, 133–134, 136–145

Outcomes: enacting systemic change, 153; envisioning systemic change, 145; preparing for systemic change, 138–139

Overindulgence, societal changes and, 7

## P

Parents: collaboration with, 103, 105; educational transformation, 163; envisioning systemic change, 149–150; responsibility of, 165*n2*; as source of complaint, 13

Payzant, Tom, 207
Perception gap, 6
Performance standards:
ecology of change and,
139–140; educational
transformation, 163–164;
enacting systemic change,
154; rigor and, 40; shared
vision, 29–30; systems
thinking about, 104
Perini, Matthew J., 39
Personal change. *See*
Individual change
Personal management, 5
Personal regard for others,
136, 165*n2*
Peters, Mark, 28
Phillips, Vicki, 28, 31,
69–70, 146
Plant management, 198–199
Politics, teachers and, 65
Povrecito culture,
197–198, 219
Preparing phase (systemic
change), 133–134,
136–145
Principals: autonomy and, 71;
culture and, 103, 113–114;
developing competencies
of, 112–113; encouraging
new links of leaders, 210;
"growing two heads," 216;
as instructional leaders, 77,
198–202; power structure
and, 165*n2*; reporting
structure, 68; Research
Center study, 199
Priorities: education reform
as, 1; educational
transformation, 163;
envisioning systemic
change, 149; focusing on,
198–207; for goals,
100–101; improving test
scores, 65; setting, 102

Problem statement, 26
Professional development:
communities of practice
and, 75; competencies
and, 99; as discipline,
31–32; effective meetings
and, 64; enacting systemic
change, 154; envisioning
systemic change, 145, 147;
infrastructure for, 111
Progress, identifying, 169–173
Project Zero (Harvard), 75
PS 198, 111–118
Public Agenda Foundation,
3–4, 6, 43
Public education system:
envisioning systemic
change, 145–146; identifying problems, 18–19,
231–232; obsolescence of,
9–10; reframing, 1–20;
shared accountability for,
140–141
Public perception,
managing, 207–208

## Q

Qualitative data: envisioning
systemic change, 146;
instructional improve-
ments using, 28; value of,
134–135
Quantitative data: envisioning
systemic change, 146;
instructional improve-
ments using, 28
Quantum Leap Project, 142,
146, 158

## R

Random acts of excellence, 16
Relational trust, 136, 165*n2*
Relationships: as change lever,
134–137; educational
transformation, 162;

enacting systemic change,
157–159; envisioning
systemic change, 149–151;
need for, 7; preparing for
systemic change, 141–143;
renegotiating, 206, 209;
respectful, 38, 42–45,
135–136
Relevance, as framework, 38,
41–42, 44–45
Respect: accountability and,
136; for authority, 7–8;
culture and, 103; demand
for, 4, 28; envisioning
systemic change, 150;
horizontal accountability
and, 135; modeling, 111;
preparing for systemic
change, 142; trust and,
136, 165*n2*
Respectful relationships, 38,
42–45, 135–136
Responsiveness, 12
Rigor: defining on learning
walk, 45–48, 235–237; as
framework, 38–41, 44–45;
importance of, 113
Risks, 15–18, 206
Rosier, Paul, 16

## S

Schneider, Barbara, 69, 136,
165*n2*
School improvement. *See*
Instructional
improvement
Scientific method, 40
Security of buildings, 199
Self-control, 7, 20*n15*
Self-discipline, 7, 20*n15*
Senge, Peter, 11, 97
Seven Disciplines for
Strengthening Instruc-
tion: ecology of change
and, 133; enacting

Seven Disciplines (*continued*)
  systemic change,
  153–154; overview,
  27–32; team exercises,
  33–34, 232–233
Shared vision: developing,
  35–38, 147; of student
  achievement, 29–30; of
  success, 171–173
Silver, Harvey J., 39
Simulated shock
  experiment, 209
Sizer, Ted, 43
Skill requirements, 3–6, 44
Snyder, W. M., 75
SoCal District, 196–197
Societal expectations, 3,
  6–8, 209
Standards. *See* Assessment
  standards; Performance
  standards
Stapes, Judy, 157
Steele-Pierce, Mary Ellen, 48
Steering committees: envisioning systemic change,
  146, 148; preparing for
  systemic change, 139, 142
Step Back Consulting, 78–80
Stigler, James, 75–76, 122*n8*
Strategies. *See* Working
  strategically
Strong, Richard W., 39
Student achievement: at
  charter schools, 25;
  ecology of change and,
  140; envisioning systemic
  change, 146–147; focused
  priorities and, 66; high
  expectations for,
  196–198; principals as
  educators and, 199;
  relational trust and, 136;
  shared accountability
  for, 140–141; shared
  vision of, 29–30

Success, defining,
  171–172, 220
Superintendents: communi-
  ties of practice and, 80;
  fostering feelings of urgency for change, 207–209;
  immunity maps of,
  203–205, 212–213;
  reporting structure, 68
Supervision. *See* Effective
  supervision
Systemic change: change
  leaders and adaptive work,
  221–227; concentrating on
  change, 218–221; developing new kind of administrative teams, 214–218;
  enacting, 133–134,
  136–137, 153–161;
  encouraging new kinds
  of leaders, 209–213;
  envisioning, 133–134,
  136–137, 145–153; focusing relentlessly on priorities, 202–207; fostering
  feelings of urgency for
  change, 207–209; holding
  high expectations for all
  students, 196–198; involving administrators in
  instruction, 198–202;
  inward and outward
  changes and, 194; mid-
  course correction, 136;
  preparing for, 133–134,
  136–145
Systems, 97
Systems thinking: assump-
  tions in, 127–129; competencies, 99–101;
  conditions, 101–102;
  context, 104–106; culture,
  102–103; defined, 97;
  4 C's diagnostic tool—
  as is, 107–110; hidden

commitments, 124–126;
  learning organizations
  and, 97; phases of organizational change, 133–134;
  transformation with,
  110–120

T
Teachers: blaming others, 8;
  coaching, 113; communi-
  ties of practice for, 75–76;
  competencies and, 99;
  culture and, 103; deci-
  sion-making and, 24;
  developing competencies
  of, 112–113; educational
  transformation, 162;
  encouraging new kinds of
  leaders, 211; envisioning
  systemic change, 145;
  leaders as buffers for, 13;
  lesson study process,
  122*n8*; power structure
  and, 165*n2*; reporting
  structure, 68; students'
  need for relationships
  with, 7; turnover rates for,
  8. *See also* Professional
  development
Teaching: changing condi-
  tions of, 112; enacting
  systemic change, 154–159;
  impact of societal changes
  on, 6; PS 198 motto, 114.
  *See also* Instructional
  improvement
*The Teaching Gap* (Stigler and
  Hiebert), 75, 122*n8*
Team exercises: Change Phase
  Diagnostic: Enacting,
  159–161, 245–250;
  Change Phase Diagnostic:
  Envisioning, 152–153,
  245–250; Change Phase
  Diagnostic: Preparing,

143–145, 245–250;
Compliance Versus
Engagement Diagnostic,
70–71, 239–240; Define
Rigor on a Learning
Walk, 45–48, 235–237;
4 C's Diagnostic Tool—
As Is, 107–110, 242–245;
Grade the Videotaped
Lesson, 35–38, 234–235;
Groupwide Approach to
Diagnosing the Immunity
to Change, 251–254;
Identifying the Problem,
18–19, 231–232; Isolation
Versus Collaboration
Diagnostic, 73–74,
241–242; Reaction Versus
Purpose and Focus
Diagnostic, 67–68,
237–239; Take Stock:
Seven Disciplines for
Strengthening
Instruction, 33–34,
232–233

Teamwork: commitment
and, 210, 218; educators
and, 72; preparing for
systemic change, 138;
team agreements, 217;
trust and, 69

Technical challenges,
adaptive *vs.*, 8–12

Technologies, 7, 10–11

Testing, 178–183. *See also*
Performance standards;
Student achievement

"Theory of change," 23

Time, challenges with, 101

Tools. *See* Diagnostic
tools/exercises

TQM (Total Quality
Management), 75–76

Transformation: adaptive
challenges and, 11; to
communities of practice,
17; competencies and,
112–113; of compliance,
68–71; conditions and,
112; context and, 111–112;
culture and, 113–119;
ecology of, 162–163;
4 C's, 110–111;
of isolation, 71–74;
of reaction, 65–68

Trombley, Donald, 141, 146,
207–208

Trust: accountability and, 136;
critical lenses, 165n2; educational transformation,
162; envisioning systemic
change, 150–151;
modeling, 111; preparing
for systemic change,
142–143; recommended
reading, 256; relational,
135–136, 157, 165n2;
team learning and, 69

*Trust in Schools* (Bryk and
Schneider), 136

Turnover rates, 8

U

Unconsciously immune,
185–186

Unconsciously released,
185, 187

Urgency for change:
envisioning systemic
change, 146; fostering
feelings of, 207–209;
instructional

improvement and, 28,
133; preparing for systemic
change, 138–140

V

Vertical accountability,
135–136

Vocabulary, lack of shared,
29, 34

W

Waller, Willard, 227

Ward, Michael, 15,
17, 207–208,
212–213, 223

Welby, Marcus, 72

Wenger, E., 75

West Clermont Public School
District: adaptive
challenges and, 212;
effective instruction and,
48; internal risks and, 15;
measuring success, 164;
urgency for change and,
28, 207

Williams, Robin, 72

Working strategically:
change levers, 134–137;
communities of practice
and, 74–80; ecology
of transformation,
162–163; focusing
relentlessly on priorities,
198–202; measuring
success, 163–165;
midcourse correction,
136; phases of organiza-
tional change, 133–134;
phases of systemic
change, 138–161

Writing skills, 4–5, 104